America's Second Tongue

America's Second Tongue

American Indian Education
AND THE
Ownership of English,
1860–1900

RUTH SPACK

University of Nebraska Press
Lincoln and London

© 2002 by the University
of Nebraska Press
All rights reserved
Manufactured in the
United States of America
∞
Library of Congress
Cataloging-in-Publication
Data
Spack, Ruth.
America's second tongue:
American Indian
education and the
ownership of English,
1860–1900 / Ruth Spack.
p.   cm.
Includes bibliographical
references (p.) and index.
ISBN 0-8032-4291-3 (cloth:
alk. paper)
1. English language—
Study and teaching—
Indian speakers—History
—19th century.
2. Indians of North
America—Cultural
assimilation—History—
19th century.
3. Indians of North
America—Education—
History—19th century.
4. Indians of North
America—Languages—
History—19th century.
5. Language and
education—United States
—History—19th century.
6. Language and culture—
United States—History—
19th century. I. Title.
PE 1130.5.A5 S63 2002
428′.0071′073—dc21
2001044414   "N"

Contents

ILLUSTRATIONS

Acknowledgments

A project like this is dependent on the kindness and expertise of numerous librarians and archivists. I was fortunate to have access to the Tisch Library at Tufts University and am indebted to three librarians who were tireless in their efforts to find even the most obscure nineteenth-century materials: Ann Marie Ferraro, Jessica Bell, and Jim Walsh. My fortune continued at Bentley College, where Lindsey White and Laurie Dewar managed to find every book or document I requested through interlibrary loan. I also am deeply appreciative of the help offered by Thomas Hamm, Lilly Library, Earlham College, Richmond, Indiana; Kristen Mitrisin, American Tract Society, Garland, Texas; Barbara Landis and Richard Pitt, Cumberland Historical Society, Carlisle, Pennsylvania; Jill Costill, Indiana State Library, Indianapolis, Indiana; Shannon Perich and Dave Burgevin, Photographic History Collection, National Museum of American History, Washington DC; Vyrtis Thomas, National Anthropological Archives, National Museum of American History, Washington DC; Alana McGrattan, Santa Fe Indian School, Santa Fe, New Mexico; Sylvia Kennick Brown, Williams College Library Archives and Special Collections, Williamstown, Massachusetts; Jack Miller, Wabash County Historical Museum, Wabash, Indiana; David Anderson, Creek Council House Museum, Okmulgee, Oklahoma; Patricia Fanning, Norwood Historical Society, Norwood, Massachusetts; and Laura Ries, South Dakota State Historical Society, Pierre, South Dakota. I also thank the staffs at the University Archives of Hampton University, Hampton, Virginia; Nevada Historical Society, Reno, Nevada; Oklahoma Historical Society, Oklahoma City, Oklahoma; Smithsonian Anthropological Library, Smithsonian Institution, Washington DC; Division of Manuscripts and Archives, State Historical Society of Wisconsin, Madison, Wisconsin; Educational Research Library, United States Department of Education, Washington DC; Beinecke Rare Book and Manuscript Library, Yale University, New Haven, Connecticut; Boston Public Library, Boston, Massachusetts; New England Conservatory of Music, Boston, Massachusetts; and Houghton Library, Harvard University, Cambridge, Massachusetts.

In addition to librarians and archivists, a number of people were helpful in providing information. I thank Ruth Ann Parker; Ellery Sedgwick; Patricia Jiron, Santa Fe Indian School, Santa Fe, New Mexico; Carrie Makin, White's Institute, Wabash, Indiana; and Janet McCarthy, Silver Burdett Ginn, Needham Heights, Massachusetts.

I am indebted to Elizabeth Ammons of Tufts University, Bill Stokes and Judith Beth Cohen of Lesley University, Jon Reyhner of the University of Northern Arizona, and most especially Vivian Zamel of the University of Massachusetts Boston for their help in shaping the direction of my research and writing. They each provided careful readings of earlier versions of this manuscript, from its inception as a course paper to its completion as a dissertation and then a book. I am also grateful for research fellowships from Lesley University, which enabled me to conduct research at the National Archives, Smithsonian Institution, Library of Congress, and United States Department of Education in Washington DC.

My husband, Norman, my daughter and son-in-law, Rebecca and Arthur Sneider, and my mother, Esther Karten, have been wonderfully supportive of my work. I must give special thanks to my son, Jonathan Spack, who spent precious hours while an undergraduate at the University of Wisconsin–Madison in the State Historical Society of Wisconsin photocopying Zitkala-Ša's letters to Carlos Montezuma.

A portion of chapter 2 appeared as "English, Pedagogy, and Ideology: A Case Study of the Hampton Institute, 1878–1900," *American Indian Culture and Research Journal* 24.1 (2000): 1–24, and it is reprinted here by permission of the American Indian Studies Center, UCLA. © Regents of the University of California.

An earlier version of chapter 5 was published as "Re-visioning Sioux Women: Zitkala-Ša's Revolutionary *American Indian Stories*," *Legacy: A Journal of American Women Writers* 14.1 (1997): 25–52.

Portions of chapter 5 appeared in "Dis/engagement: Zitkala-Ša's Letters to Carlos Montezuma, 1901–1902," *MELUS* 26.1 (2001): 173–204.

America's Second Tongue

WOONSPE VI.

(De taku he.) (Woayupte.)

wicinyanna

tipi wan

wi kin

ka	wan	cin	pi	wi	ca
na	yan	kin	ti	śun	śta

Introduction

I have tried to transplant the native spirit of these tales – root and all – into the English language, since America in the last few centuries has acquired a second tongue.
    Zitkala-Ša, preface to *Old Indian Legends*, 1901

To discuss the use of the English language in the land we now know as the United States is to become caught in a linguistic paradox. Referring to English as the native language of Americans has the rhetorical effect of making the first inhabitants of this land invisible, for they, of course, were native speakers not of English but of a multitude of indigenous languages. When English-speaking Europeans called indigenous people *native*, however, they were referring not to their language status but rather to what they perceived to be their primitive state. In the context of language learning, a rhetorical inversion occurred, such that Native people became non-native speakers of English; yet it was the Anglo speakers who were non-Native.

The paradox is further complicated by the nativist movement in the nineteenth century, which favored the interests of native inhabitants over those of immigrants. To the anti-Catholic nativists, the "natives" were English-speaking Protestants of European descent. To add to the irony, in their secret societies nativists used what they perceived to be symbols of Native life as their trademarks. They called their leaders "sachems" and "chiefs" and gave their local chapters names such as "Oneida" and "Montauk." By non-nativizing the real Natives and appropriating their identities,

Europeans were in effect depriving Native people of their linguistic birth-right.[1]

Despite the efforts of Europeans to keep Native people and their contributions invisible, Native ways of knowing have always been essential to the development of the European way of life on Native lands. Explorers, traders, pilgrims, and missionaries lacked the skills to feed and transport themselves in the territory they called the New World. They were thus dependent on indigenous people, who provided an education in survival. That education included language instruction, with initial communication taking place primarily through hand signs, pantomime, and pidgin. From the beginning, Europeans found it necessary to borrow Native words to identify unfamiliar entities such as topography, animals, plants, foods, weapons, and modes of lodging and transportation. In order to engage in trade and develop new political structures, they also learned "the language of Indian diplomacy," as Rayna Green puts it. Europeans became Americans – European Americans – as their old cultures and languages were transformed by the new.[2]

Native life too was transformed by contact, of course, and not necessarily in negative ways. For example, many communities adopted technically sophisticated goods and formed alliances with Europeans against their own Native rivals. Native languages expanded to include names for new materials and concepts. Some individuals learned one or more European languages in order to serve as intermediaries between Native people and the growing European population. These interactions were often personally and collectively beneficial. Such models of intercultural communication did not originate with European contact. For centuries many Native people across the country were bilingual or multilingual, having become fluent in the languages of their respective regions, including sign language and pidginized languages, so that they could conduct intertribal trade and ceremonial activities.[3]

On occasion, speakers of English and speakers of Native languages exchanged language lessons. In the 1630s, for example, pastor John Eliot learned Massachusett from Cockenoe, a Montauk who had acquired it as a second language while in captivity, and Eliot in turn taught English to Cockenoe. However, because such two-way lessons tended to be limited to one-on-one interactions and in any case were few and far between, they rarely led to large-scale language exchange. Furthermore, the uses to which

Eliot and Cockenoe put their new languages reflected a pattern that established the power of English and its associated culture. Eliot used Massachusett to preach the gospel and ultimately to establish several "praying villages" populated by "Christian Indians." Cockenoe used English to settle land disputes between Native and European people and ultimately to pursue a trade. Explaining why this cultural translation was essentially a one-way process, David Murray points to the unequal power relations in Eliot's interactions with Native people, noting that the latter were threatened with annihilation.[4]

As linguistic scholars Edward Tuttle and Raoul Smith have documented, once English colonists had learned enough of an indigenous language to guarantee survival, they no longer felt compelled to draw on Native sources for language, although inevitably Native words, in adapted form, continued to extend the English language. Furthermore, in the colonial era the route to Christianity was increasingly believed to be traversable through assimilation into the English-speaking world, so English began to replace indigenous languages as the conduit for conversion. And even when Native languages were deemed useful, they were typically described as defective: incapable of conveying European abstract thought. Stephen Greenblatt suggests that this deficit model was one way European Americans could account for the cross-cultural difficulty of translating the tenets and practices of Christianity without having to acknowledge the complexity of Native ways of communicating. An occasional observer provided detailed linguistic analyses that contradicted prevailing notions about the inferiority of Native languages – for example, Jonathan Edward Jr.'s *Observations on the Language of the Muhhekaneew Indians* (1787) and John Heckewelder's *History, Manners, and Customs of the Indian Nations Who Once Inhabited Pennsylvania and the Neighboring States* (1819) – but these observations were largely ignored. Native languages, like Native people themselves, were in the process of being colonized. Anglo Americans believed in the superiority of their own language and culture, and almost from the beginning they began to develop educational or civilization programs to impose the English way of life on the Native population.[5]

Margaret Connell Szasz traces the history of the education of indigenous people by the English back to the early 1600s, when charters issued to the Virginia Company included clauses requiring conversion of Indians. Like the French and Spanish before them, Anglo missionaries established schools designed to "Christianize and civilize the natives" in order to raise them above what was perceived to be a debased state. Because Native people did not subscribe to the notion of European superiority, however, they had to be pressured to attend. In some cases English colonists brought students to school as captives. In cases where parents voluntarily chose formal schooling for their children, they were typically compelled by the need to help their children survive the devastation brought on by the economic changes and diseases that accompanied the arrival of Europeans – a pattern that would be repeated throughout the centuries.[6]

The attempts to civilize indigenous populations continued after the formation of the United States of America. Promising peace and schools in return for Native land, the federal government established its first educational policies for Native people through treaties (until 1871), which included provisions for vocational and literacy education. However, although the government increasingly gained control of the land throughout most of the nineteenth century, there was little peace and virtually no government-run education. Congress established a civilization fund of $10,000 per year in 1819, but because the government had no mechanism for dispensing the money, most of the funding was given to missionary societies. Thus government-aided schools became sites for Christianization. In both day schools and boarding schools on Native lands, classes were typically conducted in the vernacular to promote understanding of biblical teachings, although most mission schools eventually added English-language instruction.[7]

After the Civil War, as increasing numbers of European Americans moved westward and wars over land rights continued to bloody the plains, the United States government undertook a peace initiative that resulted in a large-scale English-only educational reform movement, the focus of this book. This English-only initiative held sway until 1934, when Congress passed the Indian Reorganization Act, which allowed for tribal self-government and renewal of Native languages. That period of linguistic tolerance was short-lived, however. It was not until 1990, when Congress passed the Native American Languages Act, that the United States government was charged with the responsibility of working together with indigenous people to guarantee the survival of their languages and cultures. The new United States language policy calls on the federal government "to preserve, protect, and promote the rights and freedom of Native Americans to use, practice, and develop Native American languages."[8]

I came to this subject out of a practical need to learn. A few years ago I was invited to speak to faculty across the curriculum at an English-language college in Quebec on the subject of linguistic and cultural diversity. I was told that the faculty members were concerned not only about students for whom French is the first language but also about Cree and Inuit students who were dropping out at a high rate, often within weeks of starting school. I realized then that I was ignorant about the language backgrounds of indigenous people in Canada and even in the United States, the country where I was born and raised. I determined to become more knowledgeable. Shortly thereafter I was introduced to Zitkala-Ša's *American Indian Stories*. When I opened the book and saw its large print, I thought it had been created for children. But as I started to read, I began to suspect that something subversive was unfolding before my eyes, especially when the narrator began describing a nineteenth-century English-only school designed for Native children. When I finished this astonishing work – a mixture of autobiography, fiction, and journalism – I began to search for whatever material I could find on Zitkala-Ša (1876–1938) and the education she had received in the 1880s and 1890s. As a teacher of English, I was especially curious about how Zitkala-Ša and other Native students had learned the language, for it occurred to me that the acronym ESL, which has always denoted English *as* a second language in the United States, actually signifies that English *is* the second language of this country, if we understand – as Zitkala-Ša reminds us (see epigraph) – that hundreds of Native languages came first. I began to recognize the extent to which the growth and development of the field of teaching English as a second language in the United States was tied to a process by which the federal government attempted to establish linguistic and cultural control over second-language learners. This is a history that no teacher of English can afford to ignore.

There is a growing body of literature on American Indian education in the late nineteenth century, including overviews and studies of particular schools and the United States government's language policy.[9] However, as I sought material specifically related to my field, I found no full-length historical work that focused exclusively on English-language teaching for Native students or that was written from the perspective of a specialist in teaching English to speakers of other languages (TESOL). Sociolinguists have maintained an active interest in Native languages and bilingualism, but histories of the teaching of English as a second or foreign language typically deal only with Great Britain and the British Empire or do not treat American Indian education in any depth.[10] No detailed investigation exists of the way teachers taught English to Native students in the nineteenth century and how fully Native students acquired and used the English they learned in the schools. This book is a contribution to that history.

Its title notwithstanding, *America's Second Tongue* deals with only one of the many countries that compose America. When I undertook this investigation, I wanted to avoid a monolithic characterization of a hegemonic English language and culture – for example, through comparison with the ways Spanish and Portuguese supplanted indigenous languages throughout South America. I had also hoped to complicate the analysis of the English-only ideology by providing examples of empires that allowed and encouraged subjected peoples to maintain their languages (e.g., the Incas) but that did not subsequently feel compelled to refrain from slaughtering them. Finally, I had considered enriching the analysis through an examination of the roles that European languages other than English (e.g., French, Russian, Spanish, German) played in the interaction between Native people and European colonizers or immigrants in Canada as well as the United States. But it became clear early in the project that to examine these issues thoroughly would both lengthen the book considerably and shift its focus. In the interest of conserving space and maintaining unity of vision, I narrowed my focal point to the role of English in the United States. Even then, this investigation does not seek to be a comprehensive record of the history of instruction in English as a second language in the United States. As Arnold Leibowitz has documented, English was imposed as the language of instruction not only on speakers of Native languages but also on speakers of German, Spanish, and Japanese, among others. Nor is this investigation a comprehensive record of the teaching of English to Native students in the United States. Instruction took place in hundreds of venues over hundreds of years and was influenced by the interactions between myriad Native and European American communities from a variety of spheres. Each local situation informs the larger understanding of what took place in this era, yet I could not address every one. Any study compels a researcher to follow some strands of ideas and events and to abandon others.

America's Second Tongue is a study of the development, implementation, and aftermath of the United States government's language policy for indigenous people at a particular point in time and within a particular set of circumstances. The examination of the language instruction itself begins at the time when the government began to formulate its language policy (1860s) and ends at a point when the policy became more or less fixed (1900). The investigation continues into the twentieth century in order to explore retrospective accounts of nineteenth-century school experiences. Because inhabitants of the Great Plains were the earliest targets of late-nineteenth-century educational reformers, my emphasis is on that locale. However, experiences of other regions enrich the narrative and complicate the argument. As the analysis will reveal, students' acceptance of or resistance to English-only education was intimately connected to their particular family and community histories.

This is a story of language and of how people used it to further their own political and cultural agendas. To tell this story is no easy task. It is a story of linguistic ownership, and the meaning of ownership keeps shifting, depending on whether one is perceived to own English or to be owned by it. Because language can be used to justify or resist oppression, to communicate deeply held beliefs or document inexpressibility, to create positive images or exploit negative ones, it is a site of struggle over power, meaning, and representation. As Mick Gidley says of all forms of cultural expression, language does not reproduce reality but rather represents it. Nevertheless, representations function in such a way as to constitute reality for the groups that create and disseminate them. Capable of exerting this power, of shaping consciousness, representations are inevitably linked to the ideologies and belief systems of the groups that create them.[11]

As Beatrice Medicine emphasizes, the historical casting of Native life into the printed word reified images that have had long-lasting and damaging repercussions, and those images need to be deconstructed. Yet to analyze only the representations generated by European Americans would be to limit the view of what Mary Louise Pratt calls the *contact zone:* the social space where multiple discourses converged, collided, and interacted in the context of colonization. Analysis of the discourse of European Americans in powerful positions can tell us much about how they represented Native people as well as how they represented themselves. But it certainly does not tell us how Native people represented *themselves* – or how they in turn represented European Americans. Furthermore, it does not take into account the dynamic processes of translingualism and transculturation that Native students underwent as they interacted with a variety of languages and cultures over time. Nor does it attend to the extraordinarily diverse – and sometimes conflicting – ways Native people responded to the effort to impose English-language instruction on their families and communities. In an attempt to reflect this linguistic and cultural complexity, I have chosen to set this story of language in a larger sociocultural and educational context and to view it through a kaleidoscopic lens that takes in several perspectives. To that end I show various ways the English language was used by United States government officials and missionaries (chapter 1), European American teachers (chapter 2), Native teachers (chapter 3), Native students (chapter 4), and Yankton Sioux fiction writer Zitkala-Ša (chapter 5). The book thus reflects the shifting ownership of English as the language was transferred from one population to another and as its uses were transformed.[12]

Despite its multiple perspectives, this investigation does not pretend to present a balanced view of American Indian education at the turn of the twentieth century. Three of the five chapters are devoted to analyzing Native perspectives. The history and analysis in this book are themselves representations of the past as I came to understand it through careful examination of the documentary record. The documents spoke for themselves. Government officials and missionaries were not engaged in a covert operation. Practices that went underground in the twentieth century as "the hidden curriculum" (e.g., the imposition of a particular set of values) were explicitly promoted in nineteenth-century school records, as Elizabeth Vallance has shown.[13] I made every effort not to accept Native sources uncritically while applying a different standard to European American sources. Native representations can be as exoticized, exaggerated, misleading, or artful as any other representations. Still, I could not ignore the fact that government officials and missionaries situated themselves in a superior position, linguistically and culturally, and overtly expressed their disdain for Native languages and cultures. European Americans were relatively free to express their ideas – and their prejudices – to a European American audience. Native writers, in contrast, had to create texts that were palatable to that same audience and thus were compelled to express their own agendas more covertly. Although even within these two groups of texts there was variation in style and substance, inevitably I was confronted with more openly negative or exoticized images of Native people in European American texts and with more coded or equivocal images of European Americans in Native texts.

These competing images heightened my awareness of the political and cultural climate in which words reached print in this era.

Underlying the ideas in every chapter of this book is an understanding that the English-language program was situated in a colonialist context. This investigation never loses sight of the relation between ideology and curriculum or of the asymmetrical power relations between educators and students. Accordingly, chapter 1, "English and Colonialist Discourses," focuses on the way government officials and missionaries used the English language to promote their own educational agendas. This chapter shows that English signified much more than a mode of communication, for it was tied to particular religious, cultural, racial, and nationalist ideologies. Chapter 2, "Language, Pedagogy, and Ideology," looks at the role European American teachers played in implementing missionaries' bilingual programs and the United States government's English-only school system. This chapter reveals that even in the most compassionate or progressive schools, teachers were complicit in the endeavor to eradicate Native languages and cultures and thus – wittingly or unwittingly – often undermined students' potential and sense of self. While the government's language policy was promoted as an important feature of its educational and humanitarian program, it functioned as an instrument of linguistic and cultural oppression.

The unequal relations that characterized the schools extended to the production of texts on which the analysis of Native perspectives depends. Native teachers' and students' writings were sometimes reprinted in government reports and school newspapers, and they are a rich resource for investigation. However, they were typically published because they reflected the European American worldview promulgated in the schools. In order to achieve a closer understanding of Native people's representations of themselves and others, I draw on autobiographies and ethnographies of Native teachers and former students, produced after they left school, for the analyses in chapter 3, "Reproduction and Resistance," and chapter 4, "Translingual Ironies." These texts presented a challenge, however, for many of the published stories were produced in collaboration with Anglo editors, anthropologists, or sociologists. Only a few more than half of the Native autobiographical works examined in this project are original works written by the former students themselves, although presumably all of them were subject to the conventional process of copyediting. The original writers are Ah-nen-la-de-ni (Mohawk), Jason Betzinez (Apache), Charles Doxon (Onondaga), Charles Eastman (Dakota), Francis La Flesche (Omaha), Lilah Denton Lindsey (Creek), Mourning Dove (Okanogan), John Rogers (Chippewa), Luther Standing Bear (Lakota), George Webb (Pima), Howard Whitewolf (Comanche), Sara Winnemucca (Northern Paiute), and Zitkala-Ša.[14] The other texts are based on oral testimonies gathered through audiotaped and transcribed interviews with Thomas Wildcat Alford (Absentee Shawnee), Asa Daklugie (Apache), Edward Goodbird (Hidatsa), Mary Little Bear Inkanish (Southern Cheyenne), James Kaywaykla (Apache), Annie Lowry (Northern Paiute), Frank Mitchell (Navajo), Edmund Nequatewa (Hopi), John Stands in Timber (Northern Cheyenne), Carl Sweezy (Arapaho), Don Talayesva (Hopi), and Albert Yava (Tewa-Hopi).[15]

It is difficult to determine how fully texts written in collaboration reflect the former students' actual perspectives, for the Native narrators were not in control of the work. Debate persists among scholars about what to call these texts – autobiography? ethnography? biography? – and for good reason. The introductions to the texts indicate that the accounts present former students' own ideas in their own words and from their own point of view. Wherever the text is a direct transcription of a taped interview, it is possible to discern the Native perspective. But the introductions also acknowledge that editors have added background material, rearranged the narrative, and in some cases even done some rewriting. Despite these explanations of the mode of production, the Anglo collaborators are virtually absent from the narratives themselves, leaving a reader the impression that they played little or no role in generating the texts.[16] If it is at all possible to discover what Native narrators perceived as important in their own lives, and I think it is (to the extent that it is ever possible to determine intent), it is necessary to focus on how they used English to represent themselves and establish their own identities within the constraints of colonialism. Although they collaborated with European Americans, Native narrators were not necessarily acquiescent or disempowered. They were able to introduce into these texts ideas and images other than those sanctioned by European American society.

For the purposes of this investigation, I approach these works as *autoethnographic* texts, a term coined by Mary Louise Pratt to identify writings in which indigenous people in the contact zone portrayed themselves and at the same time engaged with the representations that others had constructed of them. In circumstances where Native people worked in concert with European Americans who had access to the print culture, these publications were not conventional forms of self-representation. They involved simultaneous collaboration and appropriation, accommodation and resistance.[17] Most historians of American Indian education have dealt with Native students' stories as sources of data about nineteenth-century school experiences. Many such experiential details emerge here. However, my primary goal is to analyze Native rhetorical strategies in light of the historical context in which the texts were produced. I apply a similar approach to the creative writing analyzed in chapter 5, "Transforming Women: Zitkala-Ša's *American Indian Stories,*" where I pay particular attention to representations of Native women.

Through analysis of archival documents, autobiography, ethnography, and fiction, *America's Second Tongue* examines why and how government-sponsored English-language classrooms designed for Native students came into being, how European American and Native teachers mediated the government's English-only directive, and what students did with the language after they learned it. It focuses on the ways European American and Native people used English to represent themselves and each other as they sought to fulfill their own political, educational, and cultural agendas. Through these multiple perspectives, the book reveals yet another paradox. Even as English functioned as a disruptive and destructive instrument of linguistic and cultural control, it was also a generative tool for expressing diverse ways of seeing, saying, and believing.

2. Richard Henry Pratt with three students at the Carlisle Indian Industrial School (ca. 1880). Photograph by J. N. Choate. Courtesy of National Anthropological Archives, National Museum of Natural History, Smithsonian Institution/ Choate 158.

I

English and Colonialist Discourses

In February 1900, when Zitkala-Ša (née Gertrude Simmons) published "The School Days of an Indian Girl" in the *Atlantic Monthly,* she became the first Native writer to alert a mainstream readership to the devastating effects of off-reservation, English-only boarding school education for Native children. Zitkala-Ša herself had been educated at White's Indiana Manual Labor Institute, a Quaker-run school in Wabash, Indiana. The institute's relation to American Indian education began in 1882, when its board of trustees voted to redress the school's financial difficulties by accepting federal funding to educate Native students. White's had been founded twenty-two years earlier by the Society of Friends as a school for poor children, with funds donated by a wealthy Quaker entrepreneur, on land purchased from Meshingomesia, chief of the Miamis. Now, ironically, it was time to fill the space formerly occupied by indigenous people with indigenous people. To achieve that aim, Quakers followed the pattern of other religious organizations in sending representatives directly to the reservations to recruit students. In 1884 they convinced the mother of eight-year-old Gertie Simmons to allow her to leave the Yankton Agency in Dakota Territory to attend White's Institute. Simmons (Zitkala-Ša) would later describe these Quaker missionaries as "that class of white men who wore big hats and carried large hearts."[1]

The Quakers' renowned compassion was limited, however, at least from the perspective of Native parents. Gertrude Simmons apparently went to White's Institute voluntarily, with her mother's permission (her French

American father had abandoned the family before her birth). Nevertheless, files from the school indicate that most parents were unaware that the agreement on which they had "put their mark" gave the school the right to keep the children for three years, with no vacation. In this arrangement White's Institute was typical of boarding schools in the late nineteenth century, whose underlying assumption was that it would take that long for students to absorb European American culture and learn to speak English. But against the wishes of Native parents, this process was subtractive rather than additive, to borrow the terms of linguist Wallace Lambert. Students were expected to learn English not as an additional language but rather as the only language worthy of acquisition. They were not to become bicultural but rather to substitute the Christian majority culture for their own. Ostensibly designed to ease Native children into participation in European American society, these English-only schools functioned to implement a language policy that threatened the existence of students' home languages and cultures. How and why this policy evolved in the United States in the late nineteenth century is the focus of this chapter.[2]

To understand the development of the government's English-only program, it is crucial to recognize that it was situated in a colonialist context. As in other instances of colonization, control over language served as an important instrument in political as well as cultural exploitation, for it could be used to represent indigenous peoples' lives in such a way as to weaken claims to Native sovereignty and strengthen the United States government's bureaucratic and territorial agendas. As Eric Cheyfitz notes, Europeans used language to transform Native identity by representing indigenous peoples as "barbarians" or "savages" and thereby justified (to themselves) establishing structures of domination and subordination in foreign lands. Such rhetorical constructions were manifest not only in politics but also in education. Gauri Viswanathan and Alistair Pennycook, for example, demonstrate how nineteenth-century British educational discourse in Asia represented South Asians and Southeast Asians as intellectually and morally deficient in relation to their British educators and in turn justified imposing British ways of knowing on colonized populations. Similarly in Africa, English was used in colonial schools to frame students as inferior and to denigrate their native tongues. Ngũgĩ wa Thiong'o recalls that if students at his school in Kenya were caught speaking Gĩkũyũ, they were physically beaten or forced to wear a metal plate around their necks carrying a message such as "I AM

STUPID" or "I AM A DONKEY." The English language was thus used to control the way colonized people perceived themselves and their relationship to their own languages and associated cultures. As Jorge Noriega has shown, this mission to impose values through education was not limited to the British Empire but was an ongoing concern in the United States of America.[3]

This chapter traces the evolution of ideas associated with the United States government's imposition of English on indigenous populations, from the introduction of President Ulysses S. Grant's post–Civil War Peace Policy to the end of the nineteenth century. In order to understand the process by which meaning was constructed in government and missionary texts, I examine the discourse of the educational policymakers, with particular attention to their references to the English language. This rhetorical analysis reveals the ideological universe in which particular beliefs about language acquisition were formulated and disseminated. Although various regions of the country figure in the analysis, I pay special attention to Dakota Territory, in particular the Yankton Agency, because it supplied most of the students to the earliest off-reservation boarding schools. Examining the Yankton Agency sheds light on practices and attitudes at other agencies, for government agents on all the reservations had control over virtually every facet of life, and they shared similar assumptions. The Yankton Agency is of additional interest because it was a home base of the Dakota Mission, which played a significant role in the development of American Indian education and in the struggle over bilingual versus English-only instruction. Finally, Yankton was the birthplace and early home of Zitkala-Ša, whose work I analyze at length in chapter 5.

It is easy to be judgmental about nineteenth-century ideological perspectives, especially when – in hindsight – many of the ideas are disputable or even demonstrably erroneous. But though some of the views articulated in the past were deliberate distortions of the truth, many of the established notions were seemingly logical conclusions based on what was apparently the best information available. In this book, then, I adopt Carl Kaestle's definition of ideology, which assumes that individuals embrace particular social theories that guide them in determining how to live their own lives and how to create a stable or just society. When a significant number of individuals who are positioned similarly within the social order share these theories, the theories serve to link a variety of social institutions, even if the individuals' purposes differ and even though there may be tensions and contradictions within and among them. In other words, although people do not think exactly alike, their views may reflect prevailing conceptions of how the world operates or should operate. These conceptions become accepted cultural wisdom, or what Antonio Gramsci calls "social hegemony": the consent that the majority gives to the group in power to promote a way of life and thought for the larger population.[4] The goal of this chapter is to delineate the ideology underlying the United States government's language policy and to show how the English language itself was used to sanction imposing English on the Native population.

In the early 1860s, wars occurred repeatedly between the United States military and indigenous people in the West and Southwest, largely in response to encroachment on Native lands by European Americans migrating from the eastern states. The fighting on both sides was so brutal that the public began to demand an approach different from the policy of annihilation that the military had apparently adopted. Unable and unwilling to stop the westward movement, the government turned its attention to the welfare of indigenous populations in an effort to right the wrongs committed against them, which were largely perpetrated by the government itself. President Grant instituted a peace policy in 1869 to remove the causes of hostility and thus to ensure safety for the people who called themselves settlers. He appointed as commissioner of Indian affairs his former military secretary, Ely S. Parker, a Seneca (1869–71), and he placed Quakers and members of other religious groups in positions of power at the government agencies on the reservations. As it turned out, "peace policy" was a misnomer because, as one Quaker participant noted, "while offering peace with one hand, [the nation] has grasped the sword with the other." Nevertheless, when the policy was first implemented, the idea of peace was appealing to the nation, and the findings of the newly appointed Peace Commission were eagerly awaited.[5]

The Peace Commission was headed by then commissioner of Indian affairs Nathaniel Taylor (1867–69), a former Methodist minister who, according to Francis Paul Prucha, was motivated by a genuine concern for the tragic circumstances of indigenous people in the West. Presumably to convince Congress to fund his proposal, he adopted a phrase favored by the legislators and stated that it "costs less to civilize than to kill." Couched in the language of conciliation, the commission's report represented the government as acting in the interest of humanity and national unity, which was especially important after the recent rupture that characterized the Civil War. Taylor believed that the English language would be used as a tool for erasing differences between Anglo-Saxon and Native people. However, underlying that idea was the notion that Native ways of knowing must be erased: "Through sameness of language is produced sameness of sentiment and thought; customs and habits are moulded and assimilated in the same way, and thus in process of time the differences producing trouble would have been gradually obliterated. By civilizing one tribe others would have followed. . . . In the difference of language to-day lies two-thirds of our trouble." Assuming that a uniform language could fuse the multitude of Native nations into a controllable entity – "one homogeneous mass" – the Peace Commission recommended that compulsory schools be established in which Native languages would be "blotted out" and replaced with English. Viewing Native people as a "barbarous" and "savage" race, commission members did not take into account the idea that Native languages could convey intellectual values and morals. The civilian Board of Indian Commissioners, appointed by the president in 1869 as part of his peace policy to oversee corruption in the Office of Indian Affairs and to create a "civilizing plan" for indigenous people, shared this assumption of the superiority of English. In its first report, the board recommended that the government establish schools and hire teachers "to introduce the English language in every tribe."[6]

When the Board of Indian Commissioners issued its first report in 1869, the only schools in existence for Native people, with a few inferior exceptions, were those conducted by missionary societies and by Cherokees, Choctaws, Chickasaws, and Creeks for their own communities. Many reservations had no schools at all. Overall, the government's record of fulfilling treaty promises to erect and operate schools on the reservations in exchange for land was weak at best and duplicitous at worst. The Yankton Agency is a case in point. According to the treaty of April 19, 1858 – the date Yankton was established – the United States government would provide $10,000 for schools, and children between seven and eighteen years of age would be required to attend school nine months a year. However, it would be years before a formal program was instituted. In 1863, for example, the Yankton agent complained that a school at the agency could not function because parents insisted on taking the children on their seasonal hunting expeditions. The only schooling provided from 1865 to 1868 was a summer class taught by the wife of the reservation agent. A day school did open on the reservation in 1869, but the Presbyterian mission that established it received no government compensation.[7]

In 1870 the government assumed a new responsibility toward the education of Native people, with Congress appropriating $100,000 for industrial and other schools. Congress also ended the treaty process and rhetorically denied Native sovereignty by declaring indigenous peoples to be "wards" of the United States. In 1873, through the Indian Office's new educational division, the government began to establish its own schools and hire its own teachers. Commissioner of Indian Affairs Edward P. Smith (1873–75) expressed frustration with day school programs and appealed for the establishment of government-operated boarding schools as the only way to guarantee the acquisition of English: "It is . . . well nigh impossible to teach Indian children the English language when they spend twenty hours out of twenty-four in the wigwam, using only their native tongue." The report of the government agent at Yankton, John G. Gasmann, an Episcopal minister, reflected those concerns. The only schools at his agency at this time were day schools run by the Presbyterian and Episcopal missions. Gasmann deemed these schools inadequate because of the poor attendance record, which he maintained was the result of lack of discipline in the Yankton home. His wish for a boarding school as a way to solve that problem was fulfilled when Bishop William Hare was sent to the Yankton Agency, the new headquarters of the Episcopal mission, and supervised the construction of such a building in 1873, St. Paul's School for Boys. However, in spite of the call for increased government involvement, and although a number of boarding schools were established on the reservations, most of the education for Native people was provided in reservation day schools operated by a variety of religious agencies.[8]

The focus of all mission schools, of course, was on teaching Christianity, through whatever means were feasible, and that meant teaching primarily in the vernacular. Yankton missionary John P. Williamson, who was raised at the Dakota Mission his father had cofounded, defended instruction in the Dakota language by arguing that the goal of education at the Presbyterian school was "to impart ideas, and not words": "English is an unknown tongue to the Indian children. It takes three or four years in a boarding school, and twice as many in a day-school, for them to learn enough English to make it a fit medium for the conveyance of ideas to their minds. Is it right to pass by their native tongue, the natural vehicle for the conveyance of truth, and spend half a dozen years preparing some other mode of conveyance for our truths . . . ? We say emphatically, no; the primary steps in education must be given in the mother tongue." This is not to say that English language instruction in the mission schools was ignored. However, whatever English language instruction was provided in the bilingual schools at the Yankton Agency rarely produced English-speaking students, and by 1878 agent John Douglas was fiery in his objection to the pedagogical approach of these missionaries: "In the Indian schools on this and other agencies along the river it is earnestly maintained that the Indian mind cannot be properly developed or knowledge imparted to it except through the medium of the Indian tongue. I fear as a consequence that the study of English is too much neglected, and it is very rarely spoken by the children. . . . This I regard as a serious evil." Douglas's sentiment concerning missionaries' use of Native languages to teach Native people was shared by many in the government service. His argument that the study of English was "too much neglected" soon became an even more strident call for education exclusively in English.[9]

FROM BILINGUAL EDUCATION TOWARD ENGLISH ONLY

Lieutenant Richard Henry Pratt, who had created an English-only program for prisoners of war in Florida (1875–78), convinced the government to recruit students to attend English-only manual labor boarding schools off the reservation. In 1878 the Indian Office sent Pratt to Dakota Territory to enroll students in the Hampton Normal and Agricultural Institute, a school General Samuel Armstrong had established for freed slaves. On "the principle of tak[i]ng the most pains with those who give the most trouble," Lakotas were the first to be approached because they had continued to engage in armed resistance to encroachment on their lands. A special effort was to be made to enroll girls, for Pratt believed that the goal of civilizing Native communities could be achieved only if the females were transformed into models of European American domesticity. As the recruitment project expanded, the government followed what historian James Gump describes as a pattern of imperial rule: the attempt to convert the leaders first in order to diminish the source of power in the colonized community. Accordingly, in 1879 Pratt was assigned to persuade Lakota leaders at the Rosebud Agency to allow their own children to attend the new Carlisle Indian Industrial School in Pennsylvania.[10]

Pratt had some difficulty procuring these students, however. According to Pratt's memoirs, Spotted Tail initially refused, insisting that he did not want his children to learn the thieving and mendacious ways of European American people. Pratt then used English-language literacy as the carrot to induce Spotted Tail to agree to his educational plan. Telling Spotted Tail (through an interpreter) that if he had known the English language he would not have been tricked into signing a treaty that deprived him of his lands, Pratt underscored the link between literacy, economic security, and civil rights: "Cannot you see it is far, far better for you to have your children educated and trained as our children are so that they can speak the English language, write letters, and do the things which bring to the white man such prosperity, and each of them be able to stand for their rights as the white man stands for his?" According to Pratt, Spotted Tail and the other leaders were so convinced by this argument that they offered to part with many more children than he was authorized to take from the agency. Pratt suffered a slight reversal in 1880, however, when Spotted Tail visited Carlisle and removed his own children from the school. Spotted Tail was appalled to discover that they were dressed in military uniforms, had been baptized and given Christian names, and were forced to do manual labor. Furthermore, they had not learned to speak English, nor had they become literate – which Spotted Tail had been led to believe was the main objective of the school.[11]

Despite occasional setbacks, Armstrong and Pratt took advantage of every opportunity to sharpen their public relations skills. As soon as their respective American Indian programs commenced at Hampton and Carlisle, they devised various ways to demonstrate to a skeptical public that English-only education off the reservation could succeed in civilizing Native people. Even before the first group of students arrived at Hampton, Armstrong wrote to Pratt: "Be sure to get a variety of styles of first class photographs of the Indian youth you bring, letting them appear in the wildest and most barbarous costume." For years the two men disseminated before-and-after photographs to illustrate that the students could adopt the outward appearance of European American society (see figs. 3 and 4 for the

3. Tom Torlino (Navajo) on arrival at the Carlisle Indian Industrial School (1882). Photograph by J. N. Choate. Courtesy of Cumberland County Historical Society, Carlisle PA.

4. Tom Torlino (Navajo) three years after his arrival at the Carlisle Indian Industrial School (1882). Photograph by J. N. Choate. Courtesy of Cumberland County Historical Society, Carlisle, PA

most famous and widely circulated set of photographs). School newspapers, offered nationwide by subscription, reprinted photographs of students eating and working, published anecdotes about their second-language acquisition, and reported on their attendance at religious services and conversion to Christianity.[12]

The movement toward English-only education, as Hampton and Carlisle made clear, was not designed to put an end to the Christianizing of Native people. Christianity was the dominant religion of the United States, and missionaries, government officials, and philanthropists all encouraged Christian teaching in American Indian schools because they believed in "its power as a practical element of civilization," to use the phrase of humanitarian reformer Herbert Welsh. Allowing the continuation of Native spiritual practices was unimaginable to these Christian Americans, historian David Wallace Adams has argued, for indigenous traditions encouraged and strengthened the very values the schools were attempting to erase. Booker T. Washington, a graduate of Hampton who was "house father" to the Hampton boys in the Indian Department from 1880 to 1881, later explained this civilizing project in a nutshell: "No white American ever thinks that any other race is wholly civilized until he wears the white man's clothes, eats the white man's food, speaks the white man's language, and professes the white man's religion."[13]

However, students returning to the reservations from boarding schools had few opportunities to apply the skills they had learned and virtually no employment. Reunited with their families, most resumed their former way of living and speaking. This outcome paradoxically fueled the government's determination to expand off-reservation schooling but did not inspire more job opportunities. By now it had become clear that reservation day schools were difficult to sustain because parents were reluctant to cooperate. Although school attendance was not a federal mandate (policies differed according to state), treaties with some Native communities contained clauses for mandatory attendance at schools established on the reservations. Government agents went to great lengths to enforce this policy by withdrawing rations or sending police to round up students. Even when police were successful, however, Yankton agent W. D. E. Andrus expressed frustration that parents persisted in practicing tribal customs at home and thus continued to hold sway over their children. Clearly, a battle for control over the children's minds and spirits was taking place on the reservation.[14]

The government determined to shift the balance of control by changing the site of battle, and so the Indian Office began to speed up the establishment of off-reservation boarding schools, in the interest of preventing students' "return to the blanket." According to Secretary of the Interior Samuel J. Kirkwood (1881–82), the eradication of tribal culture and its concomitant problems could be achieved only through the children's acquiring the English language and only away from their parents: "The difficulties to be overcome are mainly these: The Indians do not speak and do not wish to learn to speak our language. . . . It is not probable that much can be done in the way of teaching our language to adult Indians, but much may be done and is being done in the direction of so teaching those of school age, and our efforts to maintain and extend Indian schools should be earnest and constant." In 1880 the Indian Office issued regulations for the guidance of government agents that emphasized the importance of teaching in English, but it stopped short of demanding an exclusively monolingual approach: "All instruction must be in English, *except in so far as* the native language of the pupils shall be a necessary medium for conveying the knowledge of English, and the conversation of and communications between the pupils and with the teacher must be, *as far as practicable* in English" (emphasis added). The next year Commissioner of Indian Affairs Hiram Price (1881–85) took it one step further, calling for enforced language acquisition: "The Indian child . . . must be compelled to adopt the English language." His wish immediately became reality at the new off-reservation government boarding school in Oregon, whose first rule – after cleanliness and obedience – was "*No Indian Talk*" (emphasis in original).[15]

In the early 1880s the schools had little central control, chaos reigned, and relatively little learning was taking place. Fostering English-language literacy for Native students was, as Commissioner Price said of the entire educational endeavor, "pioneer work." English-language policies and practices were subject to trial and error; there were virtually no precedents or textbooks to follow. In 1885 Commissioner of Indian Affairs John D. C. Atkins (1885–88) placed the new superintendent of Indian schools, John H. Oberly, at the head of the Indian Bureau's new Education Division, in an effort to make the educational program more efficient, which paralleled the movement toward centralization for all schools in the United States. Oberly immediately addressed the lack of uniformity in methods of instruction and emphasized that the textbook materials were inappropriate for Native children's needs. The principal of the Haskell Institute, for one, had written to Oberly about this matter, claiming that the stories in the conventional readers furnished "as much meaning to the Indian as would stories of the actual condition of Moon-ites or Sun-ites to us." Many of the schools were modeled after the common school system, which provided free education in knowledge and skills and socialization into American mores, but Oberly recognized that Native children could not be taught effectively in the same way as "white" children.[16]

Despite the recognition that the educational program devised for English-speaking children was unsuited for Native students, virtually no one in the government up to this time suggested an alternative to English-only education. Even Commissioner of Indian Affairs Thomas J. Morgan (1889–93), who had unique insight into some of the weaknesses of the schools because he was a professional educator – the first nonpolitician selected for the post – remained committed to English-only instruction. Drawing on his expertise, Morgan pointed out that the academic expectations of the present programs were unrealistic: even the most advanced Native students were given no more than a grammar school education. He understood that it was not possible for students to acquire academic literacy in English during the three-year or even five-year term that most of them spent at the industrial schools, noting that it took fourteen to fifteen years for children in the public schools to complete a course of study. However, Morgan was as much a product of his time as were the government officials and reformers who preceded him. He never questioned the civilizing project, and thus his rhetoric reflected the prevalent assessment of Native languages and cultures as signs of "barbarism and paganism." Paradoxically, instead of calling for more pedagogical support for linguistic and cultural difference, Morgan suggested doing away with support altogether. He determined to replace Indian school education with public school education. However, this program too ended in failure because he underestimated not only the problems accompanying differences in language and culture but also the racism of public school parents.[17]

One notable exception to the demand for English-only education was Superintendent of Indian Schools William N. Hailmann (1894–98), a well-known leader of the educational movement that was based on the work of Friedrich Froebel, who stressed active learning and a balance of respect between teacher and student. Although he had no experience working with

Native children, Hailmann's background as a German-speaking immigrant sensitized him to their needs. He understood that punishment for speaking one's own language, common in the schools, was counterproductive. He argued that the vernacular enabled children to express feelings and thoughts and that it was the means through which they were "held in ties of sympathy and love" with their kin. Furthermore, he understood the personal and linguistic benefits that could accrue when teachers acknowledged the inherent value of knowing two languages: "The possession of one language, far from being a hindrance in the acquisition of another, rather facilitates it. The sympathy and respect which a teacher shows for the idiom of the child will be rewarded in a hundredfold by the sympathy, respect, and affection with which the child will apply himself to the acquisition of the teacher's idiom." In addition to encouraging teachers to learn the language and culture of the children they were teaching, Hailmann advocated an end to rote learning, the "stupid, mumbling repetition of words" from decontextualized spellers and readers, and published a lengthy *Syllabus of Language Work* to guide teachers toward more productive second-language instruction. In his annual reports, he proposed a curriculum based on conversation related to subjects of interest to Native children, arguing that teachers should take into account students' own resources and experiences and build on them to make possible the acquisition of a new language and culture. Only when students were taught to appreciate their own ways of knowing, he maintained, could they move forward as language learners. Among his accomplishments during his four-year tenure was the development of a kindergarten program staffed by teachers who spoke the children's home languages.[18]

However, Hailmann's plan was formulated within the context of the civilizing project. His goal was to inculcate "respect and love [for] what is good and best in the American civilization, to which the red children of plain and forest are to be led," which demonstrates that his bilingual approach was not devised in the best interest of Native languages and cultures. Furthermore, Hailmann privileged industrial training over literacy acquisition for Native students, leaving the door open for his successor, Estelle Reel (1898–1910), to focus exclusively on vocational training at the expense of Hailmann's educational philosophy. In 1900, the year Zitkala-Ša published three eloquent pieces in the *Atlantic Monthly*, Reel proposed a new course of study that tied virtually all learning for Native students – including the study of English – to industrial, domestic, and agricultural training, arguing that "the theory of cramming the Indian child with mere book knowledge has been and for generations will be a failure." As Tom Holm has pointed out, now that the schools had failed to assimilate indigenous populations, old representations appeared in new guise, marking Native people as incapable of intellectual advancement.[19]

By the end of the nineteenth century, even the philanthropic reformers had lost faith in residential education as a tool for assimilation. The optimism that had accompanied the opening of the first off-reservations boarding schools was gone. Government-sponsored education for indigenous people in the new century would not be intellectually based or even balanced between intellectual and practical pursuits. As Frederick Hoxie and Alice Littlefield have established, schooling was to be exclusively practical, thus officially preventing all but a very few from achieving economic prosperity. The boarding schools were geared toward producing low-paid workers to supplement the cheap labor force that had previously been drawn primarily from the ranks of immigrants and other economically deprived populations. According to this way of thinking, the English language would be useful to the vast majority of Native people only insofar as it provided opportunities for them to serve the needs of European American middle-class society. If the Bureau of Indian Affairs hoped that its failure rate would decrease when the measure of success in the schools was changed from acquiring literacy in a second language to acquiring vocational skills, however, it miscalculated. Margaret Connell Szasz shows that whatever approach to American Indian education the bureau tried met with failure. Native families were interested in education that would help their children gain skills useful in the real world. But the government did not seek input from the families. Consequently the vocational curricula designed by Reel and her successors did not prepare most students for either reservation or urban life.[20]

In blaming the students rather than acknowledging the failings of the school system, most officials failed to take into account several factors that impeded second-language and literacy acquisition in the Indian schools. The numerous archival documents I have examined reveal that these barriers included boredom and anxiety, for too often the curriculum was poorly designed and tedious, the language lessons were decontextualized, and the teachers were untrained, incompetent, and culturally insensitive. Many students spent little time in one place, moving from mission to government school, from reservation to off-reservation school, or from Indian school to public school. Sometimes their education was interrupted or even cut short because of changes in government policy. Daily manual labor – which the boarding schools depended on to help meet institutional costs – took its toll. As a 1928 government-sponsored investigation (known as the Meriam Report) revealed, many students at boarding schools experienced illness or depression, typically the result of old buildings with insufficient ventilation, crowded dormitories, low sanitation standards, inadequately trained medical staff, poor nutrition, abnormally long days, and lack of extended recreation. The military atmosphere at some schools precluded the warmth of family life that might have provided stable mental health. A significant number of students left or ran away to escape abusive treatment, including sexual harassment and assault. Largely because of the way the school system was structured, most students achieved little more than a grammar school education, if that, and consequently acquired only a low level of language proficiency. Only the rare student became fluent in the second language. Those who had maintained their first language could return home and immerse themselves in a traditional life, but too often students left school with weak skills in both English and their native tongue and suffered feelings of inadequacy related to linguistic and cultural loss.[21]

LANGUAGE, CULTURE, AND RACE

To understand how the United States government could perpetuate a failed English-only educational system, it is necessary to examine the assumptions underlying its program as articulated in the discourses related to language and culture. And here the complexity of government policy decisions is especially evident, for they were deeply embedded in strongly held beliefs informed by Christian doctrine and philanthropic approaches to education. For example, W. D. E. Andrus, the reservation agent at the Yankton Agency, framed his discussion of schooling in religious and humanitarian terms, declaring that education for Yanktons was "their only salvation" and that teachers should be "devoted to the welfare and improvement of their students." The purpose of education in his mind was to use English to inculcate European American values: "I cannot too strongly condemn the practice of teaching in the Indian language. . . . It is believed by nearly every one of experience that it is both time and money thrown away. The day-schools should be in charge of competent, practical, self-reliant, *white* teachers, who would devote all their energies to teaching in the English language, and in *English only*" (emphasis added). Andrus's rhetoric reflected the prevailing notion that the English language represented an entire culture and functioned as the conveyer of mainstream "practical, self-reliant" values. According to Charles and Mary Beard, this nineteenth-century celebration of self-reliance was tied to the doctrine of individualism, which was more than a mere extension of the democratic notion of individual rights. Reinforced by the spread of a popular form of Darwinism, the tenets of individualism held that society was an aggregate of competing individuals and that only the most ambitious and industrious would survive and succeed. The primary signifier of success was the accumulation of private property. Because individualism as understood by European American society was not evident in communal tribal life, David Wallace Adams argues, its lack was viewed as a barrier to Native peoples' acculturation.[22] As the language of individualists, English was believed to be capable of breaking that barrier and thus of improving students' lives.

Andrus's racial emphasis on "white teachers," too, was compatible with the notion of cultural improvement, according to the colonialist discourses of the day. According to historian Alden Vaughn, Anglo Americans had not always viewed Native people as essentially different in color. In the seventeenth century, for example, their hue was typically thought to be a result of environment. However, as Vaughn has shown, once the color line was drawn and indigenous people were identified as "red," race prejudice was added to existing prejudice against Native languages and cultures. By the late nineteenth century, few people could accept the idea of Native peoples' full participation in European American society. Andrus's insistence that the teachers transmitting the culture be white reflected a nineteenth-century construction of race as a concept that determined not only ethnic stock but also character. As Robert Berkhofer Jr. explains, outward characteristics were believed to mirror inner qualities. Andrus's pedagogical theory dictated that English should be taught to indigenous people but should not be taught by them, thus keeping European American society in a position of control. In essence, he subscribed to what Reginald Horsman has identified as a European colonial view: the belief that Caucasian people were destined to exert dominion over other races.[23]

Underlying these notions about language, culture, and race was a view of civilization that was linked to the popularized version of social Darwinism – biological determinism – that had gripped the country. The colonialist discourse that permeated the culture infused even the language of the growing number of humanitarian reform groups, known collectively as "Friends of the Indians." Although they objected to the government's duplicitous relations with Native communities, these Protestant reformers shared the government's views about what acquiring English as a second language signified. For example, after visiting several Episcopal schools in 1882 – including St. Paul's School at the Yankton Agency – reformer Herbert Welsh would write: "The children gain a knowledge of the English language, which is an absolute necessity to any future *progress in civilization*" (emphasis added). In tying the English language to the notion of progress in civilization, Welsh's rhetoric reflected a theory of social evolution that viewed civilization as developing in a series of stages. Popularized by United States ethnologist Lewis Henry Morgan, this theory proposed that a society could advance from "savagery" (hunting and gathering) through "barbarism" (making crafts, cultivating crops) to "civilization" (developing a written form of language). In Morgan's account, most indigenous people had already developed naturally from a savage to a barbaric condition, but he emphasized that movement to the next stage would be slow. Likening their progress to that of the once-barbarous Anglo-Saxons, Morgan maintained that it was unrealistic to expect Native people to "jump ethnical periods," and he proposed a slow process of initiation through agricultural education. It should be noted, however, that reformers typically deviated from the latter view. For example, although Herbert Welsh subscribed to Morgan's overall paradigm, his writings also show that he believed the boarding school experience could speed up the evolutionary process: "[The Indian] has already shown himself capable of effort . . . and has given promise of increased capacity in the future could but a fair chance be accorded him."[24]

At the same time, paradoxically, some reformers questioned Native peoples' innate ability to learn English. A few months after the government boarding school opened at the Yankton Agency in 1882, an article appeared in the *National Journal of Education* – later reprinted in the Dakota Mission's bilingual newspaper – explaining why the students in this school had trouble learning English: "If their *inherited observation* gives them remarkable facility in learning to [hand]write and perform other simple constructive exercises, *other inherited characteristics* make the acquisition of the English language a task of peculiar difficulty" (emphasis added). The article's emphasis on innate characteristics reflected a prevailing view that heredity was an important aspect of race. In major periodicals published from the mid–nineteenth century on, as Horsman has shown, the American public was informed repeatedly that mental and physical differences between the races could be proved scientifically. Those who subscribed to this view did not necessarily think that traits were transmitted genetically, which would mean that change could take place, if at all, only at a natural evolutionary pace. References to heredity instead usually denoted cultural transmission, which allowed for more rapid acculturation through education. Still, as Alexandra Harmon has argued, underlying this belief was a sense that racial identity was inherited, more a matter of ancestry than of culture. In the minds of many educational reformers of the time, ability to learn language was linked to racial identity.[25]

ENGLISH, NATIONALISM, AND IMPERIALISM

To the Indian service, the advantages to the country of Native people's acquiring English outweighed any benefit to Native people themselves. Superintendent of Indian Schools John B. Riley (1886–88) dropped the humanitarian rhetoric long enough to state explicitly that it was in the nation's best interest to foster the use of English among indigenous populations in order to prevent social degeneration: "More than twenty thousand of their children now of school age are without school privileges. They are growing up without knowledge of our language and consequently with an imperfect conception of our institutions, learning the vices rather than the virtues of our civilization. Our self interest, as well as the higher sentiments of justice and humanity, demand that the subject be considered in the light of its great importance." Riley's link between language and behavior demands special attention, for it suggests that to know English is to be virtuous and that to be ignorant of English is to be susceptible to vice. At the same time, Riley's words implicitly acknowledge that the human models of debauchery were those for whom English was a first language, a reality that Native leaders and enlightened reformers remarked on repeatedly in their criticism of government policies.[26]

During this period, the rhetoric surrounding English-only instruction reached a peak as it became more explicitly ethnocentric. And there was no more patriotic spokesperson for this view than Commissioner of Indian Affairs J. D. C. Atkins, who declared: "There is not an Indian pupil whose tuition and maintenance is paid for by the United States Government who is permitted to study any other language than our own vernacular – the language of the greatest, most powerful, and enterprising nationalities beneath the sun." Atkins's view of the superiority of English-speaking people was linked to the national sense of the country's "manifest destiny" to dominate territory. In a lecture titled "Manifest Destiny," published in *Harper's New Monthly Magazine* in 1885, for example, historian John Fiske used what he called "the doctrine of evolution" to conclude that the "English race" would colonize every land that was not already controlled by a civilized body. He even predicted that a century hence the world's business would be "transacted by English-speaking people to so great an extent" that everyone in the world would "find it necessary sooner or later to learn to express his thoughts in English." Commissioner Atkins's rhetoric, then, reflected the late-nineteenth-century British and United States yearning to establish linguistic domination worldwide: "True Americans all feel that the Constitution, laws, and institutions of the United States, in their adaptation to the wants and requirements of man, are superior to those of any other country; and they should understand that by *the spread of the English language* will these laws and institutions be more firmly established and widely disseminated" (emphasis added).[27]

In the past most officials in the Indian service saw acquiring English as only one – albeit a crucial – component of the civilizing mission. But Atkins raised the stakes when he declared that it was the main purpose of education, linking this goal to the country's other colonizing projects: "Nothing so surely and perfectly stamps upon an individual a national characteristic as language. So manifest and important is this that nations the world over, in both ancient and modern times, have ever imposed the strictest requirements upon their public schools as to the teaching of the *national tongue*. Only English has been allowed to be taught in the public schools in the territory acquired by this country from Spain, Mexico, and Russia, although the native populations spoke another tongue" (emphasis added). Native leaders might well have agreed with Atkins on the role (their) language played in forming a national character. But a major flaw in the logic of Atkins's argument was that the United States had no national tongue. As Shirley Brice Heath reminds us, the United States Constitution makes no mention of an official language because early national leaders chose not to designate one. Recognizing the plurality of American society and reluctant to be coercive, they allowed for the maintenance of multiple languages in the United States. Thus bilingualism could flourish in private life and in more public spheres such as newspapers, religious societies, and social institutions. Although there were periodic and persistent efforts to impose English as the sole medium of instruction in public educational institutions, many states permitted instruction in languages other than English in the public schools even well into the twentieth century. English was not mandatory as the medium of instruction in most states until after World War I.[28]

Acceptance of particular languages was dependent on their political or social favorability, however. For example, the 1880s witnessed an anti-German fervor that was linked to the anti-Catholic movement. Most of the new immigrants to the United States were Catholic, and combined with the entrenched German-speaking population, they were considered a threat to the political balance in several states. Legislatures in Illinois and Wisconsin passed laws requiring that elementary subjects be taught in English in both public and private schools but later repealed these acts. Four cities – St. Louis, Louisville, St. Paul, and San Francisco – discontinued use of German as a medium of instruction in their public schools. Some German communities responded by creating their own private school systems.[29]

Language policy in the public schools could be made only on the local or state level, but the reservation schools were subject to the edicts and whims of the federal Indian Bureau. On December 14, 1886, Atkins ordered that "in all schools conducted by missionary organizations it is required that all instruction shall be given in the English language." On February 2, 1887, he followed up with a clarifying statement: "I have to advise you that the rule applies to all schools on Indian reservations, whether they be Government or mission schools. The instruction of the Indians in the vernacular is not only of no use to them, but is detrimental to the cause of their education and civilization, and no school will be permitted on the reservation in which the English language is not exclusively taught." Not surprisingly, Atkins's dictum created an uproar among the missionaries. According to Thomas L. Riggs, although all instruction was in English at the Episcopal mission's boarding school at the Yankton Agency, Bishop William Hare protested vigorously, proclaiming that the government had gone "too far": "In its present shape [the English-only order] is tyrannical and officious; tyrannical because it is a wanton measure, uncalled for and unjustifiable by precedents; officious because it is not within the province of anyone to dictate to me the methods I shall employ in disseminating knowledge." The July 1887 issue of the *Word Carrier,* the bilingual newspaper of the Dakota Mission, carried this front page opener: "*It has come!* The government has begun its work of breaking up missionary work among Indians" (emphasis in original). In the following issue, editor Alfred L. Riggs intensified his rhetoric: "NO MORE INDIAN SCHOOLS! NO MORE INDIAN BIBLES! NO MORE MISSIONS! These are the logical results of the present policy of the Indian Bureau, as shown in its astounding rules against the use of the Indian language."[30]

Some reservation agents had interpreted Atkins's order to mean that religious services in the vernacular would not be allowed, and in September Atkins addressed this misconception by explaining that he had no intention of preventing the preaching of the gospel in the churches or of hindering the efforts of the missionaries. But the *Word Carrier* was not satisfied. Atkins was guilty of what one writer called "imperial absolutism," and the Dakota Mission wanted to chastise him publicly. In November it drew on the power of the eastern establishment by publishing an editorial from the *New York Times,* which stated in part: "The truth is, it is outside the province of the United States Government to interfere in a matter like this. Even Indians have some rights, and among them is the right to the use of their own national tongue. For the Government to offer them the advantages of schools on condition that they give up their language, is not an act of kindness, but a piece of stupid tyranny." In December the *Word Carrier* resorted to outright mockery when it published a letter to the commissioner of Indian affairs from a young Native teacher who himself had learned English as a second language and was now critical of the grammar used by a clerk in the Indian service: "[The] clerk wrote this sentence: 'I cannot *in no case determine* whether they continue or not, except they are taught exclusively in English.' Will you please tell us what he means? Mr. Riggs said he could not, it was such *bad* English. Even Mr. Cross, our new Missionary, could not tell us, and he says he played Third Base on the Yale nine which beat Harvard. And will you tell us if we must teach English which no one can understand? This is very bad" (emphasis in original).[31]

This chapter came to a close after the Reverend John P. Williamson, among others, went to Washington to present the missionary case to President Grover Cleveland, who favored Christian missions for Native communities. Although the order was never officially rescinded, the Indian Bureau published a pamphlet in 1888 titled *Correspondence on the Subject of Teaching the Vernacular in Indian Schools* to correct the impression that reading the Bible in the vernacular was forbidden. Because the issue had not yet faded away, the new commissioner of Indian affairs, John H. Oberly (1888–89), reiterated the clarification in December 1888: "It is not the intention of the Indian Bureau to prohibit the reading of the Bible by any Indian in any language, or by anybody to any Indian in any language or in any Indian vernacular, anywhere, at any time."[32]

The mixed effects of the exclusion order defy a neat analysis. From the Dakota missionaries' point of view, the order turned out to be beneficial. As a result of being told they could not study in their own language, the missionaries said, Dakotas gained a deeper appreciation for the Dakota Bible. The crisis also inadvertently contributed to a renewed pride in Dakota literacy: Dakotas increased their demand for books written in Dakota and resolved to perpetuate the language. Reports from the reservation documented continued resistance to speaking English, even when the population was known to be capable of using the language. According to the government agent at Yankton, whatever approach was tried in order to transform the residents into an English-speaking community before 1890 had met with failure: "Of those who can speak English, the majority of them don't care to use the language if they can avoid it. Even the school children will not speak it away from the school building without being forced to do it."[33]

This resistance to the commissioner's English-only order deepened the conviction of English-only proponents that Native languages must be eradicated, leading to some drastic approaches to forced language acquisition. The Yankton agent, for example, suggested that students caught speaking the vernacular "ought to be punished." This punitive view was not limited to the reservation agents. Disciplinary measures, including solitary confinement and beatings, were used at many off-reservation schools when students violated the rule forbidding use of Native languages. Anyone seeking support for such an approach could find it in Commissioner Thomas J. Morgan's insistence that "the Indians must conform to 'the white man's ways,' peaceably if they will, forcibly if they must."[34]

By the 1880s educational systems in cities across the United States were compelled to respond to the growing number of immigrants from eastern and southern Europe for whom English was not the first language. The strains produced by this linguistic and cultural diversity intensified the call for homogeneity, now identified as "Americanization." As early as 1882, Yankton agent William M. Ridpath linked this concept to the Native students who were learning English: "Besides teaching the rudimentary branches the children are taught to speak English; taught the manners and ways of the whites; in a word, *Americanized*" (emphasis added). By the 1890s the massive immigration had changed the public school system, and the apparent Americanization of immigrant children confirmed for Commissioner Morgan the necessity of pursuing this goal with Native children:

> The children of foreigners taken into our public schools, where they learn the English language and associate with our children, imbibe their ideas and grow up to be in all respects Americans in spirit, in habits, and in character.
>
> The process now going on by which nearly 20,000 Indian children are gathered into English-speaking schools, where they are taught by English-speaking people, where they learn the correct use of the English language, and come into relationship with American life and American thought, and have begotten within them new hopes and desires and changed ideas of life, is certain to work a revolution in the Indian character and to lift them on to a higher plane of civilization *if it can be allowed to operate long enough.* (Emphasis added)

For Morgan, Native peoples' acquisition of English was just a matter of time. In his mind, their lower stage on the civilization continuum could account for the differences between their slow progress and the more rapid progress of the "foreigners." But he neglected to take into consideration the crucial differences between immigrants, who made a choice to come to the United States, albeit under duress in many cases, and indigenous people, who were already here. Immigrants who arrived in the late nineteenth century perceived English to be America's birth language, and they accepted America as their new country. Native people knew that English was America's adopted language, and they understood that America had imposed itself on their land.[35]

Underlying the Americanization movement was the assumption that Native languages could make no meaningful contribution to United States society. The annual reports of the secretary of the interior throughout this period reveal that almost none of the government officials, missionaries, or humanitarian reformers involved in American Indian education at the turn of the century could appreciate the inherently positive value of Native ways of expressing and communicating ideas and beliefs. Despite his detailed "Rules for Indian Schools," Commissioner Morgan was unable to create a successful English-language program, in part because he never understood what language signified to Native people. Likewise, his superintendent of Indian schools, Daniel Dorchester (1889–93), considered Native people's "strong prepossession in favor of their own language" to be only the result of their prejudice, "varying from mere suspicion and dislike up through all the grades to animosity and furious hatred against the white race." Not even missionary John P. Williamson, who had been bilingual in English and Dakota since childhood, could understand the significance of first language in the lives of the people he served. In a retrospective account of his twenty-five years at the Yankton Agency, Williamson reported that although the Yankton Sioux had acquired many of the outer trappings of European American society – for example, its clothing and lodging – they were slow to adopt its language. Williamson saw their persistence in speaking Dakota (or Nakota) primarily in negative terms, as an "innate determination *not to learn* the English language" (emphasis added).[36]

Americanization was not a neutral process. Given that the acquisition of English was predicated on the elimination of Native languages and cultures, Americanization was designed to stamp out tribal identity. Given that English functioned as a conduit of American institutions and laws, Americanization through English-language teaching was designed to end tribal sovereignty. Given that tribal sovereignty was tied to the land, Americanization signified loss of territory. Paradoxically, although the rhetoric of Americanization implied that students would be allowed into American society as Americans, the reality of the Americanization movement was that Native people were being asked to reject the ways of their ancestors and families without being offered the benefits of full participation in the European

American way of life. In the end, the concept of Americanization through English-language teaching served to reinforce the United States government's linguistic, cultural, political, and territorial control over Native people.

The story of English-language instruction for Native people in the nineteenth century was not a simple matter of European Americans versus indigenous communities, or even of English-only education against the will of all Native people. The intersection of language, culture, race, class, and politics influenced every sphere of American Indian education in the late nineteenth century. A case in point is the school system of the Cherokee Nation.

Recognizing the threat to their survival, Cherokees accepted government and missionary assistance to educate their children in English as early as 1817. They developed their own written language early in the nineteenth century – at the time the only written Native language in the country – and subsequently achieved an extraordinarily high rate of first-language literacy, higher than that of the surrounding English-speaking population, in fact. They had their own constitution, elected officials, and legal system. They published the bilingual *Cherokee Phoenix* in 1828, the first Native newspaper, and supported bilingual and English-only mission schools. In spite of their willingness to accept many aspects of European American life, and against the will of the majority, Cherokees were forced to leave their homelands in the Southeast in 1838–39. Those who survived the Trail of Tears eventually established a new life in what is now northeastern Oklahoma. Supported largely by money received from the sale of lands to the federal government, the Cherokee Nation established a national school system in Indian Territory.[37]

Reports to the commissioner of Indian affairs in the 1870s reflect the tension in the Cherokee community between Cherokees who promoted English-only instruction, Cherokees who demanded Cherokee-only education, and missionaries who advocated bilingual education. The bilingual federal government agent, John B. Jones, a Baptist missionary, decried the English-only schools run by the Nation. With a few exceptions, he claimed, only the children from English-speaking families flourished in English-only programs, while children of Cherokee-speaking families regularly dropped out of school. The situation was complicated by perceived racial differences, for the English bilingual speakers typically had intermarried with European Americans whereas Cherokee monolingual speakers had not. And it was further complicated by socioeconomic differences, for many in the bilingual English-speaking community were wealthy or at least economically secure, whereas the Cherokee-speaking community included many more poor families.[38]

Although Cherokee was used as a language of instruction in schools in Cherokee-speaking neighborhoods, according to scholars William McLoughlin and Devon Mihesuah the leaders of the nation were interested primarily in demonstrating their achievements in accordance with the standards of European American society. The main beneficiaries of the Cherokee Nation's elite educational system in which English was the language of instruction were the children of wealthy Cherokees who had intermarried with European Americans. However, this educational program was different from the system created by the United States government in two important ways. First, it grew out of the necessity for Cherokees to survive and to maintain sovereignty. Second, even though Cherokee culture typically was not taught in the English-only schools, pride in Cherokee identity was assumed and fostered, and bilingualism was encouraged.[39]

THROUGH PARENTS' EYES

In 1880 a Yankton parent wrote to the head of the Hampton Institute: "Perhaps you don't know that Indians think of their children a great deal, and don't know how to have them out of their sight one day."[40] Parents and guardians were reluctant to send their children to boarding schools because they wanted to keep their families together and maintain the primacy of their own forms of education. Without the children, the continuity of their cultures and traditions would be disrupted. Some Native communities engaged in organized resistance to enforced English education; others had little or no choice but to comply with formal schooling. Native responses to schools and experiences with them were so different across cultures that it is impossible to describe them all. A few examples, though, can give a sense of the diversity that complicated the educational movement.

On the Great Plains, some elders continued to resist any interaction with

European Americans. However, in response to the growing European American population, parents increasingly sensed that the children would need to learn English to ensure survival and economic opportunity. As an Omaha parent expressed it: "Before many years have gone, our dealings will be mostly with the white people who are coming to mingle with us; and, to have relations with them of any kind, some of us must learn their language and familiarize ourselves with their customs." Letters written in 1880 from Dakota adults to students at the Hampton Institute – admittedly used for propaganda purposes – reveal that some families were enthusiastic about the prospect of the younger generation's learning a new language:

> My son, . . . I am glad that you are trying to learn. . . . Learn to talk English; don't be ashamed to talk it. (Crow Creek Agency).

> I want you to learn to talk English. . . . I hope some of the boys will learn to be a teacher, when they come back that they can teach the boys and girls. This is the only chance you have; get all the good you can. (Fort Pierre, Dakota)

Support for English as a second language was often linked to an appreciation of the value of knowing more than one language to communicate across cultures. Many adults were themselves bilingual, bidialectal, or multilingual in Native languages, including sign language.[41]

In response to Apaches' continued armed resistance to the encroachment of European Americans on their lands, the United States government broke a treaty agreement in 1876 by forcing all Apaches onto one reservation. The next few years were characterized by a series of conflicts that repeatedly ended in Apache surrender, followed by periods of peacefulness. After the last surrender, in 1886, the United States government sent Apaches to Florida as prisoners of war – including those who had not participated in the fighting and those who had served as scouts for the United States army. The next year Richard Henry Pratt arrived in Florida to recruit for the Carlisle Indian School. At first he had no volunteers, so he lined up potential candidates and made selections. Geronimo told at least one future leader, Daklugie, to go to Carlisle to learn European American ways and thus how to cope with the enemy.[42]

After a devastating four-year imprisonment at Fort Sumner (1864–68), Navajos (Diné) signed a treaty that required them to send their children to school, a treaty that guaranteed their return to a portion of their ancestral homeland. Nevertheless, the United States government failed for many years to fill its classrooms with Navajo students. Parents told their children to hide whenever one of the school representatives appeared. In the 1880s, when the government agent sent police to pick up the children for the boarding school at Fort Defiance, miles away from home, the situation became violent. Parents were not persuaded to send their offspring to school until they were promised food and supplies for a ten-year period. Even then, according to Frank Mitchell, they resisted by sending children only selectively.[43]

In 1680 the Pueblo-Hopi revolt resulted in the temporary expulsion of Spanish colonizers and missionaries. Given this history of resistance to colonization, there was predictable opposition in the 1890s when the federal government ordered all the children at the Hopi Mesas to attend school. According to Albert Yava, the conservatives, known as "the Hostiles," feared that Hopi traditions would be undermined. The progressives, or "Friendlies," were willing to cooperate only because they believed survival depended on learning European American ways. The villages were also divided over whether the children should be sent to day schools or boarding schools. When the government boarding school at the Keams Canyon Agency was opened several miles from the mesas, the government agent attempted to lure families with clothes, tools, and other supplies. Parents who refused to cooperate had their children removed by force – sometimes right out of their arms – by policemen who arrived periodically to round up children and carry them off to school.[44]

By the end of the century, enough children had gone to government schools for all parents to have an understanding of the relative economic benefits and emotional costs of formal education. Parents could acknowledge the advantages of having a family member who could speak English and thus find employment, if any employment was available. But they also understood that they might be separated for years at a time. They had to struggle with the knowledge that their children might be subjected to corporal punishment, might have to struggle with a loss of identity and confidence, and might even forget their first language. Certainly parents knew that their traditional way of life was under siege in the schools, for it was clear that more than language was being taught.

Although some Native parents had themselves adopted or begun to adopt the ways of European American society, most of those who finally agreed to send their children to school wanted them to learn English and *only English* – not *English only.* For the English-only policy as articulated by the United States government meant education in a new life and religion, with no vestiges of traditional ways, and virtually all the parents objected to that uncompromising stance. Whereas the government's immigration policy left room for newcomers to speak their home languages in their local communities, its Indian policy attempted to deny this right to indigenous people. As it turned out, it was the very attempt to impose English through eradication of Native languages – and then to limit its usefulness – that created the most resistance. Without coercion, as the creators of the United States Constitution understood, and as Heinz Kloss's research establishes, people are more willing to learn whatever language provides the greatest opportunities for personal and economic security and advantage.[45]

Influenced and even blinded by their preconceptions about language and culture, government officials remained insensitive to the desires of Native people themselves or the context in which they were seeking, or not seeking, education in English. The government's failure to achieve its goal of turning the entire Native population into speakers of English by the end of the nineteenth century was inevitable, in part because of government officials' own ignorance, indifference, and colonialist mentality. More significantly, the Indian Office underestimated the life-sustaining strength of linguistic and tribal identity. The United States government was able to wrest most of the land from the original inhabitants by the end of the century. It was even able to accelerate the annihilation of some Native languages and to compromise the existence of many others. But it did not succeed in removing Native people – or their ways of knowing – from the tribal or American landscape.

5. "Labor Conquers All Things" at the Carlisle Indian Industrial School. Courtesy of Cumberland County Historical Society, Carlisle PA.

2

Language, Pedagogy, and Ideology

When the government embarked on an educational program to teach Native students in English and English only, there were few if any trained teachers of English as a second language in public schools in the United States, despite the influx of immigrants who did not speak English. Language groups that wielded some political power, such as German speakers, were able to create their own schools, staffed with teachers who spoke the students' languages. In contrast, poor immigrant children, if they attended school at all, were typically drilled in English in the same material as English-speaking children, by the same teachers, even though they could not understand what the teachers were saying. The limitations of the teaching profession itself further hampered the development of effective pedagogy for these students. Before 1900, future teachers were trained primarily as apprentices or in normal schools that did not necessarily require high school diplomas for entrance. Thus many teachers who entered the Indian school system were poorly educated. Some could not speak English correctly themselves, even though it was their first language.[1]

The problem of attracting good teachers was exacerbated by Congress's refusal to allocate funds to ameliorate the appalling conditions on the reservations – for which the government itself was largely responsible – or to erect school buildings and provide desperately needed supplies to the schools, thus failing to honor treaty obligations to educate Native people in exchange for ceded land. The inability to staff a school adequately existed off the reservation as well. At one point the Albuquerque Indian Industrial

School had only two teachers for 130 students. Even the Carlisle School in Pennsylvania, whose conditions for teaching were among the best in the Indian service, occasionally suffered from a lack of staff.[2]

Even if worthy teachers had been available and willing, they might have had little chance to secure positions in the Indian service, given its political patronage system. In 1885 the first superintendent of Indian schools, John H. Oberly, initiated reform by suggesting that, at the very least, applicants should be required to provide proof of their qualifications for the job. In 1891 civil service rules were extended to cover the administrators and teachers in the schools in the Indian service. However, not even the civil service could guarantee that qualified teachers would be found. Under the aegis of the Indian Office, schools in the Indian service typically followed the standard public school curriculum and emulated conventional teaching methods. Most teachers were ignorant of the languages and cultures of the students they were hired to teach. This ignorance was so extreme that some were not even aware that there were multiple Native languages. According to Albert Kneale, when he and his wife undertook to learn the language of the people they were teaching on the Pine Ridge Reservation in 1899, "we thought we were studying Indian only to learn that we were studying Sioux."[3]

There was no doubt in the mind of anyone with any experience in the field that teaching in the Indian schools was quite different from teaching in the regular school system and that specially trained people were needed, largely because of the issues related to communication. As Indian School Superintendent John B. Riley put it in 1887: "To teach Indian children successfully requires the highest talent. . . . The work is more difficult than in a school composed of white children, for the reason that the pupils do not understand our language." With one exception in 1884, however, there were no institutes to prepare teachers for this new kind of teaching until 1890. These institutes finally gave isolated teachers an opportunity to make contact with others in similar situations and to learn new approaches. They could hear and discuss papers on such issues as "how to teach language," "methods of securing pure English in Indian schools," and "the most successful way to ensure the use of English by the Indian children." However, given the distance they had to travel and the lack of sufficient funding, relatively few teachers could take advantage of the training provided at the institutes. Lack of preparation for this specialized teaching contributed to the high turnover of teaching staff in the Indian service throughout its turn-of-the-century history.[4]

This chapter focuses on the actual classroom experience from the perspective of European American teachers who were pioneers in late-nineteenth-century bilingual and English-only programs on and off the reservations. There is a paucity of evidence about what took place in the various classrooms across the country. Few instructors who taught in nineteenth-century schools designed for Native students wrote autobiographies, and those few accounts I am aware of were written by people who taught very late in the nineteenth century, beginning their work from 1899 to 1901.[5] My goal was to learn how English was taught at the time the government was increasing its involvement in American Indian education and to determine how the teachers made sense of their own experiences while they were actually teaching. To that end I turned to a number of contemporaneous sources, including government documents, mission and school records, periodical articles, and autobiographies. The first part of this chapter examines some early schools: the Dakota Mission's bilingual education programs (1860s to 1870s), Quaker-run schools for Caddos and Kiowas (1871–73), and Lieutenant Richard Henry Pratt's classes for prisoners of war in Florida (1875–78). I then turn to the heart of the chapter: English teaching at the Hampton Normal and Agricultural Institute (from 1878 to the end of the century).

Founded as a school for freed slaves, the Hampton Institute was not designed exclusively for Native students. Unlike the government boarding schools, it had access to private financial resources and – as a contract school – was relatively free of the control of the Indian Office. Even though Hampton was not representative of all off-reservation boarding schools, I focus on it for several reasons, the most obvious being that it was the first eastern boarding school to accept large groups of Native children from the reservations in the late nineteenth century. More important, of the school principals, who were all required to submit annual reports to the commissioner of Indian affairs, Samuel Armstrong provided the most detailed accounts of instruction. Combined with vivid descriptions of actual classrooms in Hampton's newspaper, *Southern Workman,* the school left an extensive record of the earliest English-language teaching at a boarding school. In addition, the Hampton material reveals the complexity of the teaching and learning process for Native students. Other school principals either put a false positive spin on the educational outcome or, if they mentioned language instruction at all, focused on the negative. Perhaps most significant, underlying Hampton's work was a commitment to put into practice what it considered to be the best educational philosophy of the time. The school made a concerted effort to create a program in which the English language became a "flexible instrument," to borrow Armstrong's term.[6]

Despite its pedagogical innovations, however, the Hampton Institute was similar in one important way to other schools that provided American Indian education. It subscribed to the idea that the English language sustained and transmitted a superior culture. The teachers at Hampton assumed that Native students were in need of conversion to the European American way of life. The language these teachers used to discuss students' progress often reflected deeply ingrained stereotypes of Native people. Nevertheless, to see education at Hampton solely as a tool of cultural and linguistic imperialism would be to deny that the teachers considered here strove to create a supportive teaching environment. At the very least the story of English-language teaching was riddled with contradictions and inconsistencies. On the one hand, these teachers were motivated by a desire to teach well and to improve students' lives. On the other, they were a product of their virulently ethnocentric times. Their pedagogy inevitably reflected these conflicting views.

To ascertain the purpose for which English was taught and to demonstrate the ways knowledge was conveyed about – and through – language, my analysis goes beyond mere description of the course of study in the various schools. As Michael Young argues, curriculum is not simply a set of courses but a social construct that reflects the ideological framework of those who have the power to administer education programs.[7] The teaching of Native students was shaped by the government's English-only mandate and by the associated discourses of colonialism that permeated the dominant European American culture. This chapter examines how teachers consciously and unconsciously transmitted their beliefs and assumptions about language and culture to their students.

The first mission for the Sioux was established in 1834 by the American Board of Commissioners for Foreign Missions (ABCFM). These missionaries created a written form of the Dakota language using the roman alphabet and – because they were first in contact with the Mdewakanton (Santee) Sioux – translated English into the Santee (Dakota) dialect. Having rendered Dakota in their own image, they then used the language to convey their own values, for example, by translating a primer and the Bible. Dakotas, it turned out, were not unfamiliar with the concept of texts, though they had created them in a different form. Thus, according to one of the missionaries, Dakotas had a relatively easy transition to literacy instruction:

> Among the Dakota a book was a marvelous thing. It was *wowape*. Heretofore the *wowape* had consisted of rude paintings and hieroglyphs. The figures of men and horses, of battle axes and scalps, drawn with coal or cut in bark, told the story of a war-party. Rude pictures of pipes and horses' feet, with other such hieroglyphs, told a man's history. So when the hieroglyphs of language were first introduced among them, and arbitrary signs made in the ashes with a stick, or drawn with chalk on a board, spelled out words which they had been accustomed to speak and to hear, that also they called *wowape*.

From 1837 on, missionary Stephen Riggs ran a school in the Dakota language, having found that teaching classes in English bore little fruit. Students had linguistic ability, he noted, but were not willing to speak, even when they had learned to read. Teaching in Dakota, he maintained, produced entirely different results: "It was their own language. The lessons printed with open type and a brush on old newspapers, and hung round the walls of the school-room, were words that had a meaning even to a Dakota child. It was not difficult. A young man has sometimes come in, proud and unwilling to be taught, but by sitting there and looking and listening to others, he has started up with the announcement, 'I am able.'" Years later, at the Crow Creek Agency in Dakota Territory, missionary Thomas Williamson's son, John, used Riggs's bilingual method to teach the Mdewakanton exiles from Minnesota during their imprisonment after the Dakota uprising of 1862. John P. Williamson found the captive populace "eager to learn."

Perhaps because of the school's large size – more than one hundred students (actually prisoners of war) – he developed a mentor system of education in which more proficient students taught Bible reading to the less advanced.[8]

In the long experience of the ABCFM, educational advancement for Dakotas came through first-language literacy, the missionaries having discovered that the "quickest way to teach them English is to give them a start and set them to thinking by the study of their own language first." And so when John P. Williamson established a mission school at the Yankton Agency in 1869, the students – mostly grown or nearly grown young men and women – were first taught to read and write in their own language: "Our course in instructing Indians . . . is to prepare primers and a few books in the most simple and necessary truths, including the Bible in the native tongue. We expect every scholar who understands no English to complete this primary course first. Most Indian children are able to do this in six months. Then we introduce them to the English language." Williamson developed bilingual materials that added to biblical studies. He translated English-language texts such as *The Nursery,* published versions of which appeared side by side in the newspaper of the Dakota Mission, *Iapi Oaye – The Word Carrier:*

WAIHAMNAPI QA WAECONPI
1. Amy he wicincana waste
tehindapi heca, taku ota en;
tuka ohan wanji sica yuha: taku
econ kta ihanmnapi ecen anpetu
ihauke ecee.

DREAMING AND DOING
1. Amy was a dear,
good girl in many things;
but she had one bad habit:
she was too apt to waste
time in dreaming of doing,
instead of doing.

At the Santee Agency (Nebraska), Stephen Riggs's son Alfred established a school that one of its students, Charles Eastman, would later refer to as "the Mecca of the Sioux country." The Santee Normal School provided bilingual education, with both European American and Native teachers. Alfred Riggs published a number of texts in Dakota, including *Wicoie Wowapi Kin* [*The Word Book*] (see fig. 1) and a translation of *Guyot's Elementary Geography.* He subscribed to the Dakota Mission's view, promoted in *Iapi Oaye,* that teachers needed to know the language of their students in order to "gain their hearts": "It is the province of the teacher to make himself understood by his scholars, and not of the scholars to expend all their strength in vain efforts to understand what the teacher means. It is sheer laziness in the teacher to berate his Indian scholars for not understanding English, when he does not understand enough Indian to tell them the meaning of a single one of the sentences he is trying to make them emphasize properly, though they have no idea of the sense." Despite the Santee School's promotion of bilingual education, however, in some of the houses where the students boarded, conversational Dakota was forbidden.[9]

The Dakota Mission's bilingual approach to education must be understood within the context of the primary goal of the mission: to convert students to Christianity. Missionaries, just like the philanthropic reformers, viewed themselves as saviors, not oppressors, and to the extent that they helped to alleviate suffering, they were. At the same time, George Tinker argues, they were complicit in a process of cultural genocide – the systematic destruction of another group's core values and traditions. Likewise, Robert Craig maintains that these Protestant missionaries undermined Dakota integrity through their participation in a colonizing project. It is important to note that a number of Dakotas welcomed the missionaries, willingly sent their children to school, gave permission for their families to be baptized, and even became missionaries themselves. For some people Christianity filled a need. However, Virginia Driving Hawk Sneve points out, the need for Christianity was created largely because Native spiritual practices were disrupted or forbidden by the United States government. Drawing on oral history, Sneve notes that adopting Christianity was necessary for survival and for peaceful coexistence with European Americans, but she emphasizes that Dakota traditions were never fully abandoned.[10]

Missionaries fostered bilingualism to promote conversion rather than to honor or maintain the Dakotas' language and culture. Moreover, missionary bilingual education was articulated in terms of the savage/civilized paradigm that consigned indigenous people to an inferior position. In the words of one of the teachers at the Santee School, the students were "being trained with a view to help bring their people *out from the darkness* which surrounds them" (emphasis added). This perspective was reinforced through biblical quotations that mirrored a colonialist construction of Native people as childlike and infantilized the adults who in fact composed much of the student body: "The teacher, with his superior mind, should be able to learn half a dozen languages while these *children of darkness* are learning one" (emphasis added). The experience of the Dakota Mission suggests that supporting the local language did not necessarily preclude reinforcing structures of domination and subordination.[11]

TEACHING ENGLISH ON THE RESERVATION:
A QUAKER EXPERIENCE, 1871–73

As part of President Grant's peace policy, inaugurated in 1869, government agencies and schools in the southern plains were placed under the direction of the Society of Friends. In 1871, in the spirit of what he called "Christian benevolence," Quaker Thomas Battey accepted a position as teacher in a new school for Caddo students begun at the Wichita Agency. As he wrote in his 1875 memoir *The Life and Adventures of a Quaker among the Indians,* Battey felt like a "novice" even though he was an experienced teacher because – from his European American perspective – these "wild children" spoke a "strange language." Battey was a product of his ethnocentric times, but he nevertheless gained insight into what a teacher at an Indian school needed to do in order to deal with the unique language situation, especially when no interpreter was available: "The teacher must get down to the very foundation of knowledge, begin at the very beginning, and work his way up through the double process of teaching the spoken as well as the written language, – adapting his system of instruction to their crude comprehensions, making use of the things they know to teach them the things they do not know." An example of Battey's approach was using the blackboard to draw pictures of animals the students were familiar with, writing the name in English along with the Caddo name (in roman characters), which the students supplied. After students had drawn several animals and printed the names on slates, Battey introduced animals that were not found in America. This process, he claimed, awakened their interest in geography, an area in which they made rapid progress. At the end of his eight-month tenure, Battey reported that two-thirds of the thirty-eight students, ranging in age from five to twenty, could read "fluently," and twelve had made "commendable progress" in writing.[12]

Under close scrutiny, however, the students' astonishing accomplishments seem less so. Like many of his contemporary teachers in the Indian service, Battey's definition of reading was essentially a decoding of words, a rote recitation. And by writing he meant primarily handwriting, which drew on the students' existing proficiency in drawing. Furthermore, as Battey admitted, the greatest progress was made by the newer students who had some previous knowledge of English, which underlines the difficulty of teaching language to students to whom it was entirely unfamiliar. Significantly, Battey omitted an assessment of the students' speaking ability, which suggests it was too limited to be worthy of mention. And eventually he came to depend on an interpreter, a student who knew both English and Caddo, which indicates that an English-only approach was too burdensome for the teacher.[13]

On his next, self-chosen assignment – teaching among Kiowas, many of whom were still hostile to the government – Battey was much less successful in implementing an English-language program. Invited to educate the children of Kicking Bird, a leader who advocated peace with the European American population, Battey received government funding for his project. He met with an immediate challenge. Given the band's nomadic lifestyle, he had to teach out of a tent rather than in a school building. His attempts to have the children repeat words from his handmade charts occasionally met with derision from the men in the camp, who periodically visited the class. School was irregular, with no attendance on some days, and opposition grew as parents began to suspect that the teacher represented a threat to their children's health. Furthermore, Battey acknowledged, many adults were unwilling to cooperate with the representative of a government that refused to comply with the terms of its own agreements.[14]

Battey realized that his school was a failure, for he could see little improvement. He eventually gave it up but continued to try to teach English. From Battey's own description of events, however, it appears that the only language learning taking place was his own. He had undertaken to jot down and memorize Kiowa words and was gradually able to make himself understood. However, his salvationist rhetoric suggests that he had no vision of an interactive language exchange. Believing that "His grace is sufficient even for their redemption, by which they must be changed . . . from this savage, heathen life to that of Christian civilization," Battey used the Kiowa language only to explain the advantages of a European American way of life. The Kiowas listened politely but continued to prefer their own customs and practices. For a short time, most of them resisted the English language and all it represented. They had temporarily gained the linguistic upper hand.

Approximately two years later, however, Kiowa leaders and warriors were forced to surrender to United States troops and become students of English when they were held as prisoners of war by the army from 1875 to 1878.[15]

In April 1875, after months of hostilities that led to surrender in Indian Territory, army lieutenant Richard Henry Pratt escorted one Caddo and seventy-one Kiowa, Comanche, Cheyenne, and Arapaho leaders and warriors to Fort Marion, Florida, and remained to supervise their military confinement. Ranging in age from nineteen to (at least) fifty years, none of them could understand or speak English. Pratt's admiration of the prisoners' comportment en route, added to his previous positive experiences working with Native scouts, made him sympathetic to their situation. Wanting to promote understanding between them and the surrounding European American community, he declared English speech a priority and soon persuaded several local women to teach the prisoners.[16]

Because Fort Marion was in St. Augustine, a winter retreat for wealthy northerners, including some leaders of the American Indian reform movement, Pratt's educational program received widespread attention. Harriet Beecher Stowe, for one, took an interest in the school and wrote an article in which she described an English-language class she had observed: "When they read in concert, when they mastered perfectly the pronunciation of a difficult word, when they gave the right answer to a question, they were evidently delighted." For almost three years, the prisoners received daily instruction. According to Pratt's memoirs, the effort was a great success: "Most of the young men learned to write fairly intelligent letters . . . and the English language became the common tongue among them, thus breaking down the wall of language which separates the tribes as fully as between them and our own people."[17]

Pratt's goals for his students were limited, however. He was satisfied with a student who "learned to express himself a little in English," but he reacted negatively when the civilizing process worked too well. When Howling Wolf returned from Boston after five months of medical treatment, for example, his awakened sense of self-dignity and consequent resistance incurred Pratt's wrath. According to Pratt, Howling Wolf "had taken on altogether too much Boston for his resources and future good. He became insubordinate and insurrectionary, and I was forced to discipline him."[18]

After demonstrating that his English-language program aimed to produce docile subjects, not independent thinkers, Pratt raised enough funds through private sources to provide another three years of education for those who wished to continue schooling after their prison term ended. General Samuel Chapman Armstrong, head of the Hampton Institute, was the only educator Pratt wrote to who agreed to accept the former prisoners of war as students. Armstrong believed that his educational philosophy could be applied to indigenous people as well as to freed slaves. But he also understood the financial advantage. "There's money in them I tell you," he wrote to his wife.[19] In April 1878 Pratt brought fifteen (and later two more) of the young men to be educated at Hampton. With the new students on display at a welcoming assembly, Pratt had to provide an honest assessment of their linguistic accomplishments, as reported in the school newspaper, *Southern Workman*: "The work grew from teaching A. B. C. to classes, to a school. We had four classes, taught by four ladies, an hour and a-half each day. . . . Now some of them read the Bible nearly as well as some that are here. They learned to sing twenty of the Moody and Sankey hymns. They got by heart many passages of scripture which they could repeat to you. They have many good things thus stowed away in their hearts and minds. It may be, as some would say, that these are parrot-like speeches, but that is the way we all learn at first." The "parrot-like speeches" were soon in evidence when two of the new students came forward to speak. After almost three years of English-language education that had been glowingly praised by none other than Harriet Beecher Stowe, the two young men struggled to express themselves:

I go school – way off. I come a school – three days, way off – sea. I go school here – I like here. Come last night, half-past one. Came not here – other house. I went school – Miss Mather. (Matches, Cheyenne)

I to-night came. Because my head don't know. St. Augustine, one year – say don't know – A, B, C, I can't talk – A, B, C, D, two years. Good womans – Miss Mather – Miss Perrit – Mrs. Gibbs, good. (Su-Cam, Kiowa)

The students clearly needed a more effective English-language program.[20]

From the beginning, Native students at Hampton had the advantage of being taught by a group of teachers who were well versed in a progressive, student-focused approach to education. Several of the teachers had attended the training school in Quincy, Massachusetts, headed by Colonel Francis Parker, a well-known educational philosopher. Parker's program placed the child and the child's natural environment – rather than the subject matter or the teacher – at the center of instruction. He advocated and put into practice a democratic approach to education, in direct contrast to schools that employed an impracticable system of rewards and punishments to force students to learn. Disdainful of school curricula that separated language skills from content learning (e.g., through drills), Parker encouraged teachers to plan lessons that could build on students' background knowledge to create curiosity about new subject matter. As one observer noted, Parker envisioned classrooms as active places, for he believed that children were "more interested in seeing how a thing is done, *after they have tried to do it themselves,* than before" (emphasis in original). Parker did not present a lockstep approach but rather taught teachers to observe the development of the child and then urged them to devise their own methods accordingly. Parker's philosophy fit well with the situation the teachers at Hampton faced when Native students first arrived. Having no experience teaching English as a second language, they had no choice but to create an entirely new program adapted to the students' varied needs.[21]

According to Helen Ludlow, a Hampton teacher, the St. Augustine students began instruction immediately, four days a week, with two days devoted to manual labor and one to church. The Hampton teachers soon discovered that although these students were able to write and understand the language, they could not speak English well. Six weeks later, while visiting the school, Pratt declared that his St. Augustine protégés had made discernible improvements, particularly in the clarity of their speech. Furthermore, everyone agreed that they were quick and motivated learners, leading Armstrong to believe that his school had found a productive way to educate Native people. The government agreed to fund the program, with a stipend for each pupil enrolled, and sent Pratt to Dakota Territory to recruit new students. Pratt returned on November 5 with forty-nine students, including nine girls, ranging in age from ten to twenty-five. Among this first group at Hampton were eleven children from the Yankton Agency, including Zit-kala-Ša's older half-brother, David Simmons. Even though an interpreter remained at the school to help with the students' transition, Armstrong had an enormous task ahead of him. One-third to one-half of the prospective students had never been to school; most of those who had been to school had been taught primarily in the Dakota language; only a few could speak or understand "some" English; and only two could speak English well.[22]

Fortunately for Armstrong, African American students played a significant role in Native students' second-language acquisition. The first party of Dakota students at Hampton petitioned within a month of their arrival for permission to room with African Americans, in order to make more rapid progress in English. "House father" Booker T. Washington reported that African American students willingly roomed with the newcomers and became valued mentors. For example, in the summer of 1878 they took turns helping teacher James Robbins, himself a Hampton graduate, during language lessons. One African American student who participated during the evening study hour observed that Native students "seemed eager to learn, and made rapid progress. After you told them anything once, they scarcely ever forgot it." While in charge of Native girls during the summer vacation of 1879, Amelia Perry, a Hampton graduate, took advantage of the opportunity to teach them English, using the dormitory rooms as the source of language. The language learning was reciprocal: Perry later reported that she had learned many of the students' words and expressions and could understand much of what they were saying in their own language.[23]

In addition to the person-to-person contact in the study halls and dormitories, students had other opportunities to interact and socialize with speakers of English. In his monthly report, Washington told of Native students who had joined the debating club or paid a social call with an African American friend. In summer 1879 the school instituted an annual "outing system" when twelve boys were sent to farms in western Massachusetts, the expressed goal being to "separate them and give them a chance to learn to speak English," as they had "complained of 'too much Indian talk'" at the school. Female students, too, went north during the summer, to do domestic work in private homes. When they returned, these "Massachusetts girls," with their stylish new appearance and improved English, became models for other students.[24]

Despite the obvious language-learning value of these out-of-classroom interactions, Armstrong found it necessary in early 1879 to create an exclusively Indian department to meet the students' unique language needs. Students who knew enough English were able to participate in regular classes. Throughout the years, Hampton divided and redivided students in an attempt to create some unity within classes, and students were promoted as they progressed. As was true throughout the Indian school system, students entered school not only at different times of the year but also with different levels of linguistic proficiency, stemming partly from the different ages at which they were first exposed to English and partly from the length and depth of their previous study. Students' own literacy and oral proficiencies varied as well: for example, some students could read and write more fluently than they could speak, and vice versa. The aim of academic education for all the students was to acquire English – spoken, read, and written – not only in the language class but also in their other courses of study, which in the first year included arithmetic, geography, and vocal music.[25]

In principle, the teaching at Hampton took place only in English. But initially at least, providing English-only education proved impossible. For any learning to take place, teachers took advantage of students who had previously studied English. One of the first was an eighteen-year-old who interpreted for the Dakotas when they first arrived, delaying his own coursework to help the boys who knew no English. Cora Folsom reported that because he had learned English at the Presbyterian day school at the Yankton Agency, thirteen-year-old David Simmons was "much in demand" as an interpreter. Laura Tileston described a reading class in which a lesson was "put into Indian by the smallest member of the class, a bright little half-breed." Harriet Holbrook wrote of a similar situation in her arithmetic classroom when a young man had the benefit of translation: "As light dawned upon his beclouded mind, he exclaimed, 'No wonder the colored boys learn faster than we; they understand what the teacher says to them.'" During the summer, some advanced-level Native students had the opportunity to teach beginners. Interpretation – as a last resort – became an essential strategy, as student teacher Zallie Rulo reported: "To be sure, I did not teach Indian, nor did I talk Indian to them, but only when it was very necessary to do so."[26]

Students' English speaking outside the classroom fluctuated, at best. In the early years, at least, students who knew sign language used that method to communicate with one another: they often captured the sun's rays in mirrors, threw the light a short distance to attract the attention of the person they wanted to talk to, and then communicated with their hands. In 1885 the rules at Hampton allowed students to use their own languages before breakfast and after supper during the week and all day on Sunday. Students received no "severe" punishment if they broke these rules. Instead, Hampton encouraged voluntary English speaking through a system of rewards. As time went on, according to Tileston, students were more supportive of one another's efforts: "One of the boys said, 'These new Indians learn English very fast . . . we teacher these boys and help them all times, and that makes encourage.'" In 1888, after the Indian Office had turned up the heat on the English-only rule, Armstrong felt under pressure to comply, declaring that English speaking "is the law of the school, and at roll-call every night each reports on his or her adherence to it."[27]

By the 1890s more students were entering Hampton with a stronger English background than in the earlier years. In 1898 Principal Hollis B. Frissell explained that recruitment had become more selective, with education at Hampton being "held out as a reward of merit to the members of the Western schools." Hampton chose only students who had been satisfactorily educated in government and missionary schools; no students came directly "from the blanket." At the end of the century, Hampton eliminated the Indian department, and all Native students were placed in regular classes with African Americans.[28]

From Bodies to Objects to Words

In the late nineteenth century, teaching language typically meant teaching grammar, and teaching grammar typically meant following a procedure of definition, example, and application. For example, students would first learn the definition of a noun, then note examples of nouns, and then apply that knowledge in exercises requiring them to select nouns from among other words. In spite of research that demonstrated the ineffectiveness of this method, it continued to hold a place in the schools because of educators' unswerving faith that grammar could train students to express themselves precisely. The teachers at Hampton discovered immediately that this method had no value in the second-language learning of Native students. Hampton thus deferred conventional grammar teaching for the first two or three years of a student's education.[29]

At first teachers used no textbooks at all. According to James Robbins,

"The best teachers for the Indians are walking blackboards, and . . . those mysterious things called books ought not to be put in their hands for months to come." Cora Folsom, inviting readers to experience vicariously the inside of her classroom, explained what it meant to teach without texts, especially when no common language existed between teacher and students: "By a series of home-made signs, which they are quick to interpret, they are made to understand that they are to repeat your greeting, and you are rewarded with a gruff or timid 'Good monink,' and thus another gate is opened to the 'white man's road.'" Instead of books, bodies became useful resources for learning. Students were taught to match action to word, for example by following directions to "stand up," "sit down," "walk softly," "speak louder," or "march out." If the action suited the word particularly well, Josephine Richards reported, "some of the tall braves [would] go through the exercises of pulling hand or sleeve, bending wrists and arms, shaking right hand or left with great gusto."[30]

Next, students were exposed to a variety of objects – including pictures and toys – that were brought into the classroom. In using this method of second-language instruction, Hampton teachers were sometimes guided by manuals designed for teaching modern languages that composed the Worman's Modern Language Series. This series was based on the "natural method" derived from the ideas of Swiss reformer Johann Heinrich Pestalozzi (1746–1827), whose work exerted a strong influence on progressive United States schools in the late nineteenth century (including Francis Parker's). Pestalozzi started with the experiences and observations of children and proceeded by means of carefully orchestrated oral instruction to systematic and organized knowledge. Proponents of the Pestalozzian method, also known in the United States as "object teaching," sought to replace the rote and passive learning that characterized nineteenth-century American classrooms. Worman's approach in his French and German books aimed to foster speaking ability in a second language, as opposed to the method of grammar drills commonly used for language teaching in the schools. Using pictorial illustrations for the names of objects, his books attempted to show teachers an immersion approach for teaching a second language without the help of the first. In this monolingual approach, teachers presented the new language in a particular order, for example, beginning with the name of a thing, such as *boy,* and leading up to actions described or positions of objects, for example, *The boy* is under *the table.*[31]

Although in theory Pestalozzian-based lessons enabled classrooms to flow naturally according to the students' cognitive development, in many United States classrooms the lessons often became little more than rote learning, adding little to students' knowledge and understanding. Given that in the first years Hampton relied partly on Isaac Lewis Peet's *Language Lessons [for] Deaf Mutes and Foreigners,* the tedium that often accompanied object teaching may well have characterized some of the Hampton classrooms. Peet claimed that his monolingual method for second-language students was preferable to their learning from a bilingual instructor, for it enabled the child "to think at once, without any process of translation, in the new language upon which he is fixing his mind." But he described an approach that was numbing at best, with the teacher presenting twelve objects at a time, writing their names on the blackboard, touching an object, requiring a student to pronounce its name, pointing to the name, repeating the exercise until the student understood that the written word represented the thing, then pointing to the name and requiring the student to touch the corresponding object, and so on.[32]

Despite the drawbacks of object teaching, it led to some productive teaching approaches. By using materials based on principles of the oral Pestalozzian method, such as Guyot's Geographical Series, the teachers at Hampton were able to integrate oral language lessons into a content-based course, discovering through practice what late-twentieth-century second-language researchers would deem an invaluable approach to acquiring language and literacy. In one class, for example, the teacher used Guyot's method of locating things in the room and the school grounds and then having students make picture maps of their own surroundings. They then brought objects into the classroom, one teacher beginning with a watch for the purpose of studying time. Once students learned that lesson (it took two months), they were shown a globe and taught the seasons, climates, and motion of the earth. After lessons on the zones, which used pictures of life in Alaska, the United States, and South America, students made a hemisphere, complete with lines for the equator and tropics, and placed in each zone pictures of the houses, animals, and vegetation they thought would be found there. Given the special linguistic circumstances of the Hampton classroom, the Pestalozzian method proved invaluable, inasmuch as it called for dealing first with observation and direct participation rather than definitions and abstract rules.[33]

Some of the seemingly conventional methods followed in the public schools had actually been pedagogical innovations in their time. For example, "recitations," in which the teacher asked a question and the students responded with predetermined answers, had been introduced into nineteenth-century schools as a reform designed to improve instruction by reducing teachers' lecture time and increasing students' speaking time. At Hampton these recitations were sometimes referred to as "conversing in English." However, a transcription of a classroom observation reveals that that did not necessarily signify authentic communication: " 'Good morning. What a pleasant day it is. Yes; it is very pleasant. Are you glad? Yes; I am very glad.' " But even these dubious innovations were transformed by the second-language nature of the project and by the Hampton teachers' openness to developing new methods. For example, the teachers explored the differences between English and the students' own languages, at least in terms of phonology and prosody. They discovered that certain sounds were extremely difficult for students to articulate and that the lack of the rising inflection at the end of a question in Dakota presented a stumbling block. Helen Ludlow noted that "the Indian gutturals do not open the mouth and give the free play of muscle that clear cut English requires." To attempt to solve this perceived problem, teachers drilled students constantly in phonetics and worked on their enunciation. They noticed that students were more comfortable expressing exclamations or questions when they performed aloud in concert and could support one another in their efforts, and so they provided more opportunities for group recitation. These interactions with students helped to counteract some of the stereotypes teachers held of Native people. In the words of Josephine Richards, "however little they can say in English, [they] have very speaking faces, remarkably free from the stolidity generally considered a characteristic of their race."[34]

The traditional technique of memorization, too, took on a new life in the context of second-language acquisition. When Native students memorized complex texts such as poems, a common practice in the public schools, the results were questionable, for they often did not understand what they were saying. A case in point was the following verse:

Yield not to temptation, for yielding is sin
Each victory will help you some other to win
Fight manfully onward, dark passions subdue,
Look ever to Jesus, He'll carry you through.

The teacher who assigned this passage maintained that she had carefully explained the meaning of the words, but "notwithstanding it all, the verse was misapplied," as she soon discovered when a female student proudly told her, "one Indian girl she get mad with me, I no like, she big temptation; I no yield to temptation; I fight her, I was victory!" Teachers eventually found short dialogues that students memorized and repeated daily to be more "useful in giving confidence in speaking, by familiarizing the pupils with common expressions." They also discovered that when the texts to be memorized grew out of students' direct participation, the students were more likely to comprehend. After her students had drawn, molded, and talked about the subject of a geography lesson, for example, Laura Tileston gave them definitions to memorize: words first and then sentences. Students would commit these definitions to memory and at first recite them aloud in concert. Tileston found that, with this method, students' interest soon became "strong enough to overcome their natural distrust of trying to speak English" and they became "anxious to 'say it alone, that good way.'" Though "hardly the method we would take for white children," Tileston's experience suggested to her that this was "what the Indian needs most."[35]

Francis Parker's student-centered approach was evident in the choice of stimuli for the "talking class." One teacher, for example, brought in pictures that related to the students' former life, in one case a depiction of a man on horseback hunting buffalo. Through these pictures and through objects, students were taught to make sentences and put them together. As a result of her classroom teaching of geography, Tileston noted the link between students' interest in their past experiences and their willingness to speak: "Mountains, rivers, hills, lakes, and all physical features are their dearly loved friends, and they often come out of their shells, and tell of scouting parties among the mountains or hunting on the prairies." Observing that geography and natural history classes were particularly effective in prompting students to talk, the teachers brought live animals, stuffed specimens, globes, and sand tables (to mold divisions of land and water) into the classroom. Classes often took walks during school hours to learn the names associated with the natural environment. Teachers relied on role playing to promote spoken English, especially to help guarantee that students understood. For example, after Tileston realized that students had many single words in their vocabulary whose precise use they were unsure of (e.g., *where, when*), she created sets of playing cards, half of which had questions (e.g., "Where are you?" "What are you doing?") and half of which had answers (e.g., "Here I am"; "I am sewing"). Students broke into two groups to ask and answer one another. Or sometimes teachers devised a more elaborate scenario, with one student playing the doctor and others coming to complain of illness, request medication, or get a written excuse from work.[36]

In addition to classroom activities, the staff also offered opportunities for speaking in the evenings. Students met for games conducted by teachers, such as Clap in and Clap Out, Go Bang, and Simon Says. They also practiced oral language in song. One of the Hampton Student Singers transcribed several Dakota love songs and then taught students to sing "simple exercises by note in time and tune." Many Native students also learned by ear the hymns and plantation melodies sung by their African American schoolmates and sang them while they worked. In 1884 the school formed a debating society, which presented recitations and poetry readings as well as debates on student-selected topics such as "Shall the white man be allowed on the Indian reservation?" and "Ought Indians to be permitted to vote?"[37]

Despite their efforts to foster speaking, the teachers found it very difficult to induce Native students to converse in English, even when the students understood what they heard. Although some spoke readily, most did not. Teachers noted that even advanced students were more willing to produce words in written compositions than to say them. At a farewell event for departing students, for example, one girl said, "If I had had time to write I would have spoken. I had many words to say." Some younger students spoke English only outside class and only to their (white) dolls, perhaps because the dolls could not criticize them, as Helen Ludlow suggested. Repeatedly, teachers referred to their pupils as "bashful" or "shy" and singled out Dakota students for their "excessive reserve." According to Tileston, teachers had difficulty accepting the silence, especially of the older students: "They are all eager to learn, but being ready to *learn* does not always mean ready to *use* a word, and it is not unusual to 'Stand awhile on one foot and then awhile on t'other,' while the noble Red man calmly makes up his mind about answering your 'How do you do?' and there is no need to try to keep cool, for a chill of uncertainty creeps up and down your back bone as you consider that he may decide not to say it at all" (emphasis in original).

Even in the more advanced classes, teachers had to fight the temptation to talk rather than to have students do so, especially since the students were "excellent listeners." Tileston explained that often teachers were doing most of the talking in order to satisfy the students' requests: "One boy from Arizona was interested to hear of his own country, but when I asked him to tell me, said, 'not now; I like you talk now; sometime you not talk, I tell you.'"[38]

After reading teachers' reports, Armstrong occasionally implied that the blame for not speaking English lay with the students. On one occasion, for example, he said that students' "progress in English has been hindered by an almost insurmountable reticence and reserve, and a strong disinclination to respond to oral teaching." Armstrong recognized, though, that reluctance to speak did not correlate with intelligence and abilities: "Their minds are keen and clear, and they show in the study hour a capacity for independent and continuous mental work." After more than ten years of involvement with American Indian education, Armstrong came to a greater understanding of the inner workings of the mind of a student who was in the process of acquiring a second language, noting that "he must carry on two trains of thought at once; he must not only recall facts, but think of the English words in which to clothe them." Perhaps because he himself had learned another language growing up in Hawaii as a missionary's son, Armstrong understood how slow acquiring a second language could be and that some people learned more easily than others. He also acknowledged that uncommunicativeness was often linked to students' desire not to embarrass themselves: "The Indian, having himself a keen sense of the ridiculous, stands in mortal terror of furnishing it to others, and . . . unless he is morally certain he has the right answer he often prefers to relapse into utter silence."[39]

For public relations purposes, the public was largely spared confrontation with this troubling reticence. At events sponsored by Hampton, visitors were treated to displays of English-language oral proficiency by Hampton's best students. In the 1886 anniversary exercises, for example, students presented a recitation in costume, titled "Indians of To-day," written by Elaine Goodale. Beginning with a stanza recited by Charles Doxon (who would later become a manual training teacher at Hampton), the performance was designed to reinforce the notion that Hampton was successful at achieving its aim:

My friends, I shake your hands! I'm ready
To do the work I once despised,
I've thrown away my bow and arrow,
I've taken up the plough and harrow,
I'm willing to be civilized![40]

Samuel Armstrong's approach to education at Hampton often ignored Native students' own needs and desires. As early as June 1879, the St. Augustine students expressed impatience with the lack of books. One complained that he would be the object of ridicule if he returned home without knowing how to read, and the teachers became aware that the "Floridas" needed "a more nourishing mental diet." As a former slave who had been denied the right to read, Booker T. Washington understood their frustration as well as their determination to grasp the opportunity to learn. In 1880 Washington reported that students longed to attend study hour and to have "a pile of books," just as the African American students did, but had not yet been "permitted" to do so. Postponing book-based teaching made sense in light of language differences, but the record shows that there was a hidden agenda. The focus on object learning in place of reading was linked to Armstrong's tendency to infantilize the students, for he believed that "the Indian is a child." He explained that "knowing the reaction sure to follow gratifying a childish desire for school books, we kept them back, to their discontent, gradually allowing their use in class hours thus gradually increasing their eagerness to know more."[41]

Once schoolbooks were introduced into the curriculum, however, new problems arose. Repeatedly, teachers decried the lack of texts adapted to their particular student population. The standard readers, used throughout the history of the Hampton Indian program, assumed a knowledge of language that many Native students simply did not possess. For example, the authors of a text used at Hampton, *Appletons' Second Reader,* stated that "the longer words to be met with in this Reader belong to the common vocabulary, and the child should learn to recognize them in print as he does in speech." Teachers were concerned not only about the level of lexical or linguistic difficulty but also about the appropriateness of content. The problem was acute with students who were already adults. Ludlow noted the absurdity of having grown men recite lines from a text designed for elementary pupils: "We smile to hear the braves taming their tongues to tell us how the naughty boy pulled the poor cat's tail, but the only doors into the royal domain of the English language seem to be measured for children at present, and so the six foot pilgrims must stoop."[42]

As was true throughout the duration of the Indian department, ill-conceived or inappropriate methods were regularly offset by the Hampton teachers' innovativeness and desire to help students learn. Because the primary reading books were ill suited to these adult learners, teachers initially distributed instead a series of leaflets whose contents included short historical anecdotes, facts of science, and simple Bible teachings. However, the teachers acknowledged that the pamphlets lacked the "charm" of books. The students' "worship of books" manifested itself when Helen Ludlow gave them a geography text after they had been taught orally from maps for several months. Ludlow found their gratitude "really touching." With the more advanced students, *Southern Workman* itself served as a reading text. Ludlow made a point of stating that these students read the items related to Native people with great pleasure and relatively little help. Washington noted that students had a "special fondness" for newspapers in their own languages, which were provided in the reading room.[43]

However, having committed to a monolingual approach and having no special training in English as a second language, teachers were often stymied by the challenge of teaching students to read. They had little trouble explaining the meaning of words representing physical phenomena, for they could bring objects into the class, draw them on the blackboard, or make gestures until the students understood. But the most basic words defied definition, as Harriet Holbrook reported: "'What that word *had* mean? I not know,' said a tall Omaha. *Which* proves another stumbling-block. Alas, that English should be such an unexplainable language!" (emphasis in original). History teacher Josephine Richards's anecdote reveals that true understanding could elude a student even when the context of the reading was familiar: "Not long ago, reference was made in a book to a league formed by Native tribes against the United States government, and when the definition of league was called for, the answer came very promptly, 'three miles,' that meaning of the word having just been acquired in their Reading class."[44]

Over time, with experience, teachers developed different methods to teach reading skills. In some classes, for example, students read aloud in concert, then took turns reading individually and taking correction from the whole class. Teachers supplemented reading lessons by asking students to draw the action depicted in the texts. Students also acted out scenes from the books. As the years progressed, teachers began to discover that the right content could foster reading skills, even in the lower division. As Cora Folsom theorized, "To read well with an Indian means that he must be *interested,* and to be interested he must have something think about and study over out of school" (emphasis in original). Subjects related to plants and animals were particularly appealing to students, according to the teachers. They also enjoyed numerous children's magazines, such as those used at the Quincy schools, which the teachers brought to class. After the passage of the Dawes bill in 1887, which offered land allotments in exchange for citizenship, advanced students in the "civilization class" read about current events in daily newspapers to prepare them for their "new rights and duties."[45]

Teaching writing at Hampton initially meant teaching penmanship, in large part because students could do it well. The former prisoners from St. Augustine, for example, had drawn in ledger books while incarcerated, a process that undoubtedly contributed to the development of their literacy, for they had also learned to write "handsomely" before they came to Hampton, as Ludlow noted. At Hampton the teachers used the Spencer method of handwriting instruction, the most popular system in the latter part of the nineteenth century. Spencerian copybooks included charts that indicated specific heights, lengths, and slants as well as guidelines on which students could correctly copy and combine letters. By April 1879 the St. Augustine students had filled three copybooks and shown great improvement.[46]

Teachers approached the nontechnical aspects of writing according to Francis Parker's philosophy: they designed purposeful lessons to develop thought and expression and to deepen students' enthusiasm for their work. Letter writing not only helped students practice what they had learned but also kept them in touch with family and friends at home and would be useful to them after they returned to their reservations. Students also wrote letters to people outside their inner circle. For example, after studying ants in an advanced science course, the class wrote letters to the donors of the microscopes to share what they had learned. Students who received aid from private sources were required to write "scholarship letters" to their patrons, to express gratitude and to report on their progress.[47]

Teachers regularly published students' letters in *Southern Workman,* and excerpts often appeared in Armstrong's annual reports to the commissioner of Indian affairs. To certify the letters' authenticity, students' errors were not edited out, as the following example shows: "I will trying to talk English and try to be good man, I know some of the white mans way, and I want to know some more so when I get my home I will try to teach my people thats way I want to do. . . . [T]he Indian people some are good those remember the Church but some are bad those did not remember the Church and did not like to go to school and did not like to be try good man and not work." Despite its apparent authenticity, this letter did not necessarily represent the student's own sentiments. For this student's views – typical of those published in the school newspaper – are remarkably similar to those expressed by Samuel Armstrong: "Put yourself in the place of these young Indians when they shall go to their homes. The grace of God only can save them. Without careful Christian culture our work will come to naught."[48]

The stated objective in reprinting student writing in *Southern Workman* was to give students pride in their work and to help them understand the purpose of writing. However, it also served as a propaganda tool for the Hampton Institute. One purpose of publishing student texts was to establish the legitimacy of Hampton's work in order to justify its federal funding and to increase philanthropic donations. In the words of teacher Elaine Goodale (Eastman): "Public support was slow to develop and imperatively needed. It was our part to stage a popular demonstration of the red man's innate capacity." Before they reached publication, the letters home were subject to what today would be called spin control. When reformer Alice Fletcher visited Hampton, for example, she advised students to send only positive messages about life at school: "Don't spend your time saying to your parents 'I want to see you.' . . . Try to make little pictures in your letters of your happy, busy life here." Armstrong noted that "some misstatements ha[d] been made and mischief done," undoubtedly because some students had written home to complain about the school experience and their parents had become upset. Despite the occasional setbacks, Armstrong promoted the weekly correspondence. From his public relations perspective, children's letters gave parents confidence that the school was indeed teaching English, and thus it helped in recruitment.[49]

Cultural and Linguistic Domination

Armstrong understood the unsettling effect of schooling, noting that "training the head and the heart creates a wholesome discontent." But his solution for addressing that discontent did not aim to provide most students with opportunities to achieve at high levels in society or even to attain equality. Literacy education for Native students at Hampton was central to its mission but was not its central mission. Armstrong focused instead on "training the hand." Accordingly, students spent much of their day doing manual labor. Insistence on vocational training as a goal of education was already an institutionalized goal in American education for freed slaves, the very population for whom Hampton was created, as well as for other minority and poor populations. This development coincided with a prevalent belief that backward peoples could slowly advance through a process of evolution. The purpose of education was to help students overcome hereditary deficiencies by building moral character through hard work.[50]

Like many other educational reformers of the time, Samuel Armstrong viewed heredity as an important aspect of race and saw language-learning ability as linked to racial identity: "Our northern Indians are slow in gaining facility in conversation . . . partly because of the[ir] race characteristics." However, racial attitudes did not necessarily categorize Native students as inferior. Comparisons with African Americans were inevitable at Hampton, and Native students fared well in these contrasts when the focus was on speaking English. According to Helen Ludlow, Native students had an advantage over African American students with a corresponding knowledge of English because African Americans had "race peculiarities" that Native students did not share. One peculiarity, she claimed, was a "musical ear" that led African American students to (mis)interpret words by their sound or to select melodious words that made little sense in context. Ludlow's linguistic theory was also governed by assumptions about class. She asserted that Native students had a "sharper habit of thought" than African American students, which she believed was "in great part the result of careful English training from the first, with nothing to unlearn; as one of any race learns a foreign language from regular instructors more correctly than the lower classes of its natives speak it."[51]

Despite its elevation of Native people over African Americans in at least this one linguistic category, Hampton's racialized outlook situated the English language in a position superior to Native languages, according to the colonialist discourses of the day. An imperialist attitude surfaced at Hampton even in a project as apparently innocent as a grammar game, as Helen Ludlow's report reveals:

By turning it into a game, and not demanding very severe order, I have succeeded beyond my own expectations. To the active imagination of my Indian pupils the English verb will ever hereafter appear, I suppose, under a somewhat military aspect. Its "principal parts" we know as "chiefs"; the different modes, as so many reservations, in which each chief has a certain number of bands (tenses) that follow him. These bands are numbered as companies, doing valiant service in support of the King's English – or the President's American. For many weeks company drill progressed with unflagging interest and patience. To marshal a company on the blackboard for inspection, send it marching into the ears of the audience, and finally to set one or more of its members to work, building sentences, was fun enough for a long time.

In her grammar lesson, Ludlow figuratively enlisted Native leaders in defense of the federal government's nationalistic agenda. Her mention of the "King's English" in the same breath as the "President's American" linked the two great imperial powers of the time: Great Britain and the United States of America. Grammar was thus placed in the service of the growing United States empire. Ludlow's linking of grammar learning with a military endeavor established a connection between the two predominant approaches to the enforced assimilation of Native people: education and armed conflict. Grammar (standardized English) ultimately had to be taught because it would help to produce a new crop of learners whose use of language would obliterate their old identity and reflect their new social status as (standardized) Americans.[52]

Time and again the Hampton teachers imposed their own social values and asserted the superiority of their own culture and language. The schoolbooks used at Hampton – for example, William Swinton's *Introductory Geography* – reflected this ideology of European American dominance:

> There are differences among men far greater than differences in complexion and features. We ask which kinds of people are the best educated, and are the most skilled in finding out and doing things which are useful for all the world? Which are making the most progress? And, when we find a people very much noted for all these, we say that they are a highly *civilized* people.
>
> When we find people who are not so enlightened, but who still are not savages, and seem to be on the way to become civilized people, we call them *semi-civilized*, which means half-civilized.
>
> The races who, in their way of living, are the least civilized, – who have no written language, and only the rudest arts, – are called *savage* races. (Emphasis in original)

Teachers at Hampton did not challenge the racial theory represented in the textbooks they used. Rather, they reinforced Swinton's racial paradigm in the classroom through recitation lessons, whose purpose, according to Swinton's preface, was to "emphasize and fasten." A sample recitation at Hampton – teacher asks, whole class answers – was reprinted in *Southern Workman* (the fifth race is not identified in the article):

9. To what race do we all belong?
9. The human race.
10. How many classes belong to this race?
10. There are five large classes belonging to the human race.
11. Which are the first?
11. The white people are the strongest.
12. Which are next?
12. The Mongolians or yellows.
13. The next?
13. The Ethiopians or blacks.
14. Next?
14. The Americans or reds.[53]

Having internalized lessons that placed them at the bottom of a scale of human beings, students then reproduced what they learned in classroom compositions, which were subsequently published in *Southern Workman.* One student wrote:

> The white people they are civilized; they have everything, and go to school, too. They learn how to read and write so they can read newspaper.
> The yellow people they half civilized, some of them know to read and write, and some know how to take care of themself.
> The red people they big savages; they don't know anything.

The teacher who published this student essay reported that nearly all of the students in this geography class received an "excellent" mark. When students expressed criticism of their own cultural practices, it was considered a positive sign that they were becoming civilized, as history teacher Josephine Richards's comment indicated: "It was pleasant to note *the growth of modern thought* in the history class one day, when, after studying an illustration of 'ye ancient times' among Indians, where the chief was taking his ease at the door of his lodge while his wife toiled at the fire, the boy who had been reading remarked, 'Give him zero'" (emphasis added). The students internalized the school's demoralizing views on civilization vis-à-vis Native life in many other spheres as well. In the debating society, for example, the link between language acquisition and civilized behavior was underscored, as the following excerpt from student Joseph Estes's *Southern Workman* article reveals: "I teach scholar this sentence: 'My friends I want to learn how to talk English and I want you all to help me,' which he and I went to his room after supper and have him stand against his room door and first make his bow and then say it. . . . And when the time I called on him to recite his piece, he bravely got up and said: 'My-Friends: – I – want – to – learn – to – talk – English – and – I – want – you – all – to – help – me,' without stammering at all which made me think that we could be raised from that degradation."[54]

Donal Lindsey notes that Hampton typically pointed to its graduates, and especially to those who had entered the professions, as proof of the efficacy and value of its approach to education. Yet the school's own published reports about students, gathered in *Twenty-two Years' Work of the Hampton Normal and Agricultural Institute* (1893), reveal that only thirty-one students had earned a graduation diploma by 1892. Lindsey's analysis of later accounts shows that of the total of 1,230 Native students educated at Hampton from 1878 to 1912, only 158 graduated. Relatively few of those attained degrees in higher education, and even fewer went on to professional careers. Admittedly, college and even secondary school education was rare among United States residents in the late nineteenth century. Nevertheless it is also true, as Robert Francis Engs documents, that the achievements of Hampton's Native students paled in comparison with the accomplishments of African American alumni. Most Native students became subsistence farmers on the reservations or wives of such, whereas most African Americans entered the teaching profession. Even if they were living in dire poverty, Hampton assessed Native students as successful simply by virtue of their Christian marriage, European-style dress, or abstinence from alcohol. Lindsey's discovery of numerous empty student files in the school's archives suggests that many students did not in fact make any gains at Hampton.[55]

The reason so many Hampton students failed to thrive is, of course, related to factors that plagued all off-reservation boarding schools, including homesickness, overwork, and susceptibility to disease. These difficulties were in turn linked to the larger problem of cultural and linguistic displacement that resulted from the colonialist context in which American Indian education was situated. It would be easy to explain away the Hampton teachers' denigrating attitudes toward Native cultures by saying that the teachers were so much a product of their own culture that they could not step outside it to analyze their lessons from another cultural perspective. But the situation was much more complex than that. For some teachers did in fact look at their pedagogy from the students' perspective. They were not unaware of the troubling implications of their work. When she considered American history lessons from the viewpoint of Native students, for example, Josephine Richards wondered "how the graphic descriptions of the Aborigines, with scalping knife and tomahawk (so entertaining to a white child), will strike their descendants." Cora Folsom expressed ambivalence about the school's cooperation with the duplicitous United States government: "The teacher has . . . the sins of her fathers to answer for before her class. She wants to encourage her pupils to be *civilized* like the white man, to embrace his religion, and follow his example, and yet has to put into his hands a history of broken promises and of a civilization as far from Christianity as the Indian himself is" (emphasis in original). The learning process at Hampton was to some extent a two-way street; education transformed not only the students but also the teachers. As Elaine Goodale (Eastman) expressed it: "Much hung on our sympathy, ingenuity, and quick appreciation of the struggle to relearn, in maturity, such fundamental tools as a new language, new conventions, new social attitudes. It was a struggle of the will and the emotions, no less than of the intellect, in which both teacher and pupils engaged as pioneers." As they sought to help students learn English, the Hampton teachers reexamined their practices in light of students' experiences, experimented with pedagogical approaches, and tested new theories, some of which would become tenets of second-language acquisition theory in the late twentieth century. In the process they replaced many conventional methods with more productive strategies for working with second-language learners.[56]

Nevertheless, the Hampton teachers' own monolingualism and monocultural outlook caused them to miss fertile opportunities to foster second-language learning. Alternatives to the Indian Office's English-only approach regularly suggested themselves at Hampton, but they were largely ignored or misunderstood. Through their own experience, for instance, some Hampton teachers became aware of the advantages of bilingualism and bilingual approaches to teaching. Language teacher Cora Folsom, for one, noted that if students were already literate in their own language, it was a great help; and if a teacher was able to translate an English word, it was of even greater assistance. At the same time, they became aware that the students' cultural backgrounds could be useful resources for learning to speak English. Despite these discoveries, the language curriculum at Hampton remained resolutely monolingual and Eurocentric because all the teachers understood that their mandate was to displace Native languages and cultures.[57]

The Hampton teachers' good intentions and innovative teaching strategies were not sufficient to counteract the negative effect of their own unexamined prejudices. Although in reflecting on their pedagogy these teachers transformed their understanding of language methodology, they never questioned or abandoned their assumption that English was a superior language. Although the teachers respected the intelligence of Native students and claimed they exhibited advantages over African American students, they continued to make cultural judgments that relegated Native people to a lower evolutionary scale than Europeans. Although the teachers' own experiences often refuted the existing negative representations of Native people, they continued to perpetuate damaging stereotypes. Finally, although the teachers viewed themselves as separate from the colonizing authorities who created the Indian schools, they participated in cultural oppression in their efforts to persuade students to replace the Native way of life with European American Christian culture. This ideology continued to inform the work of their classrooms, weakening the link between students' home languages and identities and consequently undermining many students' sense of self-worth.

Teachers repeatedly commented that the students seemed to take the European American version of history "calmly" and that students even smiled at "any allusion to the 'savages.'" But the Hampton records suggest that students were not always passive participants, as the following excerpt from Zallie Rulo's graduation speech reveals:

During last year in Dakota, there was one white man killed by the Indians. How many Indians do you suppose were killed by the white men? There were six Indians killed by the white men. Of which savage out West do you think you would be most afraid, the red savage or the white savage?

The Hampton teachers did not recognize – or at least did not acknowledge in the school reports examined in this book – the underlying student resistance to the misrepresentations of Native people that were disseminated in the school. The language the teachers used to discuss students who did not meet Hampton's criteria for success reveals that prevailing attitudes toward racial and cultural determinism shaped the teachers' conceptual framework. Brief biographical accounts of "returned Indian students" filled more than 150 pages of *Twenty-two Years' Work* in 1893. Included in those accounts is a paragraph about Zallie Rulo. The teacher who wrote the biography stated that although Zallie had left Hampton with "advantages," she "drifted about from place to place, doing well at times but on the whole . . . made a bad record." The teacher attributed these failings to Zallie's "heredity and early associations."[58] This reliance on heredity to explain student failure effectively absolved Hampton of responsibility. Zallie's subversive commentary at her graduation and Hampton's subsequent disparaging remarks about her life demonstrate that, far from being a neutral vehicle for communication, English was a site of struggle over meaning and representation. Given the unequal power relationships in the school and in the world beyond the school, even students who had mastered the language were not guaranteed access to the benefits of European American society. The language, and all it signified, more typically mastered them.

6. Luther Standing Bear and his father. Photograph by J. N. Choate. Courtesy of National Anthropological Archives, National Museum of Natural History, Smithsonian Institution/Choate 428.

3

Reproduction and Resistance

By the time the United States government embarked on a large-scale program to replace missionaries' bilingual education programs with enforced English-only instruction in the late nineteenth century, indigenous people had long been implicated in the civilizing mission. As soon as missionaries had willing converts, they prepared them – typically in their first language – to be ministers and catechists whose primary role was to convert other Native people. After the missions erected school buildings on the reservations, these converts were often enlisted as assistants in the schools. Beginning in the 1870s, the Dakota Mission provided teacher training for young men and women at the bilingual Santee Normal Training School. The school then hired educated Dakota teachers to instruct younger students. Students who returned from off-reservation boarding schools were especially valuable employees in English-only mission schools if they spoke enough English, for they could act as interpreters. From a Native perspective, hiring Native teachers or teaching assistants supported more than the proselytizing agenda of Christianity. As Virginia Driving Hawk Sneve point outs, it also provided much-needed employment on the reservations.[1]

Missions were not the only source of employment for Native teachers. Toward the end of the nineteenth century, an increasing number of Native people were hired to work in the government schools. By 1896, for example, 28 percent of the 493 employees were Native, among whom were 60 classroom teachers and 19 industrial teachers. The total was up 3 percent from the previous year. According to Superintendent of Indian Schools William N. Hailmann, these teachers were doing as admirable a job as their European American counterparts – a backhanded compliment, perhaps, given the incompetence that typically characterized instructors in the Indian school system. Some of these Native teachers had been trained in normal schools as part of their off-reservation schooling. The Hampton Institute, for example, taught selected Native students "fundamental educational principles" and showed them how to apply those principles to the classroom. The student teachers observed actual classes of young children and gave lessons they themselves had prepared. It is difficult to get a meaningful picture of the accomplishments of students in such training programs, however. In 1892 there were fifty-seven Native students in Hampton's Normal School, but only one graduate was said to be prepared to teach in any common school.[2]

Most of the information that exists about Native teachers who taught in the late nineteenth century is found in mission, school, and government records. The documents I examined portray these teachers as faithfully promoting the civilization project. Dakota teacher James Garvie, for example, defended the teaching of European American culture in his translation and writing class, even though students found texts such as the following "sometimes rather puzzling":

When I say "Trust," you know dear Spitz,
Your honor is concerned
You would not gobble up the cake,
Because my back was turned.

This is not to say that Native teachers were passive participants. In some cases they played an important role in developing school curricula. At the Dakota Mission, several Dakota teachers created a book that contained translations of *Aesop's Fables* and a life history of Abraham Lincoln. But their choice of texts demonstrates that they were using the Dakota language to reproduce European and United States literature and history rather than to foster Dakota values and ways of knowing.[3]

Missionary and government records are valuable resources for learning about Native teachers' experiences. And it is important to acknowledge their acceptance of European American approaches to education. However, because these documents were published primarily to promote European American and Christian values, they constrain an effort to achieve a more complicated perspective on how Native teachers made sense of their own lives and teaching. I therefore sought autobiographies of Native teachers themselves, limiting my search to works of educators who taught English to Native students in the late nineteenth century and later wrote about pedagogical issues related to language and language instruction. Using those criteria, I located accounts of four teachers: Lilah Denton Lindsey (Creek), Thomas Wildcat Alford (Absentee Shawnee), Sarah Winnemucca (Northern Paiute), and Luther Standing Bear (Lakota).[4]

The life experiences of Lindsey, Alford, Winnemucca, and Standing Bear were remarkably diverse, and their different linguistic and educational backgrounds in turn shaped their educational philosophies, as this chapter will show. Nevertheless, these four educators also had many common experiences that may account for their own achievements in learning English as a second language so well that they could teach it. They each had at least one parent or grandparent who encouraged them to acquire an education in English. They also developed relationships with European Americans, including teachers, missionaries, reformers, and even businessmen who supported their desire to learn. Individually, they were determined and self-motivated learners. Although their schooling was interrupted or terminated for tragic reasons such as illness, a death in the family, or racism, they all learned to speak English well after multiple interactions with speakers of English, in and out of school. Finally, they shared a commitment to use English to help their own communities.

Hired by Christian missions or the United States government, Native teachers were expected to advance a European American worldview. However, they were not mere agents of reproduction. Even in the ideological environment that gave birth to the government's English-only policy, there was room for negotiation and resistance, as Alice Littlefield notes of students' boarding school experiences. In general, the pedagogical approaches of Lindsey, Alford, Winnemucca, and Standing Bear ranged from attempts at reproducing a European American model of language instruction (Lindsey, Alford) to efforts at resisting English-only approaches (Winnemucca, Standing Bear). Yet it would be an oversimplification to say that their pedagogy fell into any one category. All four teachers maintained pride in their own tribal identity and values and at the same time guided their students to acquire English, learn European American ways, and adopt Christianity, just as they had done. This pattern demonstrates that Native teachers did not necessarily reject or subvert all the goals of the civilizing project. But their stories also show how these teachers mediated the English-only approach, precisely because they shared the students' cultures and their experiences as language learners and understood the need to preserve the integrity of Native identity. They taught language within the context of students' background knowledge, interpreted the target culture so it was comprehensible, and functioned as role models for the productive use of language and literacy.[5]

In analyzing the cultural choices these Native teachers made, it is worth remembering that Native cultures, like European cultures, were never static. D'Arcy McNickle suggests that all of Native history can be seen as a process of cultural change, which has never meant abandonment of culture or identity. Over the centuries, indigenous people have drawn from other Native cultures as well as from European American ways of life, adapting traditional practices to accommodate changing social, ecological, and economic conditions.[6] By the time they became teachers, Lindsey, Alford, Winnemucca, and Standing Bear had long been undergoing a dynamic transcultural process that compelled them to decide which new ways of knowing to adopt and which to transform or reject. They articulated ideas and made choices based on a complex set of issues, needs, and desires. Having learned English, they opened themselves up to personal growth and engagement in a wider community. Their own biculturalism and bilingualism or multilingualism gave them insight into the implications of the interactions between cultures and of the domination of one over another. Ultimately they took ownership of English to reach a European American audience with new representations of Native people, including their own roles as intellectuals. In telling their stories, they showed not only what it really meant to be Native in America but also what (the) Native has really meant to America over the centuries.

LILAH DENTON LINDSEY, 1860–1943

Lilah Denton Lindsey was raised in the Muskogee (Creek) Nation, and thus English played an important role in her life, for by the time she was born this language had long been a source of power in her own community. Many of those who were educated in mission schools had gained leadership partly as a result of their bilingualism in Creek and English. Until early in the nineteenth century, Creeks had lived a relatively peaceful life in Alabama and Georgia, primarily as farmers and ranchers. However, through political manipulation and overt intimidation, by the 1830s Creeks were compelled to sign treaties with the federal government through which they surrendered land east of the Mississippi. When they arrived in the newly formed Indian Territory after their removal, Creeks discovered that the United States government's promises of protected land rights and sufficient rations were false. Traditional Creeks were so distrustful of European Americans that they called for the expulsion of all missionaries. Christian Creeks agreed, fearing the missionaries' objection to their slaveholding. In 1839 they formed a united government, the National Council, and began to plan an educational program so their children could learn to deal effectively with speakers of English. They soon discovered, however, that the only qualified teachers available were missionaries, and so in the 1840s the National Council allowed several European American missions to open schools. By the time Lilah Denton Lindsey entered a mission school in 1872, even Creek parents who had once opposed education and Christianity were eager to enroll their children.[7]

As Lindsey relates in "Memories of the Indian Territory Mission Field," her mother – herself a mission school graduate – had prevailed on a well-connected family member to use his influence to get her daughter into the Tullahassee Manual Labor Boarding School, for she was under the age limit. The Tullahassee School had been founded in 1850 and was run by the Presbyterian mission, sustained in part with funds from the Creek National Council. At first no teachers spoke the Muskogee language, and the school used bilingual Creek children as interpreters. After its principal teacher, Reverend William Robertson, learned Muskogee, he created first and second readers in that language. Robertson's daughter, Ann Augusta, who was to become Lilah Denton Lindsey's teacher, reported that "in an hour a bright pupil could and did learn to read these books. I myself have taught them." In 1870 the school published the first newspaper in the Creek Nation, *Our Monthly*, which included lessons in English, poems, and bilingual essays.[8]

Lindsey loved the Tullahassee school despite its "monotonous" English lessons based on memorization and the McGuffey Primer, but she had to leave in 1877 to care for her sick mother. When her mother died in 1878, leaving her orphaned (her father had died in the Civil War), she lived with leading families in the Creek Nation. In 1879, she reports, the wife of the Tullahassee missionary arranged for her to attend the Synodical Female College in Missouri, which had an opening for "a deserving Indian girl." When the school closed in June 1880, one of her former teachers got her into the Highland Institute in Ohio, a boarding school that prepared girls to become teachers and missionaries. She was the first Creek woman to graduate from that school. After she received her diploma in 1883, she returned to Indian Territory to teach at the Wealaka Mission and then at the day school in Okmulgee.[9]

Lindsey narrates the events of her education and teaching career without apparent sarcasm about European Americans' condescending attitudes toward Native people. In fact her own rhetoric occasionally reflects that stance. Having received a commission from the Presbyterian Board of Home Missions in 1886 to teach at a new school in Tulsa, she describes her experience as "teaching the little Indian children as they came from their homes on foot, on horse-back and in buggies." But her efforts were admirable. She developed her own method for teaching English, which eschewed what she calls the "punishing" approach of memorizing the alphabet and focused instead on teaching whole words. After the principal teacher had to depart suddenly, Lindsey was left in the classroom with sixty students from 9:00 in the morning until 4:30 in the afternoon. She was charged with teaching not only English but also the Bible, housekeeping, and gardening, and it was difficult for the students to learn all these things at the same time. She used some of the older and more advanced students as assistants but was still overwhelmed by the task of teaching, for she often "heard sixteen classes a day." The next year two more teachers were added as the school grew (partly by adding settlers' children), but the work continued to be exhausting because the teachers were responsible for every facet of school life, including religious services. After three years she resigned. After a year of rest, she spent the next two years as principal of the Coweta Indian Boarding School, under the direction of the Creek National Council, and then returned to Tulsa.[10]

Lindsey's next teaching choices and the language she uses to describe them reflect her prominent position in the Creek community and her own elevated sense of her mission. At the "earnest request" of the Broken Arrow community, she taught at their newly established day school, for which she received a teaching certificate from the Creek Nation school board. She left at the end of the year, however, feeling that day school work was "beneath my dignity." She resigned and returned to Tulsa. "Bankers and business men's wives" soon asked her to open a private subscription school because "they did not want their small children mixing and mingling with *undesirable* children of all *classes!*" who populated the public school (emphasis in original). Lindsey fulfilled their wishes, which suggests that she shared their social class discrimination. She created what she calls "a delightful school" on her own property. She later taught in various settings, including public school, until she ended her teaching career in the mid-1890s.[11]

Lindsey's subsequent work in the Tulsa community earned her a place in the Oklahoma Hall of Fame. She was tireless in her efforts on behalf of the First Presbyterian Church, of which she was a charter member. Among her numerous political and social contributions were her organization of the Humane Society, the Women's Christian Temperance Union, and the Women's Relief Corps. Revealing how fully she had embraced a European American lifestyle, she ends her narrative with details about her 1884 marriage to a European American who had come to work in the Creek Nation after serving in the Civil War. She refers to "the pomp" of the ceremony and the "ever popular wedding march" and describes the reception that followed as "a sumptuous wedding banquet with the beautiful wedding cake in the center of a lovely decorated table." Clearly she encouraged her students to follow her lead, for the ceremony took place in front of the schoolchildren in order to "give them an idea of a well arranged wedding."[12]

Lilah Denton Lindsey's memoirs suggest that she reproduced European American teachings without ambivalence. Her attitude may be traced to the fact that she studied and taught in schools supported by the government of her own nation, which had already adapted to change in order to guarantee survival. She also studied in a school whose teachers were bilingual. Her parents each were half Scottish; her grandfather was an ordained minister. Her mother had attended mission schools, could speak English, and had become a devout Christian. Even as a child Lindsey was one or two generations removed from total immersion in Creek culture. Some of her attitudes reflected the view of the elite class of the Creek Nation. None of this is to say, however, that Lindsey adopted a singularly European American worldview. She was proud of her Native identity, which is reflected, for example, in her membership in the Tulsa Indian Women's Club, one of her favorite associations according to J. O. Misch. This Native state of mind undoubtedly

7. Lilah Denton Lindsey. Courtesy of Oklahoma Historical Society.

influenced Lindsey's students' own sense of self in a positive way, for, she says, she fulfilled "the longing of my soul" by serving "my own (Creek) people as a teacher."[13]

THOMAS WILDCAT ALFORD, 1860–1938

Thomas Wildcat Alford, too, attempted to provide a European American–style education for the children of his own community. Unlike Lindsey, however, Alford would encounter resistance to his desire to teach English and its associated culture. Like Creeks, Shawnees experienced extreme geographical change as a result of contact with European Americans. As he reports in *Civilization and the Story of the Absentee Shawnees,* Alford was born into a peaceful community that had come to live among Creeks in Indian Territory after Shawnees' forced removal from their reservation in the state of Texas. Because of the Civil War, this group moved again in 1862, this time to the Shawnee reservation in Kansas. After the government forced Shawnees to sign a treaty guaranteeing them land in Indian Territory (a treaty the government ultimately did not honor), they moved back to Indian Territory in 1868. Despite these disruptions, Shawnee leaders had not made the accommodations to European American society that characterized the Creek community into which Lilah Denton Lindsey was born.[14]

Alford's early memories reveal the ways European Americans were represented in his Shawnee community. Long before he had laid eyes on European American people, Alford reports, he learned negative things about them around the campfire at night. In addition to the "histories, traditions, codes" of his own people taught by the elders, he heard about "deceptions and encounters that were not any more conducive to a feeling of trust and confidence in the white race than were the stories told to white children at that time of Indians and their treachery and warfare." As Alford explains it, the only reason tribal elders supported education in the local mission school was that they saw it as a militaristic strategy. The Absentee Shawnee leaders thought children should go to school in order to "fight the white m[a]n with his own weapons – words" so that they would be better able to speak for themselves in the ongoing controversies between the people and the United States government. Thus Alford's first publicly sanctioned image of the English language was as an implement of war.[15]

However, at home Alford was exposed to a competing representation of language and language instruction. His experience within his community was unique in that his father, known in English as Wildcat, had acquired "some understanding of English" during his Union Army service and was one of the few Shawnees who believed in the inherent value of formal education. Wildcat therefore cooperated with Quaker missionaries to build a day school near the Sauk and Fox Agency in 1872 and encouraged his son to enroll. Alford had developed a taste for the material goods of European American society even before he started school. Contrary to the wishes of the tribal elders, he acknowledges, he had a "yearning desire for things which civilization represented," many of which his father had already purchased for him. He thus welcomed his English-language education: "We used McGuffey's readers, and they opened to us many wonderful visions of the life of white people, especially white children." Contrary to the tribal leaders' negative representations of European Americans, in Alford's eyes the Quaker missionary teachers modeled "an example of honesty and uprightness that did much to strengthen our faith in their lessons."[16]

By his own testimony, Alford's education in the program was beneficial, even after the government took control of the school in 1874, and he shows no ambivalence. Having studied arithmetic, geography, physiology, grammar, and natural philosophy, he had "a consuming thirst for more knowledge." Because of his father's ill health and the need to supplement the family income, however, Alford found it necessary to leave school in 1876. Although his ability to speak English was "somewhat limited," he was able to find a position as interpreter for a store manager in Shawnee Town. Unfortunately, Alford's thirst for knowledge was difficult to satisfy, for it was almost impossible to find books: few people owned them, and there were none for sale or even available to borrow. One trader for whom he served as translator encouraged his pursuit of learning and arranged for him to subscribe to *The Youth's Companion,* a weekly magazine published in Boston. The limitations of his English-language education became evident as he began to read, for he could comprehend very little. Nevertheless, through frequent practice, motivated by genuine interest, he achieved a higher level of literacy: "I knew absolutely nothing of life as it was depicted in the stories, but I always was keenly interested in the pictures, and gradually I learned . . . not only a better use of English, but a better knowledge of the conditions of life and the ways of the world." When his father died in 1877, Alford's dream of gaining more formal schooling was temporarily shattered. But the

Quaker missionaries persuaded the chiefs that more people needed to be educated in order to negotiate with Washington. Alford and another young man were chosen to go to an off-reservation boarding school because they already knew English and were future chiefs. They agreed to the demand that they "*not accept the white man's religion*" (emphasis in original) but only learn how "to read in books, how to understand all that was written or spoken to and about our people and the government." In 1879, at age nineteen, Alford received a scholarship, provided by Alice Longfellow, to attend the Hampton Institute.[17]

At Hampton, Alford's interactions with European Americans continued to be affirmative. Accordingly, he continues in his autobiographical account to use language that extols the virtues of European American society. His positive outlook clearly enabled him to deal with his long and intense days, which began at 5:00 in the morning with a march to breakfast and ended at 9:00 in the evening, after a period of study. Even the classroom that first year was a model of military efficiency: "We dressed, we ate, we drilled, we studied and recited our lessons with a precision that left not even one minute without its duties." The extraordinarily sympathetic teachers at Hampton helped him make the adjustment not only to the strict regime and classwork but also to the more casual, unfamiliar social activity: "The mutual exchange of ideas, the sympathy and encouragement we received from our teachers, their politeness and dignity, helped us to understand this phase of civilization, which was as delightful as it was new to us." Devoted to these teachers, Alford fully embraced the Hampton gospel, even succumbing to the "continual pressure" to convert to Christianity, although he knew he was breaking his promise to the Shawnee leaders and eliminating his opportunity to become a Shawnee chief. By then Alford had become one of Hampton's star pupils and was even mentioned in the Minutes of Indiana Yearly Meeting of Friends as "among the best Indian scholars of that institution." One of his own classmates referred to him in an article in *Southern Workman* as "one of the leading Indian boys here." At the end of his three-year term, as he was preparing to return home, he felt a "yearning desire to impart to [Shawnees] some of the good and pleasant things I had learned." As his 1882 graduation speech from Hampton reveals, he had acquired the language of the civilization project, for his plan was to "lead them [Shawnees] out of the darkness of barbarism and ignorance into the path of peace and prosperity."[18]

However, Alford's English-only education would create problems for him. When he arrived home in 1882, he was received "coldly and with suspicion." Even his closest relatives turned their backs on him because he had adopted a European American style of dress and Christian beliefs. Alford was isolated except for his relationship with the missionary who hired him as interpreter. Ultimately he left the reservation to search for work elsewhere. After a series of disappointments at several agencies and towns, he landed his first teaching job for the Indian service at a day school near a Pottawatomie village. At the end of the year he was transferred to the Shawnee government boarding school as principal, "full of ideas for teaching, eager to try out some of the newer methods I had learned at Hampton."[19]

By this time Shawnees were more receptive to Alford's ideas, having recognized his commitment to their welfare and his interest in tribal affairs. Once he had their attention, he extolled the virtues of schooling; and when the Shawnee school opened in September 1883, he was pleased to see the largest student enrollment ever. Alford was influenced in his work by his former mentors. He received a letter from his benefactor, Alice Longfellow, who suggested that he "try to improve the educational opportunity of Indian girls," and he made this one of the goals of his teaching. His "old white chief," General Samuel Armstrong, visited his school, congratulated him "heartily" on the work he was doing, and gave him some suggestions for improvement. This feedback left Alford with "renewed courage and determination" to fulfill his dream. His "theories about teaching" included vocational education along the Hampton model. He anticipated that it might be difficult to get students to adopt a new way of life because their parents discouraged them from learning what he calls "civilized manners," but he discovered that the students "adapted themselves to the new environment even before they could speak the language."[20]

To a great extent, Alford's rhetoric reflects the European American educational discourse of the era. His pedagogical goal, he says, was to teach students "the advantages of civilization." As he sees it, his background experience served as a source of empathy: "Like them I had been ignorant of all these things, and I was in a position to sympathize with them. I could in reality 'speak their language' and understand their problems." Ironically, in his use of quotation marks, Alford emphasizes the figurative rather than the literal meaning of the expression *speak their language*. As a teacher, he viewed his role primarily as interpreting European American culture for the students in order to make it comprehensible. His way of achieving this goal was anathema to the Indian service, however. In his work with students, he says, he did not want to "seem to be critical of their old way of living." From past experience, he had learned that it was wrong to force students to deny the virtues of their own culture.[21]

Alford's view of European American educators as paragons was severely tested by his experience as a school principal in the Indian service. He began to realize how unusual his experience with Quaker missionaries and Hampton educators had been, for he was forced into contact with untrained or uncaring teachers who had been given their positions through the political spoils system. These people, he explains, often had "little consideration . . . for the real welfare of the Indians." Unfortunately, sometimes teachers who did have a contribution to make were discharged to create a place for the loyal supporter of a successful candidate: "A teacher would formulate a plan that might have resulted in great good, when snap! Off would go his head, or at least his job, and someone would be put into his place who had neither knowledge of nor interest in his work."

Alford himself was a victim of this system when he was removed as principal and replaced by a friend of the agent, on the charge that he was not living on the school premises. Technically the charge was correct, for he was living in a house adjoining the school, but only because no provision had been made for his quarters on the school grounds. He was soon reinstated, but at the end of the term he resigned, and "this finished my career in the schoolroom."[22]

Despite the drawbacks of working for the government school system, Alford did not question the goal of providing an education in English and in European American ways, at least while his career in the schools was active. He credits the European American teachers he admired with contributing to what he saw as the much-needed uplift of Native children: "Some of them have left the imprint of their fine natures, their true personalities on the lives of the children with whom they labored; their influence will live on and on, down through the ages, bearing rich fruit in the years to come." Nevertheless, his bicultural experience reinforced his sense of the value of the Shawnee approach to life. Alford offsets negative representations of Native people by making the point that learning was as important in his own community as it was in United States society: "Our people appreciated skill or knowledge of any kind. . . . [T]he knowledge of warfare, of history, and

8. Thomas Wildcat Alford. Courtesy of University Archives, Hampton University, Hampton VA.

of nature . . . all these things . . . called for a good memory, keen observation, and close application, and with these gifts one naturally would learn much in other fields. Endurance and self-control were taught so rigidly that those qualities had become a part of Indian character." Alford also challenges the notion of European American superiority by pointing out the similarities between the two approaches to life: "At Hampton we were taught the usages of polite society in vogue at that time, the so-called Victorian era . . . and in this we found the foundation of good breeding to be just the same principle as the simple teaching of our own people, namely, consideration for the rights of others, respect for our superiors (elders), and unselfishness. There were different ways of expressing this principle which is considered social culture, and which I contend is after all only the difference in social ethics."[23]

In the end, Alford's attempt to provide a European American–style education for Shawnees often did not produce the desired result. Alford notes that many young people were so enculturated that they had "lost the tenacious, underlying strength of their forefathers" but had not in return adopted Christianity or acquired what he perceives to be a high level of European American culture. This state of affairs causes him to question what is being taught in the schools. Inverting the stereotypical view of Native people's face paint and style of dress as signs of savagery, he (perhaps unwittingly) turns the rhetorical tables on European American society:

Our girls of today wear a different kind of "paint" to that used by their ancestors, they wear their hair short, dress in Paris fashion, and get their finger nails manicured, just exactly like their white friends do.
But is all this civilization?[24]

SARAH WINNEMUCCA, ABOUT 1844–91

Despite her lack of formal education, by the time she reached adulthood Sarah Winnemucca could speak five languages: three Native tongues in addition to Spanish and English. Winnemucca's knowledge of English and the uses to which she put that knowledge situated her in a precarious, paradoxical position. As an interpreter for a former enemy, the United States military, she initially incurred the suspicion of Paiutes. In her book *Life among the Piutes: Their Wrongs and Claims* (1883) she justifies her role by explaining that Paiutes needed and wanted to understand what was happening to them and had been victimized by too many corrupt interpreters. She was determined to apply her linguistic strengths to rectify the injustices done to her people. In writing about those injustices, she had to be careful not to alienate her target audience: the educational reformers whose political and financial support she needed to achieve her goal. What emerges in the book as a result of this dilemma are competing representations of European Americans. Winnemucca juxtaposes those who acted out of cruel or self-serving intent against those she viewed as well-intentioned folk. As it turns out, the former held so much power that she was thwarted even in her attempt to provide English-language instruction to the Paiute community.[25]

The first opposing images of European Americans came to Winnemucca early in her life, through her own community. She was born in what is now Nevada at a time when there was no sign of European American civilization there. That situation changed when prospectors rushed through Paiute territory after gold was discovered in California in 1848. Her grandfather, a leader of Paiutes, welcomed the European Americans who settled in the area as "long-looked for white brothers." But news began to spread that some of the newcomers were killing all the Native people who were in their way. Inverting the savage-cannibal myth, Winnemucca describes the fear that infiltrated her community: "Our mothers told us that the whites were killing everybody and eating them."[26]

Winnemucca continues to present competing images as she addresses the acquisition of literacy. When her grandfather returned from his long stay in California among European American people, she relates, he showed her a "wonderful thing . . . a paper, which he said could talk to him." Her grandfather's admiration of European Americans' use of language led him to place his own family in close contact with their society. In 1858, for example, when Winnemucca was approximately fourteen, she and her sister were sent to live with a European American family. It was there she learned to speak English fluently, she says, a process that was "very fast, for they were kind to us." But again, tensions between European and Paiute communities engendered negative experiences, forcing a separation from that family. Later her opportunity to become formally educated in English was cut short by racism; in 1860 she and her sister were removed from the "Sisters' School" in San José, California, after three weeks because "wealthy parents" complained about having their children educated with Native children.[27]

In describing her work on the reservations, Winnemucca again represents European Americans as both good and bad and links their behavior to Native people's access to English language and literacy. In 1875 she became the interpreter for Sam Parrish, the new government agent at the Malheur Agency in Oregon, a man Winnemucca fondly refers to as "our good agent." When Parrish built a schoolhouse on the reservation (which had been established in 1867) he asked her to be a paid assistant to the teacher, his sister-in-law, whom Winnemucca calls a "dear, lovely lady." According to Winnemucca, on May 1, 1876, when the school opened, it was an immediate success, with 369 boys and girls and 42 young men and women in attendance. With all this positive energy and because of the Mrs. Parrish's kindness and Winnemucca's assistance as interpreter, she says, the students "learned very fast, and were glad to come to school." A spokesperson for the Native community told her they were pleased with "the white lily [who] is teaching our children how to talk with the paper." However, in a move that subverted its own educational program, the government allowed the political patronage system to override success. By June 1876 the Parrishes were gone, replaced against their wishes by a new agent whose appointees, including the schoolteacher, were "the poorest-looking white people" Winnemucca had ever seen. The agent, whom Winnemucca sardonically refers to as "our *Christian* agent" (emphasis in original), discharged Winnemucca as interpreter when she told the army he refused to distribute rations, letting the community starve. Her first teaching job, which had started on such a hopeful note, ended almost as abruptly as her own formal education in a mission school.[28]

Winnemucca repeatedly provides evidence that European Americans resisted providing Native people with productive English-language skills. In 1879, at the end of the Bannock war, during which Winnemucca served as a scout and interpreter for the army, her community was arbitrarily separated. She arrived with a group at the Yakima reservation, Washington Territory, after a trek during which many froze to death. They were placed in the care of the agent, Father Wilbur, who treated them "as if we were so many horses or cattle." Winnemucca served as Father Wilbur's interpreter, helping him in the schoolhouse and during church services, but he never paid her. Furthermore, like the agent at Malheur, he deprived her people of rations and instead sold them supplies for personal profit. Although Father Wilbur appeared to be kind to the people he had already "civilized and Christianized,"

Winnemucca criticizes his treatment of this group as well because he kept them from learning English, which she knew could give them access to economic opportunity: "Right here, my dear reader, you will see how much Father Wilbur's Indians are civilized and Christianized. He had to have interpreters. If they were so much civilized, why did he have interpreters to talk to them? In eighteen years could he not have taught them some English? I was there twelve months, and I never heard an Indian man or woman speak the English language except the three interpreters and some half-breeds." In her effort to help these people escape this untenable situation, Winnemucca soon discovered that the written word in English was useless. She managed to procure a letter from the secretary of the interior, Carl Schurz, guaranteeing her people's return to their homeland, but Father Wilbur refused to cooperate.[29]

Winnemucca's experiences continued to be characterized by disruptions of English-language educational efforts. She left Yakima when an army friend, General O. O. Howard, invited her to go to the Vancouver Barracks in 1880 to be an interpreter and teacher. General Howard reported that, using her translation skills, Winnemucca developed a bilingual approach to promote understanding. According to her this was the first school the children had ever attended, but they "learned very fast, because they knew what they were learning." By March 1881 they could "all read pretty well" and were "desirous to learn." But again Winnemucca's teaching career was shortened by government intervention, for the people were ordered to move to a reservation. She wrote to the secretary of the interior asking that they be allowed to remain under military supervision, where they were "contented" and which she knew from experience was more beneficial than being under the aegis of a reservation agent. In the letter she used language she knew would appeal to the federal government, suggesting several ways of "enlightening and Christianizing them." But her call was ignored. Much to her frustration, when she later wrote to her students, someone wrote back to say that the children "had forgotten what they learned, as they were not going to school any more."[30]

For Winnemucca, literacy was synonymous with power, and she now understood that the government would not allow English-language literacy to empower Native communities. By putting their own relatives in the positions of teacher and interpreter, she maintains, government agents withheld literacy from Native people and thus were able to continue to deceive them.

Seeking another avenue to help her people, Winnemucca turned to the private sector: the philanthropic reformers who were known as the "Friends of the Indians." In 1883, before writing her book, she went to Boston to try to persuade the reform community to help restore the land guaranteed by treaty to Paiutes. Writer-educator Elizabeth Palmer Peabody and her sister, Mary Peabody Mann (widow of Horace Mann), were taken with her cause and arranged numerous speaking engagements for her along the East Coast. To attract a large European American audience, and understanding their desire for exoticism, Winnemucca represented herself as "Princess Winnemucca" (see fig. 9). During that same time she wrote *Life among the Piutes,* which Mary Mann copyedited, and the New England reformers rallied to get it published. Winnemucca was able to raise money but not to obtain the rights of Paiutes. Ironically, the book had become an example of one of its major themes: the futility of using the written word in English. By 1885, having realized that even her eloquent speeches to Congress had been delivered in vain, Winnemucca decided the only way she could help Paiutes was to teach the children English in her own school, at the farm of her brother Natches near Lovelock, Nevada.[31]

Documents produced after publication of Winnemucca's book show that the education she provided in her own school differed from the English-only education typically promoted by the reformers, for she advocated bilingual teaching. As she revealed in an 1886 article in the *Silver State* (Nevada) newspaper, her experience on the reservations had made her critical of the prevailing monolingual approach, which in her view accounted for the schools' deficiencies: "Indian schools are failures at many agencies, but it is not the fault of the children, but of the teacher and interpreter. . . . The most necessary thing for the success of an Indian school is a good interpreter, a perfect interpreter, a true interpreter. . . . I attribute the success of my school not to my being a scholar and a good teacher but because I am my own Interpreter, and my heart is in my work." At the end of 1885 Elizabeth Peabody wrote to President Grover Cleveland's sister in support of Winnemucca's bilingual approach: "The expected superiority of *her* school is and must always be that as she knows both languages as *vernacular* (thinks in both) she can teach English *perfectly;* so that her scholars can grow up to be *teachers of English* also *perfectly,* and this will rend the veil that has been hanging between the two races from the beginning" (emphasis in original). To enlist government support, Peabody wrote a pamphlet that described

9. Sarah Winnemucca in her "princess" outfit. Courtesy of Nevada Historical Society.

Winnemucca's program as illustrating the principles of the new educational model of Friedrich Froebel. Based on letters she was receiving from Winnemucca, she described a typical bilingual lesson, likening the teaching to the kindergarten programs for poor children that Peabody herself had developed and promoted in the United States: "She gave them always the initiative in conversation, as the kindergartners [teachers] do their children, asking each to say something in Piute, and then telling them how to say it in English, writing in chalk upon the blackboard for them to imitate the leading words, and then find them in books. She says they never forget these words, but write them all over fences in Lovelocks and tell their meaning in Piute to their parents, delighted and proud to display their acquisitions."[32]

However, Winnemucca's bilingual program did not win the support of the government. Peabody's entreaties to powerful senators and congressmen were futile, even though she pointed to the financial advantage of funding a reservation boarding school run by a Native educator. This was the era of Commissioner of Indian Affairs J. D. C. Atkins (1885–88), who codified the English-only movement in the spirit of patriotism, nationalism, and imperialism. Virtually no bilingual education was possible through the Indian service until William Hailmann, who had translated Froebel's work, became superintendent of Indian schools in 1894 and developed a kindergarten program – and even that approach was short-lived. By the summer of 1888, without sufficient funds (partly because her husband squandered money), Winnemucca was forced to close her school.

That Winnemucca's school, which she named the Peabody Institute, did not receive support from the government may well have been connected to the fact that she had a tenuous relationship with the Indian Office, which she had so roundly criticized in her book. Nevertheless, this situation reveals how inflexible and influential the English-only policy was. For although Winnemucca's approach was bilingual, in other ways it fit well with the civilizing mission. For one thing, Winnemucca shared the idea that children could transform their own communities, as Elizabeth Peabody pointed out: "The great object she has in view is to make her scholars teachers, in their turn, of all that she teaches them; and already she can make the elder ones her assistants and substitutes, and they are also inspired to make their parents companions in their acquisition of English." And as Peabody implied, Winnemucca's school also had the potential to overcome the greatest obstacle the Indian Office faced in its attempt to educate Native children – parental resistance: "A dozen children [were] taken violently from the Pyramid Lake reservation, against the protest of their mothers, to an industrial school in Colorado, since which outrage the parents of four hundred Piute children have applied to Natches to take them to board, and go to Sarah's school, 'where they would really be taught,' as they say, 'and not whipped or separated from their parents.'"[33] Furthermore, Winnemucca's educational philosophy, as expressed in an 1886 letter to the *Silver State,* acknowledges (undoubtedly with a significant degree of sarcasm) the savage/civilized paradigm that shaped the educational reform movement: "It seems strange to me that the Government has not found out years ago that education is the key to the Indian problem. Much money and many precious lives would have been saved if the American people had fought my people with Books instead of Powder and lead. Education civilized your race and there is no reason why it cannot civilize mine." Finally, Winnemucca's program fostered the Christianizing mission of the educational reform movement. According to visitors to her school, for example, Winnemucca taught the children to sing "*gospel hymns* with precise melody, accurate time, and distinct pronunciation" (emphasis in original).[34]

It appears that when Winnemucca wrote to the secretary of the interior in 1881 of her approach to "enlightening and Christianizing" Native people in Vancouver, her words were not mere rhetoric. But it is important to note that Winnemucca's Christianity does not denigrate Paiute beliefs. Rather, in a move similar to Thomas Wildcat Alford's balanced comparison of European and Shawnee social culture, her perspective equates the two value systems: "The whites have not waited to find out how good the Indians were, and what ideas they had of God, just like those of Jesus, who called him Father, just as my people do, and told men to do to others as they would be done by, just as my people teach their children to do."[35] Given that Winnemucca could educate children in both Paiute and English and could teach European American belief systems even while upholding Paiute rights and values, her case suggests that different worldviews could interact and coexist in the schools. However, the Indian Office rejected the idea that nationhood could embrace both English and Native languages or both European American and indigenous cultures.

Well aware of the power of representation, Luther Standing Bear declares in his preface that he wrote *My People the Sioux* (1928) specifically to offset misrepresentations of Native people that had been disseminated in European American publications. In *Land of the Spotted Eagle* (1933) he continues to decry this rhetoric. He notes, for example, that European Americans used the term "massacres" to describe battles Native men had fought to protect their families and homes. He also objects to the celebration of the "pioneer," who from a Native perspective was a callous and duplicitous conqueror. In his turn Standing Bear represents Lakotas as virtual paragons, describing them as members of a "powerful nation" whose practices were so marvelous that "we grew fat with contentment and happiness." Explaining at great length how the education of Lakota children was accomplished, he implicitly criticizes European ways: "Not being under a system, children never had to 'learn this today,' or 'finish this book this year' or 'take up' some study just because 'little Willie did.' Native education was not a class education but one that strengthened and encouraged the individual to grow."[36]

The troubling aspects of European American society notwithstanding, by the 1870s Standing Bear's father had come to believe that because the European American population was spreading rapidly across the country, "the only recourse was to learn the white man's ways of doing things, get the same education, and thus be in condition to stand up for his rights." In 1879, three years after the defeat of Custer, eleven-year-old Standing Bear decided to join the first group of Sioux children to enroll at the Carlisle Indian Industrial School. In recounting his experiences thereafter, he provides one of the most detailed descriptions of English-language learning in the nineteenth century and fashions a compelling argument for bilingual education.[37]

Standing Bear's representations of European Americans are softened when he describes his schooling at Carlisle, perhaps because of his fondness for his teacher, Marianna Burgess. Miss Burgess believed that for Native people to be successful, "the children must be contented and happy," as she wrote to Richard Pratt in her teaching application, and Standing Bear benefited from her kindness. Nevertheless, Standing Bear says, he felt insecure about his linguistic ability and dubious about English-only education. For a while he refused to do schoolwork, largely because he had no idea what the teacher was saying. A breakthrough came when Miss Burgess brought an interpreter into the classroom to explain the lesson. This was Standing Bear's first taste of bilingual learning, which he refers to as the "real beginning" of his second-language acquisition. However, the English-only rule held sway, and Standing Bear found living at school difficult because students were not allowed to communicate in their own tongues. As more students arrived who spoke various languages Standing Bear was unfamiliar with, the communication barrier increased because "we knew so little English that we had a hard time to get along." Standing Bear did not become a committed learner until an 1880 visit to Carlisle by his father, who encouraged him to learn all he could in order to function in the changing world: "'Some day I want to hear you speak like these Long Knife people, and work like them.'"[38]

By 1882 Standing Bear was considered one of the "more advanced" students, although he felt he "knew but little of the English language." When he was asked to act as an interpreter for Miss Burgess when she visited the Sioux reservation to recruit new students, he was "ready to do anything" for his beloved teacher. Inducing parents to part with their children turned out to be a difficult task, however, for many children had died at boarding schools, and to make matters more tragic, parents were rarely notified of the illness until their sons and daughters were dead and buried. Nevertheless, when Standing Bear was delegated to speak on behalf of the school, he spoke (in Dakota) of the benefits of English-language literacy and European American practices. Again, Standing Bear's father supported his choice, rising to say how impressed he had been during his visit to Carlisle and promising that he would send the rest of his children to study there as well. The father-son oratory was persuasive. By the time Miss Burgess and her protégés returned to Carlisle, there were an additional fifty-two students. Standing Bear was so successful at this work that Pratt sent him back to the reservation alone to "induce more children to learn the ways of the white men."[39]

Soon Standing Bear was reaching the end of his three-year term and still bemoaning the inadequacy of his English-language skills. On several vacation trips he had spent time with English-speaking families, but he "could not understand all they were talking about and it made me feel out of place." He took every opportunity to practice his English at school. For example, on a fishing trip he stayed with Pratt rather than playing with the other boys, for he found that the principal "always talked on interesting topics, and all this helped me with my English." When he had the opportunity to leave school altogether, he decided to stay behind, even though most of the Sioux children opted to return to the reservation. He was motivated by the thought that his father was "depending on me to learn everything I could of the white man's ways." Standing Bear was able to strengthen his speaking skills further when Pratt chose him to work at Wanamaker's store in Philadelphia and thus to be "an example of what this school can turn out." Standing Bear was so successful at Wanamaker's that he was promoted to the bookkeeping department.[40]

To this point, with the exception of a reference to his resistance to working in the tin shop and learning what he considered a useless trade, Standing Bear focuses on his accommodation to his English-language education. And he presents this accommodation primarily through his own unquestioning adolescent eyes. However, when he describes his experience in Philadelphia, he shifts to an adult critical perspective. The turning point is linked to the racism he experienced in trying to find lodgings: "When I would find something that seemed suitable, and the people discovered my nationality, they would look at me in a surprised sort of way, and say that they had no place for an Indian boy." Having become painfully aware of the futility of the assimilationist ideology of the Carlisle Indian School, Standing Bear returned and told Pratt that he wanted to "go home to my people." By that time Pratt was keeping students in school against their will in order to keep them away from the reservation. In this case he was so eager to retain his star pupil that he offered to let him stay at school without working in the hated tin shop. But Standing Bear again requested permission to leave, and Pratt finally granted it, although he asked Standing Bear to promise that he would come back. In an uncharacteristically confrontational way, Standing Bear "answered that if I cared to come back I would do so."[41]

When he left Carlisle in 1884 at age sixteen, Standing Bear returned to the Rosebud Agency to get a job. Armed with a letter from Captain Pratt, he went to the reservation agent and was assigned to be a teaching assistant. Standing Bear benefited socially and economically from his position as teacher, especially when he was transferred to a school at the Pine Ridge Agency for which the government "furnished nearly everything," to the extent that he was "getting along splendidly." However, he developed a deep cynicism about the imposition of European American values as he grew aware of the problems inherent in the government's educational system. As happened with Thomas Wildcat Alford and Sarah Winnemucca, his experience opened his eyes to the poor quality and low expectations of reservation teaching: "It really did not require a well-educated person to teach on the reservation. The main thing was to teach the children to write their names in English, then came learning the alphabet and how to count." Believing that "Indians should teach Indians," Standing Bear was chagrined that Native teachers were increasingly being replaced by European Americans on the reservation, which eventually contributed to his own change of career in the mid-1890s (including employment in Buffalo Bill's Wild West Show and in Hollywood movies). Standing Bear was unimpressed with the ability of these teachers: "While they knew quite a bit about book-learning, and could pass the civil service examinations, that was about the extent of their knowledge." The new teachers' bigoted attitudes rubbed salt in his wound: "Some of these people were actually afraid of Indians, did not know how to live among them, get along with them, nor instruct them."[42]

Even if he had found the teachers competent and knowledgeable about the Lakota way of life, Standing Bear would still have disapproved of monolingual teaching methods: "The English teachers only taught them the English language, like a bunch of parrots. While they could read all the words placed before them, they did not know the proper use of them; their meaning was a puzzle." As he prepared to teach, Standing Bear recalled his own feelings of depression when he had to relinquish the "consolation of speech" as a result of the English-only rule at Carlisle. His memory of that experience led him to develop his own bilingual method: "Those of us who knew the sign language [at Carlisle] made use of it, but imagine what it meant to those who had to remain silent. In teaching, I remembered all these things, so not only allowed but encouraged the speaking of both languages at the same time." Standing Bear's pedagogical approach was to write a sentence on the blackboard in English, have the pupils repeat it over and over, each time explaining the meaning, and then have them repeat it in their own language. From his perspective, the students were "so delighted with the system that they learned very fast." Standing Bear even provided proof that his method could produce better results. When he presented his class at an agency teachers' "convention," they were the only group who could "prove that they knew what they were reading about" by translating the reader into their own language.[43]

Standing Bear left it to the judgment of his "intelligent readers" to determine which approach was superior. Today's readers might question whether having students "*read* the translations as well as they did English" (emphasis added) is an adequate marker of second-language acquisition. And today's audience would likely challenge his attitude toward the education of women: "We Indians wondered how the whites taught their girls only through books. What would they do if left alone? How would they be able to cook for a family? Book learning is very good, of course, but it strikes me that domestic science is the best thing for all girls to adopt, regardless of wealth or position in life." The limitations of his pedagogy notwithstanding, Standing Bear is eloquent in his discussion of what is wrong with American Indian education, especially in *Land of the Spotted Eagle*. His criticism of the English-only rule underscores the importance of understanding the cultural and historical ramifications of language teaching: "This rule is uncalled for, and today is not only robbing the Indian, but America of a rich heritage. The language of a people is part of their history. Today we should be perpetuating history instead of destroying it, and this can only be effectively done by allowing and encouraging the young to keep it alive. A language, unused, embalmed, and reposing only in a book, is a dead language. Only the people themselves, and never the scholars, can nourish it into life."[44]

Standing Bear contests the high status accorded to literacy and challenges European Americans' tendency to equate illiteracy with savagery, exposing the illogic of their race-based privileging of literate folk:

> The written word became established as a criterion of the superior man – a symbol of emotional fineness. The man who could write his name on a piece of paper, whether or not he possessed the spiritual fineness to honor those words in speech, was by some miraculous formula a more highly developed and sensitized person than the one who had never had a pen in hand, but whose spoken word was inviolable and whose sense of honor and truth was paramount. With false reasoning was the quality of human character measured by man's ability to make with an implement a mark upon paper. But granting this mode of reasoning be correct and just, then where are to be placed the thousands of illiterate whites who are unable to read and write? Are they, too, "savages"?

Furthermore, Standing Bear points to the irony that those Native people who managed to achieve literacy in English soon discovered how it was used to denigrate them: "Books have been written of the native American, so distorting his true nature that he scarcely resembles the real man; his faults have been magnified and his virtues minimized." Instead of giving Native people access to the benefits of European American society, Standing Bear implies, books, schools, and libraries – "the very agencies . . . that purport to instruct, educate, and perpetuate true history" – enabled literacy to be used as a tool of oppression. He insists on recognition of the legitimacy of oral cultures. So that his audience can understand the value of this heritage, he recasts Native ways of knowing in European American terms, saying that "stories were the libraries of our people." Taking issue with the primitive/ civilized dichotomy promoted in European American society, which positioned indigenous societies as lacking abstract or historical thinking, he repeatedly uses the word *philosophy* to refer to Native ways of knowing.[45]

History, Standing Bear argues, did not result from literacy, as European Americans were wont to proclaim. In his eyes, the Native experience confirms that history predated literacy. In fact, he suggests that schooling in the United States could be strengthened through history courses taught from a Native perspective, thereby highlighting the reality that no true history of the United States could exist without it. Standing Bear ups the ante when he claims that European Americans precipitated their own spiritual and intellectual decline by attempting to obliterate Native traditions. His indictment exposes the way colonialism did not just impose a European American culture on Native people but also engendered a new European American culture that was self-destructive and impoverished. He employs the salvationist rhetoric of missionaries to establish the existence of a superior Native intellectualism: "It is now time for a destructive order to be reversed, and it is well to inform other races that the aboriginal culture of America was not devoid of beauty. Furthermore, in denying the Indian his ancestral rights and heritages the white race is but robbing itself. But America can be revived, rejuvenated, by recognizing a native school of thought. The Indian can save America."[46]

Ultimately, Standing Bear promotes an equitable concept of linguistic and cultural exchange. Envisioning an inclusive approach to language teaching, he is ahead of his time in calling for education that draws on the linguistic, cultural, and intellectual strengths of all students. Understanding that languages are used in different ways in different contexts, he conceives of schools as sites where different worldviews can build on and give shape to one another:

So we went to school to copy, to imitate; not to exchange languages and ideas, and not to develop the best traits that had come out of uncountable experiences of hundreds and thousands of years living upon this continent. Our annals, all happenings of human import, were stored in our song and dance rituals, our history differing in that it was not stored in books, but in the living memory. So, while the white people had much to teach us, we had much to teach them, and what a school could have been established on that idea![47]

10. "Columbia's Roll Call" (1892). Students in a pageant on Indian Citizenship Day at the Hampton Normal and Agricultural Institute, portraying Samoset and Miles Standish (first row), "The White Mingo, friend of George Washington," Pocahontas, Columbus, Columbia, Priscilla Alden, and a Quaker woman (middle row), Captain John Smith, John Eliot, Herald of Fame, George Washington, William Penn, and "Taminend, a friend of William Penn" (back row). Courtesy of University Archives, Hampton University, Hampton VA.

4

Translingual Ironies

Learning the perspective of students who attended school in the late nineteenth century is difficult, since there are few retrospective accounts. According to official reports, approximately twenty thousand Native students – half of all the school-age Native children – were enrolled in government or government-supported schools at the end of the century. Yet my examination of the one hundred autobiographies Michael C. Coleman found for his book *American Indian Children at School, 1850–1930* yielded fewer than forty autobiographical accounts in which students who entered school during the period under investigation here (1860 to 1900) discussed their education. Of those forty accounts, fewer than thirty included ideas about language and language learning, the focus of this book. Only the most accomplished graduates wrote original reports, and typically only the most fluent or most successful – or most notorious – were chosen to tell their stories to ethnographers. It is obvious that those whose stories are examined here cannot be treated as representative of all who attended school during this era. But it is this very issue that is so meaningful. The dearth of accounts reveals that the overwhelming majority of students remained silent.[1]

There may be several reasons for this silence. The first and most obvious is that, even in the European American population, relatively few people wrote autobiographies; one should not expect a greater percentage of Native students to have written theirs. Even less should one expect many of them could have found a publisher. Another reason for the silence may be that autobiography as practiced in European American literate society was not a genre commonly generated in Native communities, especially since by definition it was produced in written form (auto/bio/*graphy* = self/life/*writing*). Traditionally, Native life stories were related orally. Even then a person typically reported on one incident at a time rather than a whole life, and in many situations only men recounted their experiences.[2] It is possible, too, that a distrust of literacy in response to broken treaties and deleterious congressional acts led former students to turn their backs on the written word in English, a distrust that has reverberated through the centuries and continues to inform the Native experience today, as Scott Richard Lyons emphasizes. This explanation notwithstanding, the silence may not have been merely an outgrowth of a reluctance to relate life stories in print. As Jace Weaver reminds us, Native writers have been representing themselves in published form for more than two hundred years.[3]

Undoubtedly the silence occurred in large part because few students had become proficient or confident enough in their English-language skills to put their stories into written form, even collaboratively. It is important to acknowledge that even under ideal conditions learning a second language is a long term and evolving endeavor. A new language entails much more than a new linguistic system. As sociolinguist James Paul Gee explains, studying language involves learning new sets of discourse practices – ways of using words that are tied to the worldviews of particular social and cultural groups. Attaining new discourse practices is not a neutral undertaking, for it goes to the heart of one's sense of self. Because students' ways with language are inextricably linked with who they are, when learners attempt to adopt new literacy practices, they are in effect trying on new social and cultural identities that are disorienting. Such shifts in identity are understandably difficult and complex. Furthermore, second-language acquisition depends on personality and cognitive factors, and thus students' emotional responses and individual learning strategies figure prominently. Even the body is implicated, for relative physical comfort affects learning. Additionally, individual factors related to linguistic background, family situation, socioeconomic position, racial identity, religion, and gender play a role in learners' educational lives, determining whether, when, how, and to what extent they learn a new language and adopt new ways of knowing. To further complicate the process, the social conditions of the sites of learning are key determinants of how and to what extent a language is acquired.[4] Without a doubt, as the student autobiographies attest, the context within which

American Indian education was enacted profoundly exacerbated the difficulties of learning English.

That we cannot fully recapture the linguistic experience through Native eyes speaks to the vulnerability and subordinate positions of students in relation to those in power. All these students shared the experience of being colonized subjects before, during, and after their schooling. A number of historians, most notably Michael Coleman and David Wallace Adams, have turned to student autobiographies and ethnographies to document the negative psychological and cultural consequences of enforced English-only teaching in the late nineteenth century. This emotional damage should not be underestimated in any discussion of the educational programs, especially since this "colonial wreckage," as Scott Richard Lyons calls it, continues to affect Native communities. The students' own words reveal the cultural displacement and linguistic humiliation of colonial domination. Bitterness about this state of affairs is implicit or explicit in most of the accounts. However, as Coleman and Adams have noted, these accounts are not solely tales of victimization and oppression. Virtually all the autobiographers are members of a relatively small group of former students who not only survived but also acquired a high level of literacy – the group most likely to tell their stories and to have positive experiences to report. Some of the autobiographies are sprinkled with humor, not only because actual classroom incidents were funny but also because the narrators bring a witty adult perspective to these events. Several of the students testify that they developed significant relationships at school, especially with other students and with responsive teachers. Some also report on meaningful language-learning experiences. When they were given encouragement and praised for their linguistic accomplishments, the positive reinforcement instilled in them a desire to improve their language skills and gain more knowledge in general.[5]

This chapter draws on the autobiographical and autoethnographic accounts of former students who entered school between 1860 and 1900 and later discussed issues related to language and language instruction. My objective is not to unearth data about the school experience and the students' lives or to measure them against documented facts, as Coleman and others have already done. Instead, I aim to examine how students used the English language once they learned it – to provide a sense of the former students as owners, performers, and negotiators of language. To that end I attend to a linguistic process the students engaged in, which I identify as *translin-*

gualism. The term *translingual* traditionally has been employed in reference to linguistic translation, but here I use it to capture the translinguistic process students underwent as they moved back and forth between languages, making qualitative decisions about which aspects of language to incorporate and which to reject or transform. Translingualism involved not only students' language use and choices but also the transformation of their linguistic and cultural identities, for their worldview was now being mediated through a new language. I also extend the term *translingual* to the work of these Native autobiographers in the same way Lydia Liu uses it in her study of Chinese literary figures: to describe the creativity of writers and intellectuals who cross-culturally appropriate, recreate, and critique a language. In many cases Native students' multicultural experiences and cross-cultural perspectives gave them insight into the ironies and contradictions embedded in European American discourses. Having had inaccurate representations of themselves imposed on them so as to negatively affect their lived existence, Native writers used English to speak for themselves and represent their own lives. Focusing on the rhetoric the former students employed to tell their stories, in this chapter I analyze how these students, as adults, manipulated the English language for their own purposes and played with it to exploit its ironic potential and invert its conventional meanings. Without ignoring the assimilationist rhetoric, ambiguity, uncertainty, and nostalgia that inform many of the texts, I have mined these works for evidence of those moments when students took ownership of English to fashion a critique of a monolithic European American worldview and to reconstruct Native social history.[6]

Given that most of the works were narrated by men, inevitably the material in this chapter is presented primarily from a male perspective. Chapter 5, in contrast, deliberately focuses on a female perspective, particularly as applied to images of Native women, for transforming females was a major goal of the Indian Office. Although the thrust of this chapter is not on male images per se, underlying the analysis is an awareness of deeply ingrained European American stereotypes of Native men. At one end of the spectrum, as Robert Berkhofer illustrates in *The White Man's Indian,* Native men were viewed as noble: brave, hospitable, and physically strong. At the other they were savage: wild, cruel, lecherous, and disturbingly naked. Whichever stereotype was applied at any given juncture, European Americans typically measured indigenous cultures against their own, which almost always resulted in identifying what was lacking in Native ways of knowing. There was little or no acknowledgment of the meaningful contributions Native males were making in the education of their children, especially their sons. The student autobiographers were speaking against this bias, providing a European American audience with new ways of seeing – through a bicultural lens.[7]

As David Murray has pointed out, there was growing European American interest in Native people at precisely the moment they were perceived to be vanishing from the American landscape.[8] Many of the student autobiographers took advantage of renewed attention to put a human face on the repercussions of the United States government's imposition of English on indigenous people. Whether or not these students succeeded in becoming fluent bilinguals, they all were able to use English (even if through a translator, in the case of Frank Mitchell) to tell their life stories and thus to make an important contribution not only to the history of language instruction but to the history of the country itself. Having studied English, they made much more complex use of the language than their teachers might ever have expected. Most of them included detailed tribal histories, correcting misrepresentations of both Native people *and* European Americans that permeated colonialist discourses. They reconceptualized popular narrative and put forth their own ideas on language and intercultural contact. In doing so they demonstrated how the past – and the present – could be (re)interpreted from a Native perspective. Furthermore, in describing their traditions, they necessarily used words from their own languages – transliterated into English – because some concepts could not be translated. Through English, then, they conveyed not only their cultures but also their languages, making them an undeniable and enduring presence in United States history, literature, and life. Their stories of resistance to linguistic violence help to explain how Native cultures have endured in spite of almost unimaginable efforts to obliterate them.

ENGLISH IN CAPTIVITY

The experience of captivity shaped the tribal and American landscape for centuries. Even before European contact, Native people took Native captives for a variety of reasons, such as demanding ransom or replacing lost community members. Europeans held other Europeans captive, for example, during the British and French struggle in North America. But the best-known captivity experience is the capture of Europeans by Native people. Held for only a few days or for years, some of the European captives were treated harshly, but many were embraced as family. Although captivity was a fearful event, a number of European Americans ultimately preferred the Native way of life. Others who chose to return home after captivity often found they had unwittingly internalized Native cultural perspectives and consequently were ostracized. Some of them were anxious to divorce themselves from any hint of a Native outlook on life. Out of this complex set of circumstances was born the captivity narrative – the story of a European American's capture by Native people – feeding the hunger of European American readers for morality tales infused with exoticism and terror. As a story of Christian faith and perseverance in the face of adversity, the captivity narrative remained a popular genre from the seventeenth century through the nineteenth. In fact one of the first best-sellers in America was Mary Rowlandson's 1682 story of her three-month captivity by Algonquian Indians during King Philip's War, *The Soveraignty and Goodness of God.* Because most captivity narratives focused on Indian savagery, Scott Lyons notes, they served to justify a continuation of colonialist policies.[9]

The lesser-known story of captivity is the capture of Native people by Europeans. Many Native men were kidnapped and sold into slavery, and young Native women were especially prey to abduction. However, as Rebecca Blevins Faery notes, these stories were rarely published, and when they were, as in the case of Pocahontas, they were not told from a Native perspective. One tragic legacy of Rowlandson's narrative, Jill Lepore documents, was the disregard of the trauma experienced by Native people at the hands of European American captors.[10] In the early twentieth century a number of Native students adjusted the historical perspective by discussing their experiences in school as though they were characters in their own captivity narratives.

As David R. Sewell says of European American captives, these Native students found themselves in unfamiliar linguistic as well as geographic territory. Often no one in the school spoke their language. Even when interpreters were available, they typically did not have bilingual fluency, so communication was compromised. Yet, as Sewell points out, the captivity experience was ultimately negotiated through language. In writing about their captivity after the fact, European Americans were liberated from the linguistically limiting environment of capture. The captor had controlled past events, but the freed captive could now control retrospective storytelling. Like these former captives, former students who chose to narrate their stories could now attempt to use written language to impose their own interpretation of events. Of course the parallels do not hold when it comes to the medium through which the different groups told their stories. Anglo Americans could use their first language (English), whereas Native students were compelled to use a second language (English) to reach an Anglo American readership. The power of English was thus sustained. Nevertheless, these two sets of captives shared many of the experiences and rhetorical moves that Gary Ebersole analyzes in *Captured by Texts,* a study of the narrative and representational practices European Americans used in making sense of their captivity.[11]

Just as the European American captives Ebersole describes were forced into an isolating and culturally foreign environment, the Native students were cut off from their social support system and thrust into an alien way of life. Their identity and the very meaning of their existence were challenged when they lost their freedom. In two of the student autobiographies, this sense of alienation was underscored by use of the third-person perspective. Although virtually all of his book, *The Middle Five: Indian Schoolboys of the Omaha Tribe,* is written in the first person, Francis La Flesche presents his first moment at a Presbyterian mission boarding school on the Omaha reservation as so traumatic that he can tell it only in the third person. He describes himself as a "little boy . . . all alone, sobbing as though his heart would break." Similarly, reflecting the distance he felt from his own self, Ah-nen-la-de-ni changes briefly from first person to third in "An Indian Boy's Story" to describe the experience of being "prevented from expressing his feelings in the only language he knew" (Mohawk) at an English-only boarding school in Philadelphia.[12]

Apache students were literally prisoners of war, so when Asa Daklugie claims in *Indeh: An Apache Odyssey* that he felt like a "prisoner" during his twelve years at the Carlisle School, the term is accurate. Other students use metaphor and symbol to convey the idea that they were trapped or imprisoned in boarding schools. The first lines of Francis La Flesche's *The Middle Five,* for example, suggest that the new student is positioned like a prisoner facing a firing squad, for he is "leaning against the wall of a large stone build-

ing" and crying. In "The School Days of an Indian Girl," Zitkala-Ša identifies new recruits as "little animals driven by a herder." Charles Eastman
voluntarily entered a bilingual program at the Dakota Mission with the encouragement of his father, who had been converted to Christianity and believed Native people had no choice but to adopt some European American
ways. Nevertheless, in *From the Deep Woods to Civilization: Chapters in the
Autobiography of an Indian* Eastman represents himself as a once free-
spirited creature condemned to domestication: "I was something like a wild
cub caught overnight, and appearing in the corral next morning with the
lambs." As we learn in *Mourning Dove: A Salishan Autobiography,* Mourning Dove entered a mission boarding school on the Colville Reservation in
Washington because of the family priest's "command" that she be sent. Because Mourning Dove knew no English, she did not understand the conversation between her father and the "woman in black," the mother superior.
Her reaction was to scream and kick and cling to her father. The nun responded by putting her in a dark closet.[13]

Escape from captivity, too, is a common theme. Because he had learned
so little English at the reservation day school in New York, Ah-nen-la-de-
ni's mother encouraged him to go away to a government contract boarding
school. She thought that education would be a valuable asset, "as white men
were 'so tricky with papers.'" But Ah-nen-la-de-ni himself was tricked by
the "honey-tongued" agent who came to his reservation to recruit students
for the Lincoln Institute in Philadelphia. Two years after he started school
his mother died, and he was not allowed to go home for the funeral. Essentially held hostage at the school, Ah-nen-la-de-ni internalized that circum-
stance so deeply that at one point he opted not to return to the reservation
for a vacation even when he was given the opportunity. Initially promised
that their term would end after five years, he and other students, whom he
referred to as fellow "inmates," were forced to remain as what he called
"show scholars." He searched for a way out by applying to a nurses' training
school in Manhattan. His application went through an underground chan-
nel that circumvented the censorship of the school's regular mail. He says he
was literally in the school's "jail" when the answer to his application arrived,
being punished for something he had not done. On the Fourth of July, a
date he takes delight in remembering, he managed to flee.[14]

Don Talayesva also employs the language of captivity and escape in *Sun
Chief: The Autobiography of a Hopi Indian* to tell the story of his entrance

into a mesa day school. Before he became a student, his sister had already run away from school but had been "captured" by the principal and forced to return. When it was time for Talayesva to go to school, he says, he was "willing to try it," fear being a great motivator. He was so determined not to be handled by a policeman that he went by himself. Nevertheless, he unwittingly set the stage for his own captivity. Arriving late, and without being told, he stepped into a bathtub to scrub himself, having heard that all the boys were expected to do this. When a white woman suddenly entered the room and made the strange sounds "On my life!" he was so frightened that he jumped out and started running back up the mesa. He was pursued by boys who were sent to "catch" him.[15]

In mentioning the boys who caught him, Talayesva's story exposes a feature of colonial rule; for as historian James Gump points out, colonial powers relied on indigenous collaborators to subjugate people on colonized lands. Accordingly, Native people themselves were often hired by the schools to serve as captors. As he relates in *Born a Chief: The Nineteenth Century Hopi Boyhood of Edmund Nequatewa,* Edmund Nequatewa was "chased" by two Navajo policemen and "grabbed" by two Hopi policemen when he ran away from the Phoenix Indian School. Even relatives could be enlisted to capture their young. Albert Yava tells such a story in *Big Falling Snow: A Tewa-Hopi Indian's Life and Times and the History and Traditions of His People.* Raised in Tewa Village, Yava was five or six years old when he entered the day school below First Mesa (1893 or 1894). Although few Hopi children had adequate clothing, they did not like the "white man's style" of clothes they were given at school, so Yava and his friends stripped naked and ran back up the mesa. They were followed by the truant officer, Yava's uncle, who "had to chase us all through the village and over the roof tops to catch us." Yava himself would later be implicated in this process, when as a worker in the Bureau of Indian Affairs he was assigned to join the troops that were sent in to "round up the Hotevilla children and take them to boarding school by force."[16]

In *Captured by Texts,* Gary Ebersole notes that, precisely because they have been physically torn from their surroundings, captives become more aware of the surfaces and boundaries of the body and experience them in a more intense way than in their previous, less conscious state. Seventeenth-century captives, for example, perceived their bodies as sites of divine teaching through hunger and physical pain, forcing them to confront their human limitations and mortality. Many of the students in this book comment on the various ways the body figured in their educational experiences. Even before they entered schools, numerous students were held in a kind of captivity created by United States government policy: as victims of poverty on the reservation. The hunger they consequently experienced sometimes led them to opt for school, as Edward Goodbird sarcastically notes of the Hidatsa children in *Goodbird the Indian: His Story*: "The Indian police saw that every child was in school learning the white man's way. A good dinner at the noon hour made most of the children rather willing scholars." Transforming the body was the first order of business in the schools, especially through haircuts and uniforms, reinforcing students' sense that they were captives. As Zitkala-Ša puts it, "Our mothers had taught us that only unskilled warriors who were captured had their hair shingled by the enemy." Asa Daklugie bitterly explains that the external change altered students' sense of self: "We'd lost our hair and we'd lost our clothes; with the two we'd lost our identity as Indians. Greater punishment could hardly have been devised."[17]

Even more serious transformations occurred through disease, forcing students to confront a common experience among captives: having to view the body as a target for degradation and death. In *My People the Sioux* Luther Standing Bear says one of the hardest things about studying at the Carlisle School was that "we had to get used to so many things we had never known before that it worked on our nerves to such an extent that it told on our bodies." The year the Apaches arrived at Carlisle, Richard Pratt reported cases of scarlet fever, measles, and scrofula and the next year a high mortality rate. In *In the Days of Victorio: Recollections of a Warm Springs Apache,* James Kaywaykla reminds European American readers that these children suffered not only the "indignity" of haircuts but also the danger of "climatic conditions new to us and fatal to many." The many headstones in the cemetery at Carlisle speak to the tragedy of the era.[18]

In captivity, Ebersole shows, people become cognizant of the symbolic and cultural implications of physicality and the ways their own bodies serve as political sites. By the late eighteenth century, for example, European American captives represented their bodies as sites not of divine suffering but rather of heroism enacted for the benefit of the nation. Power relations were inscribed on the captive's body through a variety of oppressive measures, including vicious attacks and forced marches. These incidents are presented in the European American narratives not only as evidence of the inhumanity of the captors but also as tests of the captives' ingenuity and character. In the stories of the Native captives, encounters with violence play a similar role. Inverting stereotypes, these former students portray many European Americans as callous brutes while representing themselves on the one hand as sympathetic victims and on the other as shrewd, courageous, and resilient resisters. For example, Francis La Flesche recalls a series of blows executed by a teacher when the boys were caught telling stories at bedtime, but he reports that they outwitted their attacker and avoided serious harm. As punishment for refusing to debate in public because of stage fright, Don Talayesva received fifteen blows with a rawhide from the school disciplinarian. The focus of this incident, however, is on his resistance, for he proudly announces that he was not asked to debate publicly again. Ah-nen-la-de-ni recollects being made to stand in the public hall or to march about the yard for hours as a penalty for speaking in his native tongue. He remained defiant nonetheless, frequently rebelling and willingly paying the consequences. Edmund Nequatewa describes being hit across the face with a ruler because he had rushed out of the classroom, even though the reason for his leaving suddenly was that he was ill and felt the urge to vomit. He turned his anger at the teacher into an ingenious escape strategy by paying more attention to the geography lessons "because it is the only way that I can find my way out."[19]

In writing about their school experiences, several former students address what they understand to be European Americans' fear of the Native body. Some students had internalized European American views on this issue. Ah-nen-la-de-ni's discussion of the body in his 1903 autobiographical essay "An Indian Boy's Story" is useful here because shows both how a student could be influenced by the underlying racial ideology of the schools and how that ideology was linked to language learning. Even before Ah-nen-la-de-ni entered a reservation day school in 1885, he says, many residents of the St. Regis Reservation in New York dressed and farmed in a European American style. However, they all spoke Mohawk and followed Mohawk traditions. Ah-nen-la-de-ni understands returning students' decision to do the same, for the ties with family and elders were strong. Nevertheless, he offers his European American readers racial comfort by stating that "real Indians" were numerically in decline as a result of intermarriage: "On all the reservations the pure-blooded Indians are becoming rarer and rarer and the half and quarter breeds more and more common – technically they're Indians. Thus tho the tribe is increasing, the real Indians are decreasing. They are becoming more and more white. On our reserve now you can see boys and girls with light hair and blue eyes, children of white fathers and Indian mothers. They have the rosy cheeks of English children, but they cannot speak a word of English." Here Ah-nen-la-de-ni reassures his readers, apparently without sarcasm, that biology is erasing the troublesome evidence of *physical* difference. But there is still the problem of *linguistic* difference. To address that issue, Ah-nen-la-de-ni turns to the schools, which he claims are already "doing a great deal of good to the Indians and are changing them fast." He indicates that it is only a matter of time before the schools eradicate the linguistic problem. Transformation of the body is thus linked to transformation of the spoken language. The goal, Ah-nen-la-de-ni implies, is to reach the stage where the sounds of the children's words match their "rosy cheeks," so that European American society can relax.[20]

Other students are deliberately cynical as they address the expectations of European American readers in regard to the Native body. Clarifying why he presents the Native boys not in their home attire but in their school uniforms, Francis La Flesche reveals that he understands that "paint, feathers, robes, and other articles that make up the dress of the Indian" are viewed by Europeans as "marks of savagery." But his contempt for the Europeans' viewpoint is obvious, especially when he notes that, in their minds, Native dress precludes the wearer from "lay[ing] claim to a share in common human nature." La Flesche emphasizes that, contrary to European American notions, the school uniform does not alter the inner character of those who wear it. His goal is for the boys to be judged not by how they look but "by what they say and do."[21]

Luther Standing Bear, too, differentiates between the need to mimic the European American body and the need to be true to one's inner self. In so doing he inverts expectations about the role Christianity played as a source of comfort in captivity. Mary Rowlandson had pledged to die if Native captors came to take her, but instead she willingly left with them to avoid death. Rowlandson's complicity in her own capture, Jill Lepore maintains, caused her to write her narrative as a way to redeem herself. Rowlandson thus made a point of explaining how the Bible sustained her in her time of pain and suffering. Standing Bear crossed a similar path, but in writing of his own experience he subverts the captivity narrative as a story of Christian faith.

When he joined the first group of Sioux children to enroll in the Carlisle Indian School, Standing Bear pledged to follow his father's oft-given advice: "Be brave! Die on the battle-field if necessary away from home." However, instead of dying or even exhibiting courage in the Lakota way, Standing Bear became a cooperative student at Carlisle and was baptized in the Episcopal Church. Like Mary Rowlandson, he may have written his narrative as a way to redeem himself. Like her, he explains that his spiritual background was a source of strength in his captivity. But with derisive rhetorical skill he reveals that it was the Lakota way of life – not Christianity – that fortified him:

> Outwardly I lived the life of the white man, yet all the while I kept in direct contact with tribal life. While I had learned all that I could of the white man's culture, I never forgot that of my people. I kept the language, tribal manners and usages, sang the songs, and danced the dances. I still listened to and respected the advice of the older people in the tribe. I did not come home so "progressive" that I could not speak the language of my father and mother. I did not learn the vices of chewing tobacco, smoking, drinking, and swearing, and for all this I am grateful. I have never, in fact, "progressed" that far.[22]

TRANSFORMING TRANSLATIONS

A central thesis of Eric Cheyfitz's *The Poetics of Imperialism* is that translation is the colonizer's principal mode of political and cultural control. By translation Cheyfitz means not simply the process of transferring ideas from one language to another but also the power to construct cultural identity through that process. He examines various ways Western European writing translated Native cultures to the point where they were stripped of their humanity. Native languages, too, were subjected to a violent disruption in translation, whereby they were disassociated from their cultural contexts. Lawrence Venuti acknowledges that all translation is inherently ethnocentric, for foreign texts need to be made accessible to domestic audiences and are therefore reinvented for a different cultural community. But a "scandal of translation," as he calls it, is manifest in the deliberate refusal to convey the cultural values and linguistic distinctiveness of the original text. Such language use reflects and reinforces unequal power relationships, for it has the effect of subordinating the original language and culture while privileging the language and culture into which they are being translated.[23]

Most nineteenth-century European Americans gained access to Native languages only through texts and speeches in translation. In literary works such as James Fenimore Cooper's *The Last of the Mohicans* (1862), as Lawrence Rosenwald has recently shown, Native languages were represented in ways that inscribed inferiority and obscured the sophisticated means through which each language conveyed meaning. A popular sentiment of the era, articulated in an 1870 article in *Harper's New Monthly Magazine*, held that Native languages were "too limited to allow a wealth of diction." Thus did literature and journalism reproduce the ideology of hegemonic institutions such as church, state, and school, which marginalized Native lives. Yet as Venuti argues, because of the diverse and capricious effects of colonization, the practice of translation also allowed for cross-cultural resistance and inventiveness. Early in the twentieth century, several former students took advantage of the language skills they had developed in nineteenth-century mission and government schools to question the way Native languages and people had been translated into English. They used English to re-present themselves and their own languages. In doing so they also challenged European Americans' representations of *them*selves and of the English language. Their writing illustrates Luther Standing Bear's point that "all the years of calling the Indian a savage has never made him one."[24]

As a result of their interactions with different languages, many students had a better understanding of the worth of second-language learning than the monolingual teachers who were typically in charge of their education. In fact, a number of students discussed in this book report that they had been exposed to bilingualism or multilingualism even before they entered school, for they had experienced diverse ways of communicating on the reservation, including sign language. Some learned a third or fourth language after they started school, in informal settings such as summer placement with German-speaking or Spanish-speaking families or from other students. For example, as he reports in *The Arapaho Way: A Memoir of an Indian Boyhood*, Carl Sweezy learned German in a Mennonite Mission school. In describing that experience, he reveals how greatly his community on the Cheyenne-Arapaho reservation valued multilingual literacy: "Any letter, to an Indian on the Reservation, was something important, but a letter in German was something to talk about for a long time. To be able to write it was an accomplishment for a Cheyenne or an Arapaho, who had already learned, besides his own language, to talk in the sign language and to read and write in English." The English-only rule, which cut off human communication across cultures, was antithetical to this approach to language acquisition. In the classroom, many students were "harassed with words," as Charles Eastman puts it, for "like raspberry bushes in the path, they tore, bled, and sweated us . . . until not a semblance of our native dignity and self-respect was left." The frustration that resulted from the inability to use their own languages in school led to some ingenious approaches. James Kaywaykla reports that at the Carlisle Indian School, where there was a mixture of language groups, several Apache students learned sign language in order to converse with students who had been raised on the plains. With this translingual move, it is amusing to note, students were able to circumvent the prohibition against *speaking* Native languages at school.[25]

Knowing more than one language gave students a deep understanding of the variety, purpose, and power of language. No one was more eloquent about this effect than Francis La Flesche, who became a linguist and, through his work in the Bureau of American Ethnology, was instrumental in preserving the Omaha language and culture. As an anthropologist, La Flesche was aware of the ways European American texts had translated Native humanness out of existence. Undoubtedly he was familiar with popular schoolbooks used in Indian schools, such as *Elementary History of the United States* by George P. Quackenbos (first published in 1860), in which Native students could learn the following about their country: "Four hundred years ago, the land we inhabit looked very different from what it now does. There were no great cities in it then; no large farms, with fields of waving grain; no comfortable houses, with smoke curling up from their chimney tops; no horses or cattle in the meadows; no fences, no bridge, no roads; no steamboats or sailing-vessels on the rivers; no white men, to give life to the whole." In his preface to *The Middle Five,* La Flesche exposes the way English was being used to make indigenous peoples invisible so territory could be appropriated with impunity, and then he uses the language to assume historical, spiritual, and rhetorical ownership of land that was taken largely through deception and violence: "The white people speak of the country at this period as 'a wilderness,' as though it was an empty tract without human interest or history. To us Indians it was as clearly defined then as it is to-day;

we knew the boundaries of tribal lands, those of our friends and those of our foes; we were familiar with every stream, the contour of every hill, and each peculiar feature of the landscape had its tradition. It was our home, the scene of our history, and we loved it as our country."[26]

La Flesche's project is not simply to critique historical uses of the English language or even to use English to rewrite United States history. He also seeks to restore the integrity of Native languages, which have been devalued through translation. By pointing out that Native languages typically were transmitted by translators who did not have full enough command of English to convey meaning with subtlety and sophistication, La Flesche reminds readers that most of the students who studied English in the government and mission schools emerged with inadequate skills. Similarly, in *Life among the Piutes,* Sarah Winnemucca speaks to the political problems that occurred when interpreters did not "understand English enough to know all that is said." Luther Standing Bear's discussion of his own experience as a young student demonstrates how weak the link could be between the original statement and its translated version. On one occasion during an evening entertainment at the Carlisle School, when someone in the audience asked school superintendent Richard Henry Pratt to have one of the boys speak in the Sioux tongue, Pratt turned to Standing Bear, who obligingly arose and said, "Lakota iya woci ci yakapi queyasi oyaka rnirapi kte sni tka le ha han pe lo." However, when he was asked to interpret what he had just said ("If I talk in Sioux, you will not understand me anyhow"), Standing Bear was unable to do it properly. And so he made up something instead: "We are glad to see you all here to-night." Pratt was so pleased with what he thought were Standing Bear's translation skills that he took him on his next trip to Washington to act as his own father's interpreter. Meeting with the commissioner of Indian affairs to request workhorses for the agency, Standing Bear's father spoke in Lakota, Standing Bear repeated the ideas to Pratt in "broken English," and Pratt turned the words into what Standing Bear could only hope reflected his father's meaning.[27]

According to La Flesche, the poor preparation of the typical interpreter, combined with the differences between the languages, meant that monolingual speakers of English could not have the opportunity to appreciate the "beauty and picturesqueness, and euphonious playfulness, or the gravity of diction" of the Native language being translated. La Flesche recognizes that the fragmented transmission of ideas from Native languages into English contributed to the prevailing notion that Native languages were inherently primitive. To counteract that idea, he emphasizes that his first language had its own complex grammatical and communicative system: "From the earliest years the Omaha child was trained in the grammatical use of his native tongue. No slip was allowed to pass uncorrected, and as a result there was no child-talk such as obtains among English-speaking children, – the only difference between the speech of the old and young was in the pronunciation of words which the infant often failed to utter correctly, but this difficulty was soon overcome, and a boy of ten or twelve was apt to speak as good Omaha as a man of mature years." Like La Flesche, Thomas Wildcat Alford counteracts the notion of linguistic deficiency, especially as it pertained to oratory, by explaining how the Shawnee language reflected abstract concepts: "Our belief that all nature was animate, sympathetic, and responsive gave color to the speeches of orators and chiefs. When the warrior Tecumseh made his famous speech in behalf of the confederacy of the different tribes in Indiana his references to Mother Nature were considered merely poetical, but in reality they voiced the sincere belief of his people."[28]

To emphasize the sophistication of his own language, La Flesche compares it with what he identifies as the schoolboys' "broken English." Here he underlines the incongruity that the English-only rule, which made every new student feel like "a little dummy," prohibited students from speaking fluently. For he knows quite well that the boys could speak unbroken Omaha. He thus indirectly reminds readers of the boys' first-language proficiency and implies the linguistic strengths they were bringing to the enterprise of second-language learning. He illustrates his point through the boys' retelling of traditional stories when they went to bed at night. In contrast to the fragmentary English-speaking style that La Flesche transcribes – for example, "Where you live?" – the Omaha speech of the storyteller is fully developed and sophisticated: "He was so handsome a youth that whenever he walked through the village all eyes were turned upon him with admiration." In other sections of the autobiography, furthermore, La Flesche artfully demonstrates that the boys' "broken" language was not necessarily deficient, for students were resourceful in their lexical constructions, taking advantage of their knowledge of their first language to acquire the second: "William T. Sherman was quick to learn, and by the time winter was over he was speaking the peculiar English used by the boys of the school; he said, 'fool bird,' for quail; 'first time,' for long ago, and other Indian expressions turned into English." In an inventive act of translingualism, La Flesche sprinkles the text with other translations, what he calls "Indian expressions turned into English," such as his father's use of the term "house of teaching" to describe the school or the label "make-believe white-men" to describe the people who formed the Christian village on the reservation his father headed. In so doing, he simultaneously (and rather slyly) reveals the expressive and ironic potential of his own language and effectively demonstrates that the English language is enriched by Native ways of naming.[29]

Underlying La Flesche's words is his recognition that his translations are enhanced and enriched by his bilingualism, whereas his readers' understanding is limited by their monolingualism. A hint of cynicism about this state of affairs also appears in Carl Sweezy's statement that "we had to learn from people who did not speak our language or try to learn it, except for a few words, though they expected us to learn theirs." Other students employ a rhetorical sleight of hand by exposing European Americans' inadequacies when attempting to use a Native language. In telling the story of the missionary teacher who asked him in Dakota what his name was (a question, he says, that no Dakota would answer in such circumstances), Charles Eastman emphasizes the teacher's lack of cultural knowledge. And in referring to this teacher's attempt at communication as "broken Sioux," he also points to the man's linguistic deficiency. Mourning Dove recalls a priest's "way of jumbling up words from several Indian languages he had learned so that his words sounded childish." In *Navajo Blessingway Singer: The Autobiography of Frank Mitchell, 1881–1967,* Frank Mitchell takes delight in revealing the inadequacy of a visiting priest's Navajo: "He would begin his talk by saying, 'My dear children,' (*átchíni*) but instead of saying it that way, he used to say '*diichiłí*' (abalone shell)." Mitchell also implicitly criticizes the school at Fort Defiance for not being able to foster any real communication. No adult in the school – not an administrator, not a teacher, not even an employee – knew any Navajo. Nor was there an interpreter available for the weekly church services, so the children listened to sermons without comprehending anything. Mitchell surmises that the priests were "just talking to themselves."[30]

As he explains how he transcribed the nonstandard speech of the boys, La Flesche engages in another attack on European Americans' speaking ability – this time when they used English. Implying that his own language is morally superior, he turns the rhetorical tables on the educational reformers who believed that the English language would elevate Native students:

In the talk of the boys I have striven to give a reproduction of the peculiar English spoken by them, which was composite, gathered from the imperfect comprehension of their books, the provincialisms of the teachers, and the slang and bad grammar picked up from uneducated white persons employed at the school or at the Government Agency. Oddities of speech, profanity, localisms, and slang were unknown in the Omaha language, so when such expressions fell upon the ears of these lads they innocently learned and used them without the slightest suspicion that there could be bad as well as good English.

As Stephen Greenblatt has said of the sixteenth-century indigenous people who came in contact with Europeans, the students could echo Shakespeare's Caliban and say, "You taught me language; and my profit on't / Is, I know how to curse." Don Talayesva makes a point in *Sun Chief* of saying that he "learned to preach pretty well, and to cuss too" at the Young Men's Christian Association, something that was not possible in Hopi, for the language had no curse words. In *A Pima Remembers,* George Webb makes a similar point, showing how Pima provided a more creative way to express distaste: "We have no bad swear words in our language. Words like *ashu·ge-nuwi* (you stinking little Buzzard), *or alu·ge-ban,* (you sneaky old Coyote), are about the worst I can think of." Speaking of the profanity of the "white boys" he lived with in Philadelphia, Luther Standing Bear takes the opportunity to criticize European American society: "And these boys were supposed to be civilized, having had good teachers and good education." In *Cheyenne Memories* John Stands in Timber, too, mocks English speakers' proclivity toward swearing when he describes the class that a medicine man formed on the reservation to prepare children for the mission school:

> [The Indian teacher] showed us a picture of two men on horseback facing each other. "They are talking," he said. "They are saying, 'Goddamn.'" So we all said that, one at a time. And the next thing was, "You son-of-a-bitch." That was some of the first English we learned. We thought it was the way the white man said "Hello."[31]

As humorous as some of these comments may appear, they are not meant to detract from the more serious issues related to translation. The student autobiographers make it clear that the consequences of poor translation are not just communicative, not merely a problem of the inaccurate transmission of ideas. La Flesche reveals the deeper psychological repercussions when he links European Americans' lack of appreciation for the complexity of Native languages to disrespect on the part of the English-speaking listener, which in turn creates unspeakable sadness: "No native American can ever cease to regret that the utterances of his father have been constantly belittled when put into English, that their thoughts have frequently been travestied and their native dignity obscured." George Webb, too, expresses regret as he addresses the denigration of his language, as well as the efforts to eradicate it, and he offers an alternative view. In spite of having been educated in three English-only environments – a reservation day school, a government boarding school, and a public high school – Webb explains, he has continued to speak and celebrate Pima, for "anyone, once speaking the language, will not ever forget it" because it is "very gentle and musical." Furthermore, he emphasizes the vital connection between language and culture by explaining that the Pima language enables Pimas to understand their own way of life, for it conveys concepts that do not exist in English.[32]

As he describes his own career after he returned home from the Chilocco Indian School in Oklahoma, Albert Yava reveals an even more profound link between language and culture. He was in demand as an interpreter at the Keams Canyon Agency in Arizona, even though some of the other returned students spoke English better than he, because he spoke the dialect of First Mesa, which the government officials had arbitrarily deemed the "standard." He explains that his task was "not only to translate words but to translate culture," which involved attending to the contexts the words arose from: "If a Hopi spokesman said something about a certain matter, I had to understand what was back of what he said and all the things that were implied but not spoken." Yava also implies the relation between language, meaning, and power when he points out that, as translator, he "had to know . . . who were 'the moving forces'" in the community. Some of the village or clan spokesmen did not trust him with their information because he was not a member of one of the important kiva groups, so he was initiated into the One Horn Lodge. This made him a "full-fledged Hopi" and committed him to a lifetime of learning Hopi traditions. He thus reveals that his job as interpreter for the Indian Service led him toward the very life he was supposed to be moving his clients away from. The colonial power of translation was thus inadvertently subverted.[33]

However, for the students in the schools, colonizing acts were more difficult to evade. Eric Cheyfitz emphasizes that a feature of the imperial mission has always been to rename Native people, translating them into the terms of the empire as a form of cultural control. At school, teachers assigned the students European American names or translations of Native names. The name change was ostensibly carried out for convenience. However, Francis La Flesche understands that its true purpose was to fulfill the colonialist mission to eradicate Native cultures. In discussing the renaming, he exhibits rhetorical deftness when he reminds European Americans of their own barbarous past: "All the boys in our school were given English names, because their Indian names were difficult for the teachers to pronounce. Besides, the aboriginal names were considered by the missionaries as heathenish, and therefore should be obliterated. No less heathenish in their origin were the English substitutes, but the loss of their original meaning and significance through long usage had rendered them fit to continue as appellations for civilized folk." Ah-nen-la-de-ni, known as Daniel La France, also connects renaming to colonizing forces, declaring that "my family had had the name 'La France' bestowed on them by the French some generations before my birth."[34]

With unmistakable irony, La Flesche explains that he uses English names rather than Omaha names for the boys in his book so that they would not "lose their identity and fail to stand out clearly in the mind of the reader." In suggesting that the boys could "lose their identity" if they were to retain their Omaha names, La Flesche of course deliberately inverts the truth. For by *not* retaining their given names, they were threatened with loss of identity. Here La Flesche poignantly emphasizes that a student's change of name entailed more than a new sound in a new language, for it could mean a redefinition of the self, as a number of students testify. Signifying accomplishments or potential, Native names were a source of pride. When his Mohawk name was "discarded" and replaced with a name devoid of meaning, Ah-nen-la-de-ni says he was so devastated that at first he felt "lost": "I had been proud of myself and my possibilities as 'Turns the crowd' . . . but Daniel La France was to me a stranger and a nobody with no possibilities." Asa Daklugie experienced a similar bitterness. He never forgot the day when names were fired at the students like bullets from a death squad:

They marched us into a room and our interpreter ordered us to line up with our backs to a wall. I went to the head of the line because that's where a chief belongs.

Then a man went down it. Starting with me he began: "Asa, Benjamin, Charles, Daniel, Eli, Frank." . . . We didn't know till later that they'd even imposed meaningless new names on us, along with the other degradations. I've always hated that name. It was forced on me as though I had been an animal.[35]

Naming was not a one-way process in the schools, and on the other side it often took the form of resistance. Students were inventive translingualists, creating their own secret nomenclature for the personnel at their institutions. La Flesche and his classmates, for example, referred to their teacher only as "Gray-beard," thus robbing his identity of all but a removable physical feature. Frank Mitchell and his friends, at a place renamed Fort Defiance by the United States government, did their own defiant renaming: "We could not even memorize the names of the teachers. So we would give them names in our language. I had a teacher, a woman teacher, who was very slim and skinny; at times she got mean. So we named her 'Miss Chipmunk.' There was a lady we worked for in the laundry; she was a tall woman and really light in complexion; that's why we called her 'Red Corn.' Then there was another one who worked in the kitchen; she was an awful-looking thing, and we called her 'The Woman Who Makes You Scream.' "[36]

QUESTIONING CULTURAL REPRESENTATIONS

In their survey of postcolonial theory and practice, *The Empire Writes Back,* Bill Ashcroft, Gareth Griffiths, and Helen Tiffin define postcolonial literature as literature created by people in response to their colonization. This definition is especially apt for the autobiographical productions examined in this book because it takes into account that the narrators were experiencing not the aftereffects of colonialism but the situation of colonialism itself. Although each of the former students had a unique experience and each came from a unique culture, they remained grounded in their Native roots even as they were forced to – or chose to – live in a world increasingly dominated by European American culture. The United States government's stated educational goal was students' acquisition of English and acculturation to European American ways. For that goal to be accomplished, the Indian Office believed Native languages and traditional practices would have to be eradicated. On a practical level, given that few students could acquire linguistic mastery or even relative fluency in the programs that were offered, it is not surprising that the goal was not reached. Yet even in cases where students achieved a high level of linguistic proficiency, it is evident in the life stories that the government fell short of its aim. It is true, of course, that disruptions occurred that would have far-reaching implications for students' lives and communities. But a close examination of their stories reveals that, simultaneously with learning a new language, they were also engaged in a dynamic process of transculturation. As Mary Louise Pratt points out, in conditions of conquest or domination, transcultural processes are unequal and erratic. People in subordinated positions do not control what flows out of the dominant culture. However, in a variety of ways, they can choose what to incorporate into their own culture. Without sacrificing their tribal identity, virtually all of the student autobiographers considered here built a new life on what they perceived to be the most meaningful features of the communities that influenced them. These new cultural forms themselves were constantly changing, involving a complex interaction in which former students moved back and forth between languages and cultures.[37]

Like other postcolonial writers identified by Ashcroft, Griffiths, and Tiffin, many of the student narrators felt the need to question the English language's underlying assumptions about cultural difference. Some of these students recognized how extensively European American culture was socially constructed precisely because they understood how their own cultures were being misrepresented in the hegemonic discourses of the day. Even under the constraints of colonization, as Bernd Peyer demonstrates in *The Tutor'd Mind*, his study of seventeenth- through nineteenth-century Native intellectuals, the use of English could have a liberating effect on the student autobiographers, allowing them to be active constructors of meaning rather than merely passive recipients of knowledge. Students who still had access to their birth languages could, of course, use them to maintain their own cultures, as many did. Students with sufficient second-language proficiency could also use English, as Chinua Achebe did in the wake of the decolonization of Nigeria, to convey the very concepts and experiences the colonizers sought to destroy.[38]

It is impossible to do justice here to the culturally complex lives of the people whose stories I examine in this chapter. What follows is a selection of commentary that suggests the diverse and complicated ways former students represented their own cross-cultural contact. Whether they chose English or had it imposed on them, they learned the language in the nineteenth century because it was in their best interest. They now had to negotiate their identity through a new tongue and a new understanding of the world and the word.

As Ashcroft, Griffiths, and Tiffin note of the early productions of postcolonial literature, many of the students' texts reflected the colonialist discourses of the day. Perhaps not surprisingly, four of the strongest accommodationist statements were in some way connected to the Carlisle Indian School, run by the ardent and influential assimilationist Richard Henry Pratt. "A Short Story of My Life" by former Carlisle student Howard Whitewolf is a model of the popular "I was lost but now I'm found" epiphanies, telling how this Comanche "sinner" gave himself to Christ. Reflecting the assimilationist ideology, Whitewolf says his goal was for Native people to "make greater progress in civilization." In "Address by Mr. Charles Doxon," a speech at a Carlisle graduation published in a Carlisle newspaper, former Hampton student Charles Doxon tells of his Onondaga youth in New York. He then ends with some "deep woods to civilization" advice that must have had a familiar ring to the Carlisle audience: "Do not give up. You can see that I was as wild and timid as a rabbit when I went away from the reservation, but you have a good start." Despite his initial resistance, Jason Betzinez considers his selection by Pratt to have been a significant turning point, as he reports in *I Fought with Geronimo*. As a result of his experience at Carlisle, Betzinez declares that "tribal life . . . is archaic," and his words reflect Pratt's view that "the future of the Indian lies in getting out and settling down like any other American citizen." In *The Arapaho Way*, the language of former Carlisle student Carl Sweezy, too, echoes Pratt's philosophy that indigenous people need to learn "to follow the white man's road and bec[o]me good American citizens."[39]

For these men, however, acceptance of citizenship and of a European American lifestyle did not denote rejection of Native identity or belief. They identified decisively and profoundly with their respective Comanche, Onondagan, Apache, and Arapaho roots. Their worldviews had been established in diverse ways, informed by multilayered sets of needs. Howard Whitewolf and Carl Sweezy, for example, took a syncretic approach to religion, incorporating into their Christian practices the peyote ceremony, which held some of the same meaning as rites that were no longer performed. In fact, Whitewolf was active in the Society of American Indians as a member of the peyote delegation. In his autobiography, Sweezy underscores that European Americans misunderstood the religious significance of the ceremony. He likens it to communion, noting that "there are many ways to God."[40] That former students made such choices as adults points to the deepening complexities of issues related to language and identity (and belief) in this era. Although the Indian schools played a destructive role, English-only education was not a zero-sum cultural encounter.

Charles Eastman's reflections on his educational experiences provide a useful framework for understanding how transculturation could play out in a student's life. Eastman's cross-cultural identity evolved over time, from his struggle as a young student entering the European American world through a bilingual mission school to his ironic assessment of his past and his present. He had lived his first fifteen years under the influence of only Dakota practices and values before he was suddenly thrust into a new reality when his father returned home, after a long imprisonment, as a converted Christian. As Eastman confronted this new way of life, he moved back and forth in confusion between ways of knowing. As an adolescent, he was torn between a desire to learn new things and a belief that "it is cowardly to depart from the old things!"[41] The title of his autobiography, *From the Deep Woods to Civilization: Chapters in the Autobiography of an Indian*, suggests that he had become a model product of European American society and had adopted its notion that Native life in the "deep woods" was lower on the social continuum than European American "civilization." And in fact Eastman did convert to Christianity, graduate from college and medical school, marry Elaine Goodale (a former Hampton teacher), become active in the assimilationist reform movement, and write several books that exoticized his Dakota past, including an earlier autobiography titled *Indian Boyhood.* But here Eastman enacts a number of translingual moves that suggest a more subversive intent in his writing.

In *From the Deep Woods to Civilization,* Eastman covertly calls into question European American assumptions about the Native way of life when he recalls his reaction to his first English-language program at a mission day school: "The teacher made some curious signs upon a blackboard on the wall, and seemed to ask the children to read them. To me they did not compare in interest with my bird's-track and fish-fin *studies* on the sands" (emphasis added). By identifying the activities he engaged in before the mission school as "studies," Eastman counteracts the prevailing notion in European American society that Native people who had not had formal schooling were uneducated. Furthermore, by mentioning the two kinds of studies in the same paragraph, Eastman shows that any type of education can appear to be foolish or valuable, depending on the cultural lens one is looking through. When he repeats the argument his father made to convince him to continue his education, he introduces an ironic perspective, for his father created a parallel between European American schooling and the traditional Dakota way of life: "'The way of knowledge,' he continued, 'is like our old way in hunting. . . . [S]uccess lies in the choice of the right road.'" For Eastman's father, books were the "'bows and arrows' of the white man." Eastman extends the analogy to embrace its militaristic connotation when he claims that the Sioux were "entrenched . . . in the warfare of civilized life."[42]

Eastman executes the ultimate translingual irony when he refers to his education at Dartmouth College: "It was here that I had most of my savage gentleness and native refinement knocked out of me." Here he inverts European American notions of the civilizing effect of formal schooling. Conversely, he suggests that his classmates were positively influenced by his "Indian standpoint," for they often called on him to advance "a native theory or first hand observation" to help them with their work. Furthermore, in using the word "theory," he negates any notion that his knowledge was less valid than European American ways of knowing. And what he says at the end of the book suggests that there is a double meaning both in his title and in the internal references that refer to his accommodation, for he exposes the false claims of the superiority of the European American–Christian way of life: "Behind the material and intellectual splendor of our civilization, primitive savagery and cruelty and lust hold sway, undiminished, and as it seems, unheeded." Here Eastman emphasizes that the ideal spiritual life he had sought when he converted to Christianity is rarely seen in practice. Although he identifies himself an "advocate of civilization," it is important to note how he justifies that position: "There is no chance for our former simple life any more." This line suggests that if that life had still been possible he might have found it desirable. At the very least, he clings to the values of that life: "I am an Indian; and while I have learned much from civilization, for which I am grateful, I have never lost my Indian sense of right and justice. I am for development and progress along social and spiritual lines, rather than those of commerce, nationalism, or material efficiency. Nevertheless, so long as I live, I am an American." As a reflective adult, Eastman has weighed his experiences and made judgments about the relative value of each worldview. While his "I am an Indian . . . I am an American" statement can appear to be contradictory or ambivalent, it makes sense when viewed against the comments in the middle of the passage. Within the context of declaring his allegiance to America, Eastman makes the case that United States culture is enriched by Native ways of knowing.[43]

Like Eastman, John Rogers demonstrates two ways of study and of looking at the world. Writing of his life only up to his late teens, in *Red World and White: Memories of a Chippewa Boyhood* he makes no mention of his accommodation to European American society as an interior decorator (which we learn about from the editor's introduction). Instead, Rogers ends with an idealized version of the Chippewa (Ojibway, Anishinabe) approach to life and learning. Sent to board at the Flandreau School in Dakota at the age of six, Rogers initially accepted the notion that European Americans could provide him with a superior education: "I was learning much that never would have been taught to me by continuing the ways of my Indian people." But as he grew older, he says, he began to understand the implications of his schooling and to recognize the equally important value of the Chippewa education: "Nothing the white man could teach me would take the place of what I was learning from the forest, the lakes, and the river." Reunited with his father, he relearned traditional ways of thinking and began to understand why he "had never been able to believe what the white man tried to teach me as a substitute for the beliefs of my own people." When he describes the long strip of birch bark that his father showed him, Rogers suggests that, contrary to prevailing European American views of Native intellectual practices, Chippewas had a long tradition of study:

> "This is a chart," he explained to me, "that has been handed down to me through many generations of our peoples. It is said to be fully six hundred years old. Since you are the oldest of my children, it is my wish that this chart shall go to you, as will also the drum. Of the chart I shall teach you all I know. Study it closely."
>
> Bending over this ancient chart of birch bark I noticed that it was covered with many strange drawings.

As his father explained each symbol on this ancient chart, the history and future of his people emerged in pictures and (Chippewa) words. Through this remarkable scene, Rogers represents Chippewas as having their own literature, their own form of literacy, their own way of transmitting and preserving knowledge.[44]

Don Talayesva maintains a cynical perspective toward European Americans throughout much of his narrative, *Sun Chief.* Talayesva was raised on Third Mesa in New Oraibi, Arizona, where resistance to European American education was fierce. As he reports, he "grew up believing that Whites are wicked, deceitful people." Eventually the old chief and his grandfather became friendly with some European Americans. Although the chief made it clear that he would never forsake Hopi beliefs or ceremonies, he was convinced by chiefs from other villages to let the children go to school in return for much-needed tools, supplies, and clothing. At age nine Talayesva entered a mesa day school but says he learned little and preferred to listen to the stories told by elders in his own community. He soon transferred to Keams Canyon Boarding School, in part to become literate and in part to obtain clothes. He was sent to the Sherman Institute in California a few years later, where, he says, he was tricked into committing himself to Christianity. However, as a result of a near-death experience, Talayesva understood that he had a "Hopi Spirit Guide whom I must follow if I wished to live." He returned home in 1909, immersed himself in Hopi life and practices, and had little contact with European Americans for the next twenty years. He made a special point of avoiding missionaries, whom he viewed as hypocrites who denigrated Hopi beliefs and practices. Eventually his ability to speak English brought him in contact with anthropologists who came to the mesa to study Hopi life. Talayesva expresses satisfaction that, as a result of his schooling, he has learned how to survive in a European American world. Nevertheless, he mocks the European American approach to knowledge when he implicitly compares it with the Hopi way: "I had learned many English words and could recite part of the Ten Commandments. I knew how to sleep on a bed, pray to Jesus, comb my hair, eat with a knife and fork, and use a toilet. I had learned that the world is round instead of flat, that it is indecent to go naked in the presence of girls, and to eat the testes of sheep or goats. I had also learned that a person thinks with his head instead of his heart."[45]

Some students' mixed racial identity figured prominently in their transcultural process. As Annie Lowry explains in *Karnee: A Paiute Narrative,* her European American father saw to it that his daughter spoke her first words in English rather than in her mother's Paiute tongue. In fact he discouraged any use of Paiute. However, when he was away from their home in Lovelock, Nevada – which was often – Lowry would speak her mother's language and follow her mother's path. Finding this situation untenable, her father arranged for her to live with a European American family, with orders that she have no interaction with the Paiute community. At his insistence, she was the first Native child in Lovelock to go to school with European American children (about 1882). Because he saw English-language literacy as the route away from Paiute life and toward an elite existence in European American society, he helped his children with the verses they needed to memorize every week in public school. Teaching them to recite the "American Flag," he connected their ability to speak English with patriotism and stressed that it was a mark of class: "Be proud of your country and your flag. When you go to speak stand up, open your mouth. Don't slouch and act ashamed like poor white trash." Lowry was aware that her father's goal was to create an "attractive 'Indian princess' whom he could parade before his hated stepmother in Virginia." However, she refused to cooperate in his scheme, no matter how much he "cajoled, even threatened my very existence." When Jerome Lowry left Lovelock Valley for the last time, his sons went with him and "passed for white." Annie Lowry remained with her mother, having "taken the shawl," and never went to school again. Although she "associated with white people and spoke English naturally," she "believed in the Indian way of life."[46]

Mary Little Bear Inkanish's cross-cultural education was also shaped by the fact that her father was European American. In *Dance around the Sun* she explains that her transcultural struggle temporarily severed her relationship with the Cheyenne community, by her own choice. Because of her gray blue eyes, Vee-hay-kah (White Girl), as she was then known, was typically treated as a non-Cheyenne by other children. As a result, unlike most Cheyenne mothers, Inkanish's mother was adamant that she attend boarding school on weekdays. She believed that as "half a white woman," her daughter would have to learn the ways of her father, even though he had abandoned the family. Inkanish's English-language education on the Cheyenne-Arapaho reservation caused her to question Cheyenne traditions to the extent that she and her mother had a falling-out over her mother's participation in the Sun Dance ritual. Inkanish ran away to a more distant school. She eventually reconciled with her mother, married Jim Inkanish

(Caddo), and during her first pregnancy, began to return to the Cheyenne way of life, guided by her mother's teachings. Inkanish remained a Christian but saw parallels with her mother's spiritual beliefs, and she continued to speak both Cheyenne and English. She calls her bicultural life an "Indian-white puzzle."[47]

Gender, too, could influence the ways a student acquired an education, as the experience of Mourning Dove (née Christine Quintasket) illustrates. Raised on the Colville Reservation in Washington, Mourning Dove was exposed to two religious cultures: the ancient traditions of her people and Catholicism, both practiced and taught by her mother. At the insistence of her mother's priest, Mourning Dove attended the Goodwin Mission school sporadically between 1894 and 1899, at which time government funding for missionary schools was cut. Her parents then expected her to fulfill her prescribed female role as baby-sitter for younger siblings. Mourning Dove had to read "secretly" because her parents believed reading was an "idle" pastime for her. When she requested permission to go the Tonasket Indian School, her mother refused because she had observed the girls who had returned from government schools and feared that such an education would destroy Mourning Dove's "good character." Mourning Dove was frustrated but understood the role of strong family bonds: "Indian people do not like to be away from relatives and loved ones for very long." Combined with the tradition of girls marrying young, she says, these close family ties made it almost impossible for female students to finish school. However, Mourning Dove – who would eventually become a writer and publish a novel – took advantage of every educational opportunity. She learned to read from "an orphan white lad" of thirteen whom her family had adopted. Her mother objected so much to Mourning Dove's interest in books that one day she "papered our cabin with Jimmy's novels." But even that drastic action did not stop Mourning Dove, for when Jimmy came home and found that his books had become wallpaper, he "got busy and continued to read from the wall, with me helping to find the next page." Mourning Dove later attended the Fort Spokane Agency school and remained until her mother died, when she had to come home to care for her siblings. But she persistently sought a formal education and was able to complete several years of schooling. As she reflects on her dual educational experiences, Mourning Dove says she believed that both Salishan and English teachings were beneficial. Unlike the "present generation, which is too busy learning from the white man's books to study ancestral history," she had had "the opportunity to know authentically, from personal experience, a fraction of the real, ancient Indian life that existed before." She ultimately found a use for English that her European American teachers had not intended: to fulfill her goal of sharing "the wisdom of my elders" with a larger audience.[48]

Albert Yava sums up most of the students' responses to their English-only schooling when he acknowledges that formal education helped them to compete in European American society but regrettably left no room for their own traditions: "Something important is being gained, but something important is being lost." Several students offer as an alternative a multicultural perspective on learning. As Carl Sweezy explains in *The Arapaho Way*, he was raised on the Cheyenne-Arapaho reservation, where two cultures lived in one area, and thus was exposed from birth to a unique and rich linguistic situation. Although Cheyennes and Arapahos had much in common culturally, their languages were quite different, and few people knew how to speak both. To converse with one another, they used sign language, with which they could communicate as rapidly as they did in their first languages. Sweezy's schooling brought him from a reservation day school at the Darlington Agency to Mennonite Mission schools in Kansas, back to Darlington, then to the Carlisle School, and finally to the Chilocco Indian School in Oklahoma. His diverse experiences opened his eyes and mind to multicultural approaches to learning and living, which challenged the predominance of a particular European American culture: "Germans and Americans and Indians, traders and farmers and soldiers and anthropologists, Quakers and Episcopalians and Mennonites and believers in the religion of the Indian, we were all mixed up together there at Darlington. We Arapaho learned something from them all, and kept the best of our own beliefs as well."[49]

Edward Goodbird's experience, too, illustrates the impulse to embrace more than one culture. As he spent time in the mission day school on the Fort Berthold Reservation, Goodbird began to love to read Bible stories. Although his father "would not himself forsake the old ways," he allowed his son to make his own decisions about the path he would follow, and Goodbird chose to attend church. The missionary, Mr. Hall, became a model for him of Christian behavior and English-language use. Yet Goodbird's life outside school remained "wholly Indian." He played traditional games and participated in dances and hunts. As a child, he was able to accept European

American instruction without abandoning Native culture: "I thought an Indian could be a Christian and also believe in the old ways." As an adult, he began to think, "The Indian's way is hard. . . . The white man's road is easier." Nevertheless, even when he became a preacher, Goodbird did not sacrifice his Native values. He transformed European American Christianity linguistically and culturally, for example, by conducting services in Hidatsa but omitting sermons, which "we Indians do not care for." Goodbird says that he feels "no anger" for what had happened to Hidatsas and believes it was for the best. However, his words reflect the reality of the transcultural process in its colonialist context: Native people had developed a heightened awareness of transculturation, whereas European Americans' own transculturation had become invisible to them:

> I think God made all peoples to help one another. We Indians have helped you white people. All over this country are corn fields; we Indians gave you the seeds for your corn, and we gave you squashes and beans. On the lakes in your parks are canoes; Indians taught you to make those canoes.
>
> We Indians think you are but paying us back, when you give us schools and books, and teach us the new way.[50]

11. Carrie Anderson (Sioux), Anna Dawson (Arikara), and Sarah Walker (Gros Ventre) on arrival from Dakota Territory at the Hampton Normal and Agricultural Institute (1878). Photograph by William Larrabee. Courtesy of University Archives, Hampton University, Hampton VA.

12. The three girls fourteen months later. Courtesy of University Archives, Hampton University, Hampton VA.

5

Transforming Women

Zitkala-Ša's *American Indian Stories*

> Now, as I look back upon the recent past, I see it from a distance, as a whole. I remember how, from morning till evening, many specimens of civilized peoples visited the Indian school. The city folks with canes and eyeglasses, the countrymen with sunburnt cheeks and clumsy feet, forgot their relative social ranks in an ignorant curiosity. Both sorts of these Christian palefaces were alike astounded at seeing the children of savage warriors so docile and industrious.

In these lines from "An Indian Teacher among Indians," published in the *Atlantic Monthly* in 1900, Zitkala-Ša uses her consummate translingual skills to turn the field of anthropology on its head. Once an object of study whose "savage" identity was constructed by European American social scientists, she has gained the power to "see," and in her eyes the "civilized peoples" become the "specimens" to be studied. Zitkala-Ša's literary ethnography is thus a form of what Kenneth Lincoln calls bicultural play: an intercultural exchange in which the object of observation takes on the role of observer and returns the gaze. In Lincoln's own play on words "the *see-ers* . . . are see*ing* the *seen* . . . and . . . on the other side native 'seers' peer back." Truly a seer, Zitkala-Ša anticipates the remaking of social analysis at the turn of the next century. Almost one hundred years after Zitkala-Ša first published her work, cultural anthropologist Renato Rosaldo would write, "Social analysis must now grapple with the realization that its objects of analysis are also analyzing subjects who critically interrogate ethnographers – their writings, their ethics, and their politics." Zitkala-Ša's own education helped her to develop her unique talent to the point where she could use English to speak for herself and represent her own life.[1]

From the beginning, as Zitkala-Ša learned, the Indian service envisioned an outcome in which the burden of civilizing the Native populace would fall on the shoulders of newly educated children. By the time Zitkala-Ša was born, government officials were already plotting her future and planning to use children like her as cogs in what she calls the "civilizing machine." As Commissioner of Indian Affairs Ezra Hayt put it in 1879, after the children were removed from the influence of their "savage home[s]" and trained in "useful knowledge," they would return among their people and instigate change in the entire community. Richard Henry Pratt emphasized that this goal could be achieved only if the female students were transformed: "The labor and expense of educating Indian boys while the girls are left untaught is almost entirely thrown away. Of what avail is it that the man be hard-working and industrious, providing by his labor food and clothing for his household, if the wife, unskilled in cookery, unused to the needle, with no habits of order or neatness, makes what might be a cheerful, happy home only a wretched abode of filth and squalor?" To develop a middle-class Christian home, as K. Tsianina Lomawaima has shown, the girls were expected to repudiate the teachings and practices of their own mothers and grandmothers, thus breaking with centuries of tradition. And those working in the Indian service knew it was necessary to sever that mother-daughter connection, for, as Pratt put it, "It is the women who cling most tenaciously to heathen rites and superstitions, and perpetuate them by their instructions to the children." It is no wonder, then, that when female students were cast – body and soul – in the European American mold, it was considered to be among the highest possible achievements. O. H. Bales, head of White's Indiana Manual Labor Institute, wrote: "There is nothing . . . we observe with greater pleasure than the improvement of the girls in womanly grace and virtue from year to year, and their constant training in household duties." Zitkala-Ša – who was attending White's Institute at the time – was considered an exemplary student.[2]

Although large numbers of students failed to fulfill the goals of the civilizing mission, Zitkala-Ša was a success story. Her entrance record at White's Institute indicates that she attended a Yankton Agency (Presbyterian, bilingual) day school for two years before entering boarding school at age eight. Between two terms at White's Institute (between ages eleven and fourteen or fifteen), she lived in Dakota Territory and for some of that time attended the bilingual Santee Normal Training School at the Dakota Mission. She graduated from White's Institute in 1895, and from 1895 to 1897 she studied at Earlham College, a Quaker-run institution in Indiana, where she excelled academically, winning college and state prizes in oratory. After two years she left Earlham, partly because of ill health and partly "for the sake of money-making," as she wrote to a former mentor at White's. In mid-1897 she began a brief teaching career at the Carlisle Indian Industrial School. She was already a somewhat experienced instructor, having been music teacher for the primary grades at White's Institute while still officially a student and for local farm children during the two summers following her graduation. Zitkala-Ša remained at the Carlisle School for eighteen months, during which time she traveled out West to recruit children for the school.[3]

Despite her apparent complicity with the Carlisle mission and adaptation to a European American lifestyle (see fig. 13), Zitkala-Ša actively defended her cultural heritage in an effort to correct misperceptions about Native people. At opening exercises of the school in September 1897 she gave a talk, "The Achievements of the White and Red Races Compared," which, according to the editor of the school newspaper, was an effort to show that "the history of the Indian has been wrongly written, and that their motives as a people have been misunderstood." However, misrepresentations of Native life followed Zitkala-Ša to Carlisle. On the front page of the same issue of the *Indian Helper* that announced her hiring, readers of the school newspaper could learn of the "transformation of the Carlisle children from barbarism to the ways of a civilized race." Zitkala-Ša's view of history notwithstanding, Richard Pratt continued to show disdain for the Native past and Native culture. He criticized Buffalo Bill for promoting a misleading "idea of Indians" by hiring "the reservation wild man to dress in his most hideous costume . . . and to display his savagery" in the Wild West Show. Yet he himself accepted this representation as a reality of Native life:

> It is this nature in our red brother that is better dead than alive, and when we agree with the oft-repeated sentiment that the only good Indian is a dead one, we mean this characteristic of the Indian. Carlisle's mission is to kill THIS Indian, as we build up the better man.
>
> We give the rising Indian something nobler and higher to think about and do, and he comes out a young man with the ambitions and aspirations of his more favored white brother.[4]

At the end of 1898 Zitkala-Ša left Carlisle to study violin at a renowned conservatory of music in Boston, her tuition and expenses at the conservatory apparently paid by the office of the commissioner of Indian affairs. Because of her accomplishments, her name appeared in books and magazine articles of the era, and she was touted as a "representative Indian": proof that the civilizing project worked.[5] However, Pratt soon discovered that "THIS Indian" was even harder to kill than those who arrived in paint and feathers. At the beginning of 1900, Zitkala-Ša published three semiautobiographical pieces in the *Atlantic Monthly,* including "An Indian Teacher among Indians," a scathing indictment of an unnamed boarding school that looked suspiciously like Carlisle, headed by a principal whose appearance was uncannily similar to Richard Henry Pratt's.

The newspapers of the Dakota Mission and of the Carlisle Indian School gave Zitkala-Ša some praise for the "literary quality" of the three *Atlantic Monthly* pieces. But overall they criticized her for the "underlying bitterness" of her stories and labeled her a person of "infinite conceit" who was "utterly unthankful for all that has been done for her by the pale faces, which in her case is considerable." In the mainstream press, in contrast, she received accolades for her "poignant and utterly despairing note of revolt." Despite – and because of – the mixed criticism, Zitkala-Ša continued writing. She did not give up the idea of pursuing a literary career until 1902, when she married Raymond Bonnin, a Yankton Sioux, after which she spent fourteen years on a western reservation teaching and doing community service. During her time on the reservation, Zitkala-Ša occasionally wrote articles for the *Quarterly Journal of the Society of American Indians* and also collaborated on an opera, *The Sun Dance,* which premiered in Utah in 1913. In 1916 she returned east to work for the Society of American Indians (SAI), ultimately becoming editor of the society's journal. In 1921 she gathered together many of her published pieces – most written between 1899 and 1902 – into a volume titled *American Indian Stories.*[6]

It is important to acknowledge that Zitkala-Ša's career continues to be a subject of controversy. Her political activism has received high praise from such scholars as William Willard, David Johnson, and Raymond Wilson, but others have weighed in to create a more complicated perspective. Betty Louise Bell, for example, points to the accommodationist rhetoric in Zitkala-Ša's journalistic writing, particularly in articles published in *American Indian Magazine* in 1919. Robert Allen Warrior argues that Zitkala-Ša's early

13. Zitkala-Ša (1898). Photography by Gertrude Käsebier. Courtesy of Photographic History Collection, National Museum of American History, Smithsonian Institution/85-164.

politics hindered efforts to maintain Native sovereignty. Like other members of SAI, Zitkala-Ša promoted citizenship for indigenous people and integration into the United States political system at the expense of traditional Native governing structures. In her contributions to the anti-peyote campaign, Warrior further maintains, Zitkala-Ša stood in the way of Native religious freedom. Nevertheless, while it is true that she subscribed to some of the tenets of SAI, she actively attempted to transform the society into an organization that lobbied for self-determination. Furthermore, as Warrior acknowledges, she moved away from the politics of SAI and remained an activist long after the organization folded and other members abandoned political work. After 1920, like many women of her generation, Zitkala-Ša was determined to do everything she could to harness women's organizational and political power now that (white) women could vote. She worked with the General Federation of Women's Clubs to establish their national Indian Welfare Committee in 1921, and together they fought for Native rights and achieved some concrete results before she and her husband founded their own pro-tribal political organization, the National Council of American Indians, of which she was president from 1926 until her death in 1938. Zitkala-Ša continuously sought to strengthen pantribal alliances and contested reform agendas that would have the effect of erasing Native ways of knowing from the American cultural and intellectual landscape.[7]

Although Bell faults Zitkala-Ša's early journalistic writing for its assimilationist strain, she emphasizes that her creative writing can and should be interpreted much differently. And it is Zitkala-Ša's creative writing that I am examining here. Earlier critics of *American Indian Stories* have suggested that Zitkala-Ša lacks authorial control: that she struggles to express herself in a second language and to discover her own voice as she tries to satisfy the expectations of European American readers.[8] I share the view of more recent critics who argue that she is very much in command of language and audience.[9] To examine the ways Zitkala-Ša exerts rhetorical control, I apply Eric Cheyfitz's postcolonial theories (which in turn are drawn from the work of Frantz Fanon) to *American Indian Stories*. Cheyfitz distinguishes between two possibilities that language learners confront as colonized people. One is to master the colonizer's language in order to "become white." The other is to master the language in order to expose the colonizer's power position. The latter rhetorical stance challenges the notion that the colonizer has exclusive rights to the language and instead asserts that anyone can claim ownership. As a creative writer, Zitkala-Ša enacts this stance. She appropriates English to expose the (linguistic) violence and explode the myth of European American superiority that the language has perpetrated. Anyone who has been forced to speak English – or who chooses to – Zitkala-Ša affirms, can employ it to fulfill his or her own cultural and political agenda. To demonstrate how this scenario plays out in Zitkala-Ša's writing, I examine her treatment of women as a device that unifies *American Indian Stories*.[10]

Although the emphasis in this chapter is on a female perspective, I want to underscore that I am not holding Zitkala-Ša up as a representative Native woman. The autobiographical accounts examined in chapters 3 and 4 provide evidence that Native women across cultures have used English in a variety of ways. My goal here is to demonstrate how Zitkala-Ša uses the language creatively to write within the constraints of colonialism – satisfying a mass audience while at the same time infusing her work with subversive messages. On the one hand, she pitches her work at precisely the level that popular culture demanded by describing a highly romanticized Native culture. On the other, she demonstrates that imposing English had unintended results, one of which is her choice to use the language to criticize government officials and missionaries and especially to take issue with the ways women have been represented in European American discourses.

HISTORICAL REPRESENTATIONS OF NATIVE WOMEN

Most of the knowledge available to turn of the century readers about the actual lives of Native people was transmitted by anthropologists sponsored by a United States government agency, the Bureau of American Ethnology, and two independent museums. The anthropologists' work was narrow in scope both practically and intellectually, for except in rare cases a lone male ethnographer interviewed male tribal elders through a male interpreter. Such a method could not allow for a full picture of Native women's lives. Likewise, intellectual bias precluded a true picture. Anthropologists were steeped in a European American cultural tradition and shaped by a capitalist ideology that denigrated female strength and women's work. They assumed that societies lacking a leisure class whose survival tasks were performed by servants were at a lower end of an evolutionary scale. Furthermore, the developing field of anthropology itself was based on a scientific paradigm of oppositional dualism into which ethnographers had to fit their data. Using arbitrary categories, they classified societies as either "civilized" or "primitive." Native societies inevitably fell into the latter category.[11]

Thus most turn-of-the-century ethnographic studies represented little improvement over earlier descriptions of Native women's lives recorded in the journals, diaries, and letters of European American travelers and traders. In her study of these texts, Katherine Weist finds remarkable consensus about the role and status of northern plains Native women. Most of the men described Native women's work as "menial" and viewed the women themselves as "beasts of burden," "slaves," and "brutes" who were "sexually lax," "uncultivated," and "inferior" and lived a life of "barbarism" and "drudgery." Weist's study of government documents likewise reveals that government agents referred to the women's nomadic life as "degraded" and "savage," basing their judgments on their own notions of womanhood, which required a stable home and hearth – and ignoring the government's own role in indigenous peoples' removal. By the late nineteenth century, Native women's lives were almost universally seen as an affront to the "cult of true womanhood," which was characterized by the virtues of piety, propriety, and domesticity.[12]

Turn-of-the-century European American popular art and literature mirrored these attitudes. It is important to note, however, that Native women had not always or exclusively been represented in such negative terms, as Annette Kolodny's analysis of sixteenth-century explorers' accounts reveals. Because they were gracious and friendly toward the European men who landed on their shores in the sixteenth century, the women were viewed as emblematic of a landscape filled "with love and kindness and . . . as much bounty," as one English captain put it, and thus were integral to a cherished male fantasy of compatibility with nature. Even when that dream failed in reality – the land-woman was violated – it was perpetuated in the arts, with the Native woman represented as a member of royalty. Rayna Green traces the image of Indian queen back to the late sixteenth century when artists began to use her full, strong, maternal figure as a symbol of the paradoxically terrifying yet inviting New World. As the colonies moved toward independence, Green shows, the image of queen was transformed and Americanized into a more cultivated light-skinned princess, a figure who was drawn in classical lines and pictured with symbols of liberty and colonial America. Another, equally limited model of the Native woman existed at the other end of the spectrum, however. In the nineteenth century, the Native woman was often constructed as "squaw": a "dark," "savage," "fat," "lewd" woman of vice who served as a mere sexual commodity at the whim of men. These dichotomized images – princess/squaw; aristocrat/savage; virgin/whore; powerful symbol/powerless servant – persisted into the twentieth century, making it impossible for the Native woman to be seen as real.[13]

ZITKALA-ŠA'S *ATLANTIC MONTHLY* PUBLICATIONS: 1900

Against this backdrop, Zitkala-Ša entered the literary scene. Educated in English, she was able to tell her story directly rather than through a male interpreter, ethnographer, or editor, as had been the case for her tribal elders and most other Native writers. Thus she circumvented translation, the colonizer's principal mode of linguistic control. Using the Boston-based *Atlantic Monthly* as her vehicle, she published three sketches in January, February, and March of 1900 while she was at the conservatory in Boston. At least two compelling reasons may explain Zitkala-Ša's success in finding a publisher. Laura Wexler argues that Zitkala-Ša's work was deemed suitable for the genteel *Atlantic* because, having been educated by European Americans, she was able to mimic a popular sentimental style of writing. Patricia Okker suggests that Zitkala-Ša fulfilled the readers' exoticized fantasy of the Native woman, noting that her essays and stories were sandwiched between racist and stereotypical writings about Native people. Certainly it is true that into the twentieth century the *Atlantic* catered to an audience who craved romanticized tales of young women as well as savage depictions of Native people.[14]

At the same time, by the turn of the century the magazine was beginning to make changes. According to Ellery Sedgwick, when Bliss Perry assumed editorship of the *Atlantic* in 1899 he made a decision to broaden the authorship of contributions, in the interest of supplementing the expressions and opinions of the Anglo-Saxon upper-middle class with new voices and ideas. One of Perry's earliest editorial decisions was to accept Zitkala-Ša's work after it was sent to the *Atlantic* by Joseph Edgar Chamberlin, a respected newspaper columnist in Boston, in whose home she did her writing. Furthermore, even though the *Atlantic*'s readers included adherents of the missionary movement who might well have been offended by her attack on philanthropic European American Christians, Perry encouraged her to submit more writing. Zitkala-Ša was fortunate to have this particular editor for another reason: his typical approach was to let writers design their own projects, and he gave them final say over his editorial comments.[15]

Evidently Zitkala-Ša was able to define her own mission, and therefore she could decide to sign only her self-given Lakota name, without providing its English translation (Red Bird) or adding her European American birth name, Gertrude Simmons, by which she was also known.[16] Linking her Lakota name with her English-language text, Zitkala-Ša reminds readers that she has replaced a narrow monocultural European American lens with a more inclusive bicultural lens through which they could now view the life of a Native woman. With her first sentence – "A wigwam of weather-stained canvas stood at the base of some irregularly ascending hills" – she announces that the English language could and would be used effectively by a Native writer to describe Native life. Zitkala-Ša uses English for her own purposes, not those for which her English-only education was intended: obliteration of everything Native in America. Using the language of Anglo Americans, she endeavors to preserve the world they seek to destroy. In her textual evocation of Sioux culture, as Dorothea Susag suggests, Zitkala-Ša attempts to dissipate the power of colonialist discourses.[17]

The three *Atlantic Monthly* pieces that open *American Indian Stories* – "Impressions of an Indian Childhood," "The School Days of an Indian Girl," and "An Indian Teacher among Indians" – have always been treated as autobiographical works. But like many writers before her, Zitkala-Ša blurs the distinction between fact and fiction. An examination of other sources – which, of course, may be fictions themselves – suggests that the details provided in these sketches do not always match her actual life. Certainly Zitkala-Ša revises or at least obscures her father's status. Rather than identify him as a European American man who deserted the family before his daughter's birth, she exoticizes him as a victim of white oppression who "has been buried in a hill nearer the rising sun."[18] Although she implies that her mother exposed her at a young age only to tribal traditions, this information is suspect, given that her mother apparently had become a Christian even before she moved to the Yankton Agency in 1874, two years before Zitkala-Ša's birth. Zitkala-Ša claims that her brother, "Dawée," lost his job at the agency and had no source of income, but other sources suggest that David Simmons chose to leave the job in order to become a farmer, at which he was an unquestioned success.[19] In addition to the discrepancies related to her family, some of the school experiences she describes may not have told the whole story. She fails to mention, for example, that she attended bilingual schools before and between her two terms at White's Institute. Nor does she disclose that she achieved some status at White's when as a teenager she became the music teacher for the primary grades, which indicates that she was not as marginalized as she suggests, even taking into account that her appointment helped address White's staffing and economic problems at the time. According to Agnes Picotte, several of the incidents Zitkala-Ša describes were actually told to her by other Native people who had experienced them.[20]

Even if Zitkala-Ša's *Atlantic Monthly* contributions are fiction, it is important to acknowledge the autobiographical truth in the writing, for these pieces reveal the author's experience if not the exact details of her life. Zitkala-Ša may have fictionalized her account not because what she has to say is not true but precisely because it is true. Fiction allows her more freedom of expression. Furthermore, as Okker says of Zitkala-Ša's other stories, the author may well have deliberately chosen to write from a personal, emotional perspective to avoid the pretense of objectivity that characterized the writings of ethnographers. The personal discourse that shapes her work is tied to the social and political field that surrounds it. I am not suggesting that Zitkala-Ša is being deceptive in representing her work as autobiography, although if she were she would be joining a long list of autobiographical tricksters in mainstream American literature. Rather, it was the readers who made – and have continued to make – that assumption. The three *Atlantic Monthly* pieces originally appeared with no generic designation. Furthermore, when Zitkala-Ša gave a title to the book in which these sketches were later included, *American Indian Stories,* the term *stories* provided a hint that she had fictionalized her own life. I will treat the texts as fiction, for I believe that such an approach allows readers to separate the loss of control of language that the first-person female narrator sometimes experiences from the rhetorical control that the author always maintained.[21]

In "Impressions of an Indian Childhood," Zitkala-Ša turns almost immediately to women's work, the first area in need of revision: "Morning, noon, and evening, my mother came to draw water . . . for our household use." This is precisely the type of labor that nineteenth-century European American male accounts labeled demeaning and that provided alleged evidence of Native women's low status. For example, in 1872 E. D. Neill said of Dakota women: "From early childhood they lead 'worse than a dog's life.' Like the Gibeonites of old, they are the hewers of wood and *the drawers of water for the camp*" (quoted in Weist, emphasis added). In contrast, Zitkala-Ša shows that drawing water was an activity of high status, to which a young girl could aspire: "My grown-up cousin, Warca-Ziwin (Sunflower), who was then seventeen, always went to the river alone for water for her mother. . . . I admired my cousin greatly. So I said: 'Mother, when I am tall as my cousin Warca-Ziwin, you shall not have to come for water. I will do it for you.'" Likewise, Zitkala-Ša describes the women's farm work in idyllic terms, in language that has a positive connotation: "From a field in the *fertile* river bottom my mother and aunt gathered an *abundant* supply of corn. Near our tepee they spread a large canvas upon the grass and dried their *sweet* corn in it" (emphasis added). For European Americans, however, such work was evidence of the women's enslaved position and reflective of the men's debased state, as the following excerpt from a French trader's nineteenth-century journal reveals: "Beasts of burden of these inhuman monsters [Native men], they (the women) are loaded with all the work. They endure alone all the labor of farming . . . without which the men would probably not be able to live, because of their sloth and laziness" (quoted in Weist). To the narrator in "Impressions," women's farming practices, in contrast, are tied to fond "early recollections of autumn" and represent positive models that lead young girls to emulate the much respected protective female-mother role in the community: "I was left to watch the corn, that nothing should disturb it. I played around it with dolls made of ears of corn. I braided their soft fine silk for hair, and gave them blankets as various as the scraps I found in my mother's workbag." With images like these Zitkala-Ša challenges the prevailing notion that Native women without formal schooling were uneducated, for she demonstrates the experiential way a Sioux girl learned from female elders.[22]

Through a Siouan lens, then, Zitkala-Ša focuses on the traditional worth of women within their own society, revealing in 1900 what scholars have only recently begun to recognize. Through the perspective of historical ethnography, for example, Raymond DeMallie reexamines accounts written or dictated by a number of Lakota people rather than relying on previous European American interpretation of the documents and events. He finds that, within the context of a Lakota society structured around a sexual division of labor, women were respected for the work they did. Patricia Albers shows that Sioux women had rights that included control over the process and product of their labor. Explaining why this pattern was ignored, Paula Gunn Allen argues that predominant patriarchal attitudes at the turn of the century and beyond could not allow for the veneration of Native women. Because their lifestyle was ostensibly different from European American women's it was considered barbaric, as a nineteenth-century history book asserted: "The savage woman is debarred of the prerogatives, and deprived from exercising the virtues, of her sex, by her wandering life. The fireside, the family circle, all the comforts, luxuries, and enjoyments which are comprised in the word *home,* are created and regulated by female affection, influence, and industry – and all these are unknown to the savage" (quoted in Weist, emphasis in original). Zitkala-Ša discredits this myth, illustrating with affection the warm Sioux home life and emphasizing female influence and industry: "Close beside my mother I sat on a rug, with a scrap of buckskin in one hand and an awl in the other. This was the beginning of my practical observation lessons in the art of beadwork. From a skein of finely twisted threads of silvery sinews my mother pulled out a single one. With an awl she pierced the buckskin, and skillfully threaded it with the white sinew. Picking up the tiny beads one by one, she strung them with the point of her thread, always twisting it carefully after every stitch." Domestic tasks such as this were recognized as important artistic contributions by Native people on the plains if not always by European Americans at that time. Recent scholars acknowledge that beadwork designs reflected female power and prestige. According to Mary Jane Schneider, acquiring such skills was a sign of a girl's virtue and honor, which may explain why the mother in "Impressions" has "little patience" with her daughter's design mistakes. (It would appear that Native people on the plains had a "cult of true womanhood" of their own.) Zitkala-Ša later implies the power of female artistry when she describes this same daughter as a college student who is living with "a cold race whose hearts were frozen hard with prejudice" and who "spun with reeds and thistles, until my hands were tired from their weaving, the magic design which promised me the white man's respect."[23]

By the end of "Impressions," Zitkala-Ša makes clear that the weakening of female power was tied to the encroaching European American world. Contact with European American educators had helped undermine the narrator's mother's way of life, making her a stranger in her own world: "Within the last two seasons my big brother Dawée had returned from a three years' education in the East, and his coming back influenced my mother to take a farther step from her native way of living. First it was a change from the buffalo skin to the white man's canvas that covered our wigwam. Now she had given up her wigwam of slender poles, to live, a foreigner, in a home of clumsy logs." Zitkala-Ša thus makes readers aware that government policies and practices, which allowed European Americans to take land and forced Native people to move, led to a disruption of the Sioux way of life. Given that these policies had begun much earlier, that at the start of "Impressions" the family had already been relocated, and that the area in which they were forced to live was an artificially constructed community, it is clear that the idyllic, traditional life of a Sioux woman that Zitkala-Ša describes is a fiction. As Albers documents, Native women's roles and identities were always in flux, changing according to the prevailing social and historical forces.[24]

Although Zitkala-Ša's representations of Sioux women in "Impressions" are exoticized, they become useful for comparison with the "fair women" that the narrator meets at the beginning of "The School Days of an Indian Girl." In "Impressions," Zitkala-Ša has been careful to show how politeness rituals were transmitted: most important, the mother taught her daughter to avoid "intruding [her]self upon others." Now, on the train, the girl is confronted with intrusive "bold white" faces of children whose own mothers permit this "rude" behavior. The first "paleface woman" she meets at the missionary school, too, invades her private space, impolitely treating her like a toy doll. Not one woman comforts the eight-year-old child as she sobs uncontrollably. Responding to scenes like this, a reviewer in the *Red Man* criticized the Indian girl (assumed to be Zitkala-Ša herself), calling her a "passionate and ill-tempered" child and claiming that "nothing is good enough for her." But implicit in Zitkala-Ša's description of the European American women, as Margaret Austin Lukens suggests, is an honoring of Sioux women's ways.[25]

Throughout "School Days," Zitkala-Ša stereotypes European American women, and certainly it is logical to conclude that this stereotyping makes her guilty of the kind of linguistic violence she objects to. But looked at from the perspective of the ownership of English, it is also reasonable to see that she is consciously exerting linguistic control in order to overthrow linguistic domination. With several strokes of her pen, in an act of rhetorical inversion, she uses the language that previously demonized the Native woman to characterize the European American woman. The female teacher who physically punishes children – a rare event in Lakota society – is guilty of "brute force." In tying a child "fast in a chair," she exhibits uncivilized behavior. Her approach to health reveals that she is "cruel," "ignorant," and "superstitious."[26]

This last failing is worth closer examination, since medical knowledge, so important in Lakota culture, was a source of power and respect for women. Lakota women who had visions might gain the power to cure and protect children through use of herbs and charms; these women formed the Women's Medicinal Cult, which gathered annually to prepare medicines for warriors. Even women who were not spiritualists had knowledge about everyday health care. Furthermore, their medical knowledge was so specific that they could prepare medications and foods to treat distinct illnesses and conditions. That the teacher does not attend to a child's "dull headache or . . . painful cough" and that she uses one teaspoon from the same bottle to heal "variously ailing Indian children" is beneath contempt in Zitkala-Ša's eyes. In referring to this woman as "well-meaning," the narrator excuses her ignorance as the inevitable outcome of an underdeveloped society, thus implying the superiority of her own culture. When she returns to the school after a four-year hiatus, she is careful to strengthen herself with the medicinal wisdom of her own people: "In the second journey to the East I had not come without some precautions. I had a secret interview with one of our best medicine men, and when I left his wigwam I carried securely in my sleeve a tiny bunch of magic roots. . . . So absolutely did I believe in its charms that I wore it through all the school routine for more than a year." That the narrator loses this bag "containing all [her] good luck" is an omen. By the end of her "School Days," which now reflect her college years, her ability to be empowered by her own culture is waning.[27]

At the height of success in college, just when she has been chosen to participate in an oratorical contest, the narrator is confronted with racism. Several students in the audience hold up a flag on which they have drawn a "forlorn Indian girl" labeled "'squaw.'" The narrator recognizes that she is being branded as a degraded woman, a European American man's sex object. Thus at that moment, despite public recognition of her linguistic skills, she feels powerless. She fights back in the only accessible way: by succeeding on the European Americans' terms. She uses an English-language speech to regain power by winning the statewide prize in oratory. However, in her desire to use the colonizer's language "to be white," to use Eric Cheyfitz's words, she succeeds only in trapping herself in the position of a colonized subject, which inevitably leads to her alienating herself from her own community: "In my mind I saw my mother far away on the Western plains, and she was holding a charge against me."[28]

Zitkala-Ša recognizes that females were victims not only of secular discourses that essentialized Native people but also of religious discourses that disrupted the Native way of life. And it is clear in "An Indian Teacher among Indians" that one of her goals in *American Indian Stories* is to confront and attack European American religious rhetoric. Here Zitkala-Ša uses the English language to expose the power position of those who are educating Native children with missionary zeal. By the end of "An Indian Teacher," she is referring to "palefaces" as "*Christian* palefaces" and underscoring that the school in which the narrator is teaching is run by "*Christian[s]* in power" (emphasis added). Rage against the misuse of Christian power was already evident in "School Days," with the dazzling turn of phrase that describes an unsympathetic European American female teacher as standing in a "halo of authority." It also is obvious when the child destroys the Bible, after dreaming that her mother had saved her from the devil's grasp: "Stealing into the room where a wall of shelves was filled with books, I drew forth The Stories of the Bible. With a broken slate pencil I carried in my apron pocket, I began by scratching out his wicked eyes. A few moments later, when I was ready to leave the room, there was a ragged hole in the page where the picture of the devil had once been." In this scene the narrator uses a pencil – sign of a literate culture – to perform the ultimate act of revision. Symbolically, she obliterates a threatening Christianity, signified by the devil. Even earlier, in "Impressions," she had anticipated the "terrible magic power" of the tattooed cross, a mark (of Christianity) whose implied violence makes for a "fearful story." The teacher-narrator reveals her inner torment as she describes the personal cost of her religious education, which led to the dissolution of her relationship with her mother: "For the white man's papers, I had given up my faith in the Great Spirit. For these same papers I had forgotten the healing in trees and brooks. On account of my mother's simple view of life, and my lack of any, I gave her up, also." As George Tinker notes, nineteenth-century European American missionaries tended to romanticize their work, focusing on its beneficent aim and activity; but when the stories are told from a Native perspective – in this case, Zitkala-Ša's – the central theme is often anguish and loss.[29]

Through her own experience, Zitkala-Ša has come to understand the role boarding schools are playing in the subversion of Native spiritual values, for this endeavor was by no means covert. The Quakers at the school Zitkala-Ša attended as a child and teenager were actively seeking converts. White's Institute's 1887 report attests: "The religious instruction of the pupils is carefully attended to; an endeavor is made to bring them to an intelligent reception of the truths of the Gospel, a heart surrender to the Lord Jesus Christ, and to the formation of habits expressive of Christian discipleship." There was never a moment when students at White's were unaware of the evangelistic mission, for it pervaded every aspect of the school, including the students' domestic and industrial work: "The various factors of educational work are here intimately interwoven. The school room teaching, the home discipline, the industrial training, the social intercourse, the guarded recreations, the personal influence of officers, the reading of books, papers and periodicals; the effect of some outing, and much contact with visitors, *joined to the daily moral and religious training,* unite in quickening thought, moulding character, and fixing habits in pupils" (emphasis added). Believing their religion to be superior to Native spiritual practices, the Quakers made every effort to "*raise* the religious character of the pupils to a *higher* standard" (emphasis added). Students did not readily accept the notion that their spiritual values were deficient, however, and there was significant resistance to conversion. Despite their professed view that "each pupil is the object of loving regard," the staff at White's apparently hounded students until they succumbed to (the) Christian persuasion: "Marcus Pearson, the present pastor, speaks encouragingly of the religious growth among them. He states that by the daily pressure of Christian influence, many of the new pupils who seemed incorrigible at first, have been restrained."[30]

The nondenominational Carlisle School, where Zitkala-Ša taught from 1897 to 1898, was also openly complicit in the proselytizing. Wary of having his school considered "Godless," Richard Pratt assured the commissioner of Indian affairs that he kept students in constant contact with religious folk who were "on the alert to advance the cause of Christianity." Students were surrounded by Christians hoping to convert them: "There are in the school representatives of nearly all the leading churches, both among the students and instructors, and, as far as these churches are represented in the town of Carlisle, their preaching, Sabbath school, and other services are attended by the students. In addition, a Sabbath school is regularly held at the school; also a Sunday service – undenominational in its character – and a students' prayer meeting weekly. . . . No pupils come here and go away ignorant of Christian truth and morality." Zitkala-Ša's own experience as a teacher suggests how far she had become complicit in the civilizing mission before she left Carlisle and began to write. In 1898 the following scene of her (Miss Simmons's) teaching was published in a Carlisle School newspaper, the *Indian Helper*:

> One of the most interesting hours the Man-on-the-band-stand [Richard Pratt] has spent for many a day was in No. 6, last Thursday evening when Miss Simmons in the chair, conducted a debate between her morning and afternoon schools upon the subject of whether or not the treatment of the Indians by the early settlers caused King Philip to make war. There was a degree of life manifested on the part of the speakers in gaining the floor, that was refreshing, and arguments pro and con that would have done credit to the higher grades. Mr. Dennis Wheelock, Miss Wilson and Miss Burgess were appointed judges and decided that the best argument was on the negative side.

At the time this classroom debate took place, the prevailing European American interpretation of the relationship between the Puritan and Native populations was that the Puritans were humane and fair in their treatment of Native people, who self-destructively refused to embrace the norms of European American society and accept Christianity. Extensive documentation of Puritan brutality and injustice challenges this interpretation, however. A contemporary analysis holds that the primary cause of the 1675 war between the Puritans and King Philip (Metacom), sachem of Wampanoags, was the Puritans' violation of Native people's rights, especially through encroachment on their land. Given the outcome in her classroom debate, it is apparent that Zitkala-Ša was put in the position of having to support a blame-the-Indian interpretation of history. At that moment she was trapped between two cultural interpretations, but she would soon find a way to use writing to express her views.[31]

A photograph taken by the famous photographer Gertrude Käsebier in 1898, three years after Zitkala-Ša graduated from White's and during the time she was teaching at Carlisle, shows a graceful young woman in Victorian dress holding a symbol of European American culture: a violin (fig. 13).[32] As she gazed soulfully at the camera, Zitkala-Ša must have warmed the hearts of late-nineteenth-century observers like Merial Dorchester, special agent in the Indian school service, who derived so much delight "from learning how like these girls are to white girls." But as Zitkala-Ša gazes at us today, she has a different effect. For we now know that she was just beginning to realize that the traditional power and prestige of Sioux women, which "white girls" had never experienced, was being diminished by the very Christian ideology she had been convinced to embrace.[33]

"WHY I AM A PAGAN"

Zitkala-Ša continues *American Indian Stories* with an essay that extolled nature and the Great Spirit. To follow the first three pieces with "Why I Am a Pagan," she had to change the chronological order of the original publication of her works, for this composition was first published in the *Atlantic Monthly* in 1902, and the two stories that follow it were first published in *Harper's Monthly Magazine* in 1901. By rearranging the order, Zitkala-Ša makes it possible for "Why I Am a Pagan" to serve as a moment of reflection before she moves on to the stories. The selection also acts as a transition from a focus on the effort to assimilate and Christianize one individual Sioux child to a focus on the larger project of destroying all of Sioux sacred culture and, by extension, all Native cultures.

Zitkala-Ša's experience in Christian or Christian-dominated schools has opened her eyes to the political nature of religious discourse. Through her writing, she shows that she understands how much its underlying ideology has diminished the strength and status of Sioux women. To restore her own feminine power, she implies, it is crucial to turn away from the Christian rhetoric that permeates the schools. In "Why I Am a Pagan," she creates a narrator who communicates instead through the sacred discourse of her own people: "A wee child toddling in a wonder world, I prefer to their dogma my excursions into the natural gardens where the voice of the Great Spirit is heard in the twittering of birds, the rippling of mighty waters, and the sweet breath of flowers." Zitkala-Ša's narrator embraces her spiritual heritage, thus revealing that the "*Impressions* of an Indian Childhood" are not merely scattered remembrances but quite literally permanent imprints that are part of her consciousness. For it is the story her mother told at the site of the plum bush about the "*sacred* ground" and the "whistle of departed *spirits*" that has formed a "lasting *impression*" (emphasis added). By having her narrator repeat what she learned from her mother, Zitkala-Ša reconnects the links in the chain of the female-to-female tradition of storytelling. She also implies that (Sioux) ideas transmitted orally, unlike (Christian) ideas transmitted through written texts, cannot be scratched out or erased.[34]

The ideological perspective of "Why I Am a Pagan" is not as straightforward as it may seem, however. There is biographical evidence that Zitkala-Ša did not wholly repudiate Christianity. And she is careful to note here that the "pale-faced missionary" is one of "God's creatures." There is another curious factor that recommends caution in attributing an anti-Christian view to Zitkala-Ša. Two versions of *American Indian Stories* appeared in 1921, both published by Hayworth Publishing House. In one, the title of the essay "Why I Am a Pagan" remains the same as in the 1902 *Atlantic Monthly* piece; but in the other it is changed to "The Great Spirit." The endings of the two versions also differ. In "Why I Am a Pagan" the last line reads, "If this is Paganism, then at present, at least, I am a pagan." The last paragraph of "The Great Spirit," like the title, eliminates the word "pagan": "Here in a fleeting quiet, I am awakened by the fluttering robe of the Great Spirit. To my inner most consciousness the phenomenal universe is a royal mantle, vibrating with His divine breath. Caught in its flowing fringes are the spangles and oscillating brilliants of sun, moon, and stars." I have been unable to determine why the changes were made or which version appeared first. But it is possible that Zitkala-Ša had second thoughts about representing herself as a pagan in 1921. "Why I Am a Pagan," then, at least in the context of *American Indian Stories,* may best be viewed as a sign not that Zitkala-Ša turned away from Christianity itself, but rather that she rejected a Christianity that denigrated Native life.[35]

(P)RESERVATION FICTION

Strengthened rhetorically by her own spiritual roots, Zitkala-Ša now returns to reservation or even prereservation life as a resource for her fiction. The first three stories that follow "Why I Am a Pagan" are arranged according to their original publication order; the next two stories are apparently new.[36] One pattern that emerges from the arrangement of the five stories is that the three stories in the middle, which end on a hopeful – even empowering – note, are framed by stories that end in tragedy. Together they can be seen as plotted on a line graph, beginning at the bottom in tragedy ("The Soft-Hearted Sioux"), moving upward with renewed energy ("The Trial Path"), peaking at a moment of great strength ("A Warrior's Daughter"), moving downward but rising with renewed hope ("A Dream of Her Grandfather"), and finally declining toward despair ("The Widespread Enigma of Blue-Star Woman"). In short, the order of the tales can be said to mirror the mercurial history of the once-powerful Sioux in the middle to late nineteenth century, which included key moments such as the removal of Sioux communities to reservations (beginning in the late 1850s), the Sioux revolt (1862), the defeat of Custer (1876), the United States government's off-reservation education program (beginning in 1878), and the massacre at Wounded Knee (1890). An examination of the role of female characters in each story reveals the consequences of the loss of Native women's prestige and power during this period. Only in dreams, or in settings devoid of European American civilization, do women regain status and strength.

Among most Plains people, Paula Gunn Allen explains, cultural knowledge and its associated power were accumulated by and dispensed through females. It is therefore no coincidence that in "The Soft-Hearted Sioux" the narrator's first advice about his future role as hunter and husband comes from his grandmother. Significantly, the grandmother is smoking a pipe, for this links her with the Lakota creation story of White Buffalo Calf Woman, whose gift of the pipe was a gift of truth. Equally significant, in "refusing to smoke [his] grandmother's pipe," the narrator symbolically rejects the truth. He turns instead to Christianity through conversion in a mission school, where he learns that "it was wrong to kill." Thus, in yet another rhetorical inversion, Zitkala-Ša uses the language of the missionary to echo the Sioux mother's advice in "An Indian Teacher among Indians" to "beware of the paleface": "He is the hypocrite who reads with one eye, 'Thou shalt not kill,' and with the other gloats upon the sufferings of the Indian race." According to Raymond DeMallie, Lakotas believed that their society was only as strong as its women. Rejection of female wisdom, then, could only lead to tragedy, as in this story, in which the narrator is powerless to save his father from death. Thus Zitkala-Ša lays the blame not only on born Christians but also on converts who adopted a Christianity that had no room for traditional Sioux cultural values.[37]

Unlike "The Soft-Hearted Sioux," the next story, "The Trial Path," is notable for the absence of any reference to European American Christian culture. In fact, in a letter to her then fiancé, Carlos Montezuma, Zitkala-Ša said of this story, "That is purely Ancient history and won[']t bear hard on any one's pet causes." Again, a grandmother takes center stage at the beginning, as she tells a story containing "sacred knowledge" that she wants her granddaughter to understand. Unfortunately, although the granddaughter hears the tale, she sleeps through the subsequent explanation of its ritual significance. Zitkala-Ša thus symbolically points to the difficulty of transmitting cultural knowledge from generation to generation, even without the intervention of European Americans, but not its impossibility. Although the grandmother's memories may be a "dream," and thus in European American terms not real, "the guardian star in the night sky" remains, beaming "compassionately" on the two women. As long as the grandmother lives to tell and retell the "sacred tale," the hope exists that the younger female generation will hear it, learn from it, and be able to pass it on. As Allen points out, the perpetuation of the oral tradition, especially in its ritual aspects, depends on the women.[38]

Zitkala-Ša's revision of Sioux women's privileged status is most evident in the central story, "A Warrior's Daughter," whose protagonist risks her life to save the man she loves. Here the author's rhetorical inversion is nothing short of audacious, for she subverts the well-known story of Pocahontas's seventeenth-century rescue of John Smith. Rayna Green shows that the Pocahontas–John Smith rescue tale mirrors a frame story that dates back in printed form to the thirteenth century. A white Christian male is always captured by the "natives" but then rescued by the king's or pasha's dark, beautiful daughter, who, like all good princesses, defies her own people to save the white man, acting out of "Christian sympathy." The image of Pocahontas's body protecting the endangered John Smith was rendered in popular art and repeated in literary works so often that it became a national myth and set up a model for Native-European relations, making the white man every Indian princess's dream. Zitkala-Ša shatters that myth. In her story Tusee does have aristocratic roots, in Native terms: as Beatrice Medicine explains, a female's status typically reflected the warrior position of her father, and Tusee's father is "the chieftain's bravest warrior." Yet when this princess goes to rescue a man, he is Native, not European. Zitkala-Ša appropriates the language used to construct the European male hero in creating this Native male as a romantic figure whose heart "beat[s] hard and fast" when he asks Tusee's father for his daughter's hand in marriage. Furthermore, in setting the story in a society with no hint of European American culture, Zitkala-Ša undercuts religious rhetoric by eliminating "Christian sympathy" as a reason for the rescue.[39]

Nativizing the Pocahontas tale even further, Zitkala-Ša disguises her princess. Rescuing her from her captive state as the European American image of Indian princess as classical model, she dresses her instead as an old, bent woman with a bundle on her back. Jeanne Smith suggests that Tusee's disguise links her with the Lakota trickster Iktomi, who carries grass in his blanket as though it is a heavy burden in order to capture ducks. Masking her character in a "harmless" pose, Zitkala-Ša enables her to exact revenge. Employing another trickster strategy, Zitkala-Ša endows Tusee with apparently male characteristics: a "warrior's strong heart," which gives her the courage to murder the enemy, and "broad shoulders," which allow her to carry her lover safely away. Here Zitkala-Ša may have been drawing on what Beatrice Medicine identifies as the Plains tradition of "manly-hearted women," who excelled in every significant aspect of tribal life. As children, these women were favored, just as Tusee was – she was her father's "great joy" – which led to an adulthood of high self-esteem and drive. As Allen contends, powerful women were typically discredited in European American society, which perpetuated the notion that the only social system that made sense was patriarchy. In restoring Sioux women to a powerful role, "A Warrior's Daughter" challenges the assumptions of European American ideology.[40]

At the same time, Zitkala-Ša may have been challenging a Sioux tradition by creating a situation in which it is no longer necessary for the male suitor to "buy" his wife from her father: Tusee takes her man for herself. It is important to note that buying a wife did not have a negative connotation among Lakotas. DeMallie suggests that the purchase was a sign of honor, placing a high value on the woman. Katherine Weist even contends that it was not a purchase at all but rather an exchange that cemented ties between the two kin groups. Perhaps the romantic essence of the custom was captured by Zallie Rulo in her graduation speech at the Hampton Institute: "Those that are bought, as a general thing, are bought by the men they love." However, Zitkala-Ša's feminist stance is evident in "A Warrior's Daughter." In her letters to Carlos Montezuma, Zitkala-Ša challenged all forms of patriarchy and demanded a strong role and equality in their marriage: "Were you planning a Charity Hospital under the guise of matrimony? There are plenty of Charity Institutions in the cities whither proper lack of pride and respect would take me! But for one life-time at least I am not so totally depraved as to accept charity – private or public! I do not want to demoralize you! I had no thought of limiting your ambition." Even earlier, she clearly articulated a feminist ideology in her commencement oration at White's Institute in 1895, in which she condemned the inequality of all women, saying, "Half of humanity cannot rise while the other half is in subjugation."[41]

The following story, "A Dream of Her Grandfather," initially exchanges the cultural and romantic language of "A Warrior's Daughter" for political discourse and jolts readers back into a contemporary world threatened by European American power. We learn that the grandfather "came to Washington, D.C. with one of the first delegations relative to affairs concerning the American Indian people and the United States government" and that his granddaughter is doing "welfare work." Yet ultimately this story, like its predecessors, places great store in the cultural importance of the female character. Mirroring the optimism of "The Trial Path," Zitkala-Ša suggests that as long as there is a female, the Sioux heritage can be preserved, especially if she is the descendant of a great male leader. For in this story the unwritten tradition, symbolized by the picture of a Native camp, passes from grandfather to granddaughter through nature – by way of a "red wood" box that signifies the "breath of the forest" – and appears as a "vision." This heritage reminds readers that before the government banned ceremonies on reservations, Sioux women were essential participants in tribal rituals and could have visions that gave them inspiration and power.[42]

If American Indian Stories had ended with "A Dream," it could have been viewed as a paean to Native women's strength, their wisdom, and their power to sustain Native traditions. But reality intervenes again. The last of the five stories in this grouping, "The Widespread Enigma concerning Blue-Star Woman," reveals that European American power cannot be suppressed. The woman in this story is "lonely" and "poor," having had to forfeit the "unwritten law of heart" for the "white man's law." The "old teachings of her race," part of an oral tradition of which no written record remains, have meaning to her but wield no authority now that she must answer to government officials. Her very identity is in question.[43]

Before we learn how her current situation came to pass, we are given hints of the ways Blue-Star Woman's personal history evolved and how it reflects the historical relationship between Native communities and European Americans. We see that she embodies the best of Sioux tradition yet shows a willingness to change with the times. Zitkala-Ša once again suggests that Sioux were more enlightened than European Americans about women's status when she explains that because Sioux traditionally did not use family names, the newborn Blue-Star Woman was given a name "for which she would not be required to substitute another's upon her marriage, as is the custom of civilized peoples."[44]

Zitkala-Ša also reminds readers that Native women were not always viewed by European Americans as degraded – and simultaneously equates the women with the best European American civilization has to offer – when she points out that "neither the Pilgrim Fathers nor Blue-Star Woman" ever held Native peoples' traditional generosity against them, unlike contemporary critics who find this characteristic to be a "fault." Blue-Star Woman is also lauded for attending school and learning to read and write and, in direct contrast to the stereotyped squaw, is shown to be capable of "deep abstraction." Her education within European American civilization has enabled her to take a critical perspective toward what she has learned and to consider the weakness of European American Christian teachings in comparison with Sioux views: " 'The missionary preacher said he could not explain the white man's law to me. He who reads daily from the Holy Bible, which he tells me is God's book, cannot understand mere man's laws. This also puzzles me,' she thought to herself. 'Once a wise leader of our people, addressing a president of this country, said: "I am a man. You are another. The great Spirit is our witness!" This is simple and easy to understand, but the times are changed.' "[45]

Indeed, the times have changed. The literary language of this story is often transposed into harsh politicized discourse, as Jeanne Smith points out. There is a good reason for this transposition. The story is emblematic of the failure of the "sacred tale" to shatter the misrepresentations promoted in European American discourses. The personal, sacred, and cultural tales, which had infused the preceding *Stories,* are inadequate to tell the full story of Native life. Explicitly historical facts are necessary to explain the exchange of power positions, and so we come in contact with Native police whose ilk had murdered "the great leader, Sitting Bull" in 1890. We have already learned that Blue-Star Woman has been deprived by European Americans of her tribal lands and that she is deceived by some of her own people, "would-be white men," whose actions cause the tribal leaders to turn against her. In deceiving others, Zitkala-Ša tells us, these "schemers," "pretenders," "wolves," "tricksters" deceive "themselves most of all." This aspect of the story, along with the reference to the Native police, suggests that Zitkala-Ša's project does not absolve Native communities of responsibility for the devastation. Zitkala-Ša does take aim primarily at European American colonizers, but she is also critical of Native people who have participated in the deception, for she understands that the United States government depended on indigenous collaborators to diminish traditional power structures and thus subjugate Sioux communities.[46]

POLITICAL WRITING AND COMMUNITY ACTIVISM

Having mined other genres, Zitkala-Ša concludes *American Indian Stories* with a journalistic article, "America's Indian Problem," which was also published in *Edict,* the magazine of the Illinois Federation of Women's Clubs. In this article she quotes extensively from a public document, a 1915 report on an investigation of the corrupt Indian Bureau, which by implication is another "story" of Native life that is now subjected to interpretation through a bicultural perspective. But first she returns to history, reminding readers that the land that became America was inhabited by her people long before the "early settlers" arrived: "DeSoto and his Spaniards were graciously received by the Indian Princess Cofachiqui." Her reference to the princess can be no accident. She exposes the explorers' desire for a new beginning, symbolized in the virgin (land). Yet she also shows that this male fantasy had given way to the reality of the inevitable (self-)violation that accompanies colonization: "The barbaric rule of might from which the paleface had fled hither for refuge caught up with him again." Already an important activist, she is frustrated with legislation written and signed by men, legislation that has consistently denied civil rights to Native people. Now she puts her faith in the group whose potential power she understands: "The time is at hand when the American Indian shall have his day in court through the help of the *women* of America" (emphasis added). Thus *American Indian Stories* begins and ends with a focus on the value of women's work: their activity and their activism.[47]

Even after she abandoned the idea of pursuing a career as a writer, Zitkala-Ša never desisted in her attempt to reconstruct the image of Native women, even to the extent of treating herself as an artistic creation. Whenever she lectured on Native people's rights or lobbied Congress as Gertrude Bonnin, she wore a dress that signified her Native identity. Thus she linked her female Native culture (dress) to symbols of literacy and power (Congress), much as she has done by signing her Lakota name (Zitkala-Ša) to the literary work she published (in English). In using her body as text, Gertrude Bonnin was, of course, guilty of the same exoticizing of the Native woman that as Zitkala-Ša she sometimes exhibits in her *Stories,* for she fed the era's hunger for an authentic Indian, most especially an Indian princess. Furthermore, just as the Native cultural discourses in the stories could not eradicate injurious European American rhetoric, the dress itself occasionally failed her as a useful symbol. According to Hazel Hertzberg, Gertrude Bonnin inadvertently included in the costume a peyote fan and thus opened the way for her political detractors to ridicule her, for at the time she was fighting vigorously against the Native American Church's use of peyote.[48]

Nevertheless, Gertrude Bonnin's/Zitkala-Ša's choice of dress and discourse(s) functioned to achieve the goal of exploiting her transculturation. Taking her legitimate place in this new world, she set her gaze in two directions, using the English language to take a critical perspective toward the European American people who attempted to destroy Native life and also toward Native people, including herself, who collaborated with them through either deception or assimilation. Her primary audience in 1900 was European American, but in 1921, when her stories were gathered into a book, she may also have been writing for a growing Native readership, including her colleagues at the Society of American Indians. In *American Indian Stories* she created a space for bicultural play, in which the two sets of readers could look at each other and become conscious of their respective roles in the changing landscape – and in changing the landscape. Zitkala-Ša thus invited all readers to pause and reflect on the poignant question raised by "An Indian Teacher among Indians": "whether real life or long-lasting death lies beneath this semblance of civilization."[49]

Just as Zitkala-Ša indicated that the land was not the colonizers' exclusive property, so did she demonstrate that neither was the English language. If a goal of the government was to use education to impose a universal language so that the people would become "homogeneous" in thought and action, as

President Grant's Indian Peace Commission recommended in 1868, Zitkala-Ša subverted that goal. In writing the eclectic *American Indian Stories*, she refused any one voice. Previous attempts to tell the story of indigenous peoples within a single discourse or genre were oppressive, as she made clear in her implied and explicit criticism of the representations disseminated through the accounts of travelers, anthropologists, missionaries, artists, historians, and government officials. As she took ownership of the language, her act of revision merged personal, cultural, sacred, literary, historical, and political discourses. The juxtaposition of genres became in itself a tool of resistance – in America's second tongue.

14. Valedictorian Alfred Willie (San Felipe), Santa Fe Indian School (1983).
Courtesy of Santa Fe Indian School Archives.

Epilogue

In the fall of 1997 I visited the Santa Fe Indian School in New Mexico. Founded in 1890, it was established by the United States Congress as an off-reservation boarding school for the purpose of civilizing and Christianizing children of the southwestern tribes. Though still operating on United States government land, the school is controlled and operated by nineteen Pueblo governors. An appointed school board sets the educational policy and is accountable to Native people. One hundred years ago, students marched in military battalions, spent half their day doing manual work, and were punished for speaking their native tongues. The day I visited, youngsters outfitted in clothing of their choice chattered freely as they moved through the campus from class to class. One hundred years ago, most southwestern Native parents were opposed to formal schooling and refused to part with their children. Today the Santa Fe Indian School has a long waiting list of parents who seek a program that meets the needs of Native children.[1]

Ironically, as Brenda Child explains, Native families were largely responsible for keeping the boarding school system alive, even when the United States government and philanthropic reformers deemphasized residential schools in favor of reservation day schools at the turn of the century. The system endured partly because of sluggish bureaucracy but also because parents sent children to the schools as a refuge from the social problems caused by poverty, disease, and early mortality on the reservations. Today indigenous populations are growing. Many Native languages are being maintained and renewed, with the support of the 1990 Native American Languages Act. Congressional statutes such as the 1934 Indian Reorganization Act and the 1973 Indian Self-Determination and Educational Assistance Act (despite the underlying assumption of European American values and political structures), as well as Titles I and XI, have enabled Native communities to take greater control over the education of their own children. The 1978 Indian Child Welfare Act officially put an end to the policy of forcibly removing Native children from their families and placing them in boarding schools. Today many tribal governments and Native communities run locally controlled schools that in some cases embrace bilingual education.[2]

If this were the whole story of American Indian education today, there would be little left to say except that things have turned out well. But that is not the case. In her in-depth study *Sisters in the Blood: The Education of Women in Native America,* Ardy Bowker reports that school dropout rates among Native youth continue to be the highest in the United States. Following a historical pattern, Bowker documents, Native students themselves – not the educational system – are typically blamed for this state of affairs. With student deficiency at the center of such analyses, the discourses of colonialism continue to reverberate through discussions of American Indian education. Studies like Bowker's own serve as correctives to this point of view, for Bowker analyzes the systemic as well as the personal issues related to the high dropout rate. She acknowledges the role that social issues such as poverty, alcoholism, and teen pregnancy can play in students' lack of success at school. But she also provides compelling evidence that many Native students' poor records in school can be traced to discrimination on the part of non-Native teachers and administrators, many of whom refuse to acknowledge that these students are intellectually capable of academic excellence. Bowker's interviews with more than nine hundred Native women reveal that stereotypical attitudes toward indigenous peoples continue to have a negative impact on students' sense of self-worth. Teachers' low expectations enact a self-fulfilling prophecy of failure. Furthermore, resistance to the idea of incorporating Native languages and cultures into public school curricula persists. Too often, schools operate in the interest not of Native students but of those outside Native communities. In many schools, Bowker maintains, "Indian education today is no more than a continuation of the education of a century or two centuries or even three centuries ago."[3]

On the positive side, Bowker identifies several variables that contribute to student success, even within oppressive environments. The single most important factor is a caring and sensitive teacher who sets high expectations and takes the time to encourage and support students, even helping them with personal or bureaucratic problems so that they can achieve academically. As might be expected, students typically thrive when entire schools provide this kind of climate. Supportive family members, too, play a major role in helping students overcome the stresses of school, especially when they serve as mentors or role models or provide a home atmosphere in which children feel safe and loved. There is an apparent link between these factors and what Bowker calls students' strong inner sense of "spirituality," by which she means having a sense of purpose or destiny.[4]

Aiming her remarks at other Native community members, Bowker's goal is to use "the past as a path to the future," to reevaluate and redefine American Indian education. This goal is supported by numerous publications produced by Native scholars and educators. For example, the *Journal of American Indian Education,* published by the Center for Indian Education at Arizona State University, focuses on research that is initiated, conducted, and interpreted by Native scholars. Its purpose is to encourage original research geared toward helping indigenous communities develop educational programs that maximize the potential of Native youth. Articles in *Tribal College Journal of American Indian Higher Education,* published by the American Indian Higher Education Consortium, relate directly to the work of tribal colleges in the United States and Canada. Because Native people have historically had little control over their formal education in English, there is some debate within the Native scholarly community about who should write about American Indian education. In her 1996 article in *American Indian Quarterly,* "Why Indian People Should Be the Ones to Write about Indian Education," Karen Swisher acknowledges the work of sensitive non-Native scholars but argues that indigenous people need to explore educational issues in such as way as to reflect principles of self-determination and sovereignty. K. Tsianina Lomawaima insists that any scholar in the field of American Indian education must understand the larger political field in which it is situated. Tribal sovereignty, which intersects with state and federal jurisdictions, functions as a fundamental, if limited, right to self-government. Treaties that acknowledge inherent sovereign rights are legal documents and need to be treated as such. Understandably, given the history of education, Native communities want to set the terms of the debate about issues related to their own lives. For Lomawaima, self-determination and sovereignty signify not only political self-governance but also the right to shape the way educational research and education itself are conducted.[5]

To teach effectively across languages, it is essential to understand the political, sociocultural, and historical relationships that inform first and second languages. After years of imposition and adoption, English is now the only language of many, if not most, indigenous people in the United States. In that sense English has truly become a Native language of America. Nevertheless, although most Native children in the United States may speak English, many enter school with little or no proficiency in the language. And as William L. Leap's research suggests, they may use English in different ways, in part because American Indian English – actually a variety of Englishes – has been shaped by ancestral or tribal languages and by the boarding school experience, during which students' various language patterns merged. On the reservations and off, educational programs need to build on the linguistic, cultural, and intellectual strengths students bring to the classroom. *Teaching American Indian Students,* to which both Native and non-Native teachers and scholars have contributed, is one example of a text that includes discussions of programs aimed at developing linguistically and culturally sensitive approaches to educating Native children. In several chapters, various researchers and teachers demonstrate how language arts instruction can take into account Native students' knowledge of English and view it not as an marker of language deficiency but rather as an indicator of differences that signify historical change and community identity. Students in these programs are not asked to reject their home language – whether it is an ancestral tongue or a variety of English – but rather to add to their linguistic resources. The best of these schools foster cooperation among parents, elders, and teachers in developing curricula that build on the home learning environment and allow room for experimentation in academic ways of knowing. United States educational policy has typically assumed an acculturation model in which success is measured by how closely a Native student adheres to non-Native ways of life and thought. The Indian Nations at Risk Task Force concluded in their "Treaty of 1992" that Native education needs to be informed by Native culture and community. As Carl Union argues, academic discourse must now acknowledge and embrace Native discourses, allowing for multiple perspectives to be brought to bear on education for Native students.[6]

These approaches are based on an understanding that the key to language and literacy acquisition does not lie solely in well-intentioned teachers or innovative pedagogical strategies. As the case study of the Hampton Institute in chapter 2 demonstrates, students' learning and self-esteem can be undermined by teachers' unexamined prejudices even when the teaching method itself is state of the art. Hand in hand with curriculum development, educators need to address the fact that misrepresentations of Native people continue to be disseminated in schools and in the larger society. Devon Mihesuah and other Native scholars have illustrated how this scenario plays out in textbooks, literary works, visual media, and journalistic and scholarly publications. Scott Richard Lyons shows, for example, how the oral/literate binary, which Luther Standing Bear decried seventy years ago, continues to inform scholarly inquiry, relegating traditional Native rhetoric to a low rung on the intellectual ladder. Such misrepresentations persist, Lyons contends, largely because non-Native writers and scholars continue to determine the direction and content of public and academic discourse. Given the history of contact, it makes sense for Native people to assume a primary role in establishing scholarship on their own lives and literatures, as the First Convocation of American Indian Scholars emphasized in 1970. Accordingly, Robert Allen Warrior emphasizes the need for Native "intellectual sovereignty," and Jace Weaver builds on that notion to call for "hermeneutical sovereignty." Lyons extends their vision to embrace "rhetorical sovereignty": the right of the people to determine communally what they need to communicate and how they will express their concerns and desires. Lyons is not suggesting that non-Native scholars should abandon Native American studies, but he does insist that Native scholars have a voice in their own rhetorical representations. In Elizabeth Cook-Lynn's metaphorical rendering, non-Native scholars can continue to have a seat at the table, but Native scholars should sit at its head.[7]

Critical theory, once the domain of a privileged few, is now informed by the work of these and other Native scholars, who have made it clear that the Native experience in America is not an academic exercise but involves people's lived realities, which continue to be affected by colonialism. Native American studies are undertaken so that the people might live, to borrow the title of Jace Weaver's book.[8] The legacy of the United States government's language policy rests not only in the reach of its destructive power but also in the limit of its power to change the core values of Native communities. The fundamental strengths of Native cultures endure. Maintenance and renewal of first languages and literacies continue to allow for Native values and ideas to be articulated in Native terms. An ever-growing body of Native literature in English continues to enrich and transform the United States canon. English as a shared language has engendered a pantribal political and social environment that has empowered Native people in ways policymakers never imagined. In place after place there is a rich story to be told by Native people of how they have taken ownership of English and shaped it to accommodate new and powerful forms of expression. It is time for me to push my seat to the side and listen.

Notes

INTRODUCTION

1. Knobel, "Know-Nothings and Indians" 175; Knobel, *America for the Americans. Note:* With the understanding that no term is ideal, I use *American Indian* to refer to the educational programs created by missionaries and government officials. When referring to the people themselves, I use *indigenous* or *Native* for the general population and specific tribal names for particular individuals or communities. I use the term *European American* to differentiate Native people from the non-Native people who were in a position to develop educational policy, virtually all of whom in this era were of European descent. Protestants were the primary and most powerful group vying for control of the schools. For a discussion of the tensions between Protestants and Catholics, see Prucha, *Churches and the Indian Schools.*

2. Axtell, *European and the Indian* 134–35; Weatherford, *Native Roots* 198–203; Cutler, *O Brave New Words!;* Tuttle, "Borrowing versus Semantic Shifts" 602–05; Green, "Tribe Called Wannabee" 32.

3. Axtell, *European and the Indian* 253, 263; White Hat, *Reading and Writing the Lakota Language* 32; Szasz, *Indian Education in the American Colonies* 6; Taylor, "Indian Lingua Francas" 175; Leap, "American Indian Languages" 132–33.

4. Szasz, *Indian Education in the American Colonies* 111–13; Murray, *Forked Tongues* 6–7.

5. Tuttle, "Borrowing versus Semantic Shift" 603–04; Smith, "Interest in Language and Languages in Colonial and Federal America" 30; Greenblatt, "Learning to Curse" 564, 568; Murray, *Forked Tongues* 14–15; Rosenwald, "*Last of the Mohicans*

and the Languages of America" 11. Rosenwald cites the 1876 reprint of Heckewelder's book. For a discussion of linguistic work on Native languages up to the middle of the nineteenth century, see Edgerton, "Notes on Early American Work in Linguistics" 25–34.

6. Szasz, *Indian Education in the American Colonies* 46, 5–6, 59.

7. Bowden, *American Indians and Christian Missions* 167.

8. Leibowitz, *Educational Policy and Political Acceptance* 75–76; Reyhner, *Teaching American Indian Students* 62.

9. Trennert, *Phoenix Indian School;* Reyhner and Eder, *History of Indian Education;* DeJong, *Promises of the Past;* Mihesuah, *Cultivating the Rosebuds;* Coleman, *American Indian Children at School;* Lomawaima, *They Called It Prairie Light;* Lindsey, *Indians at Hampton Institute;* Adams, *Education for Extinction;* Ellis, *To Change Them Forever;* Child, *Boarding School Seasons;* Riney, *The Rapid City Indian School;* Cobb, *Listening to Our Grandmothers' Stories;* Leibowitz, *Educational Policy and Political Acceptance* 63–80; Park, "Historical Foundations of Language Policy" 49–67.

10. Ferguson and Heath, *Language in the* USA; Herriman and Burnaby, *Language Policies in English-Dominant Countries;* Howatt, *History of English Language Teaching;* Pennycook, *Cultural Politics of English as an International Language;* Phillipson, *Linguistic Imperialism;* Viswanathan, *Masks of Conquest;* Darian, *English as a Foreign Language;* Crawford, *Bilingual Education.*

11. Gidley, *Edward S. Curtis and the North American Indian* 4–5.

12. Medicine, "Anthropologist as the Indian's Image Maker" 27; Pratt, "Arts of the Contact Zone" 34. *Note: Sioux* is a Europeanized term used to describe people who speak three similar dialects of Siouan language: Teton (Lakota), Santee (Dakota), and Yankton and Yanktonai (Nakota). The Tetons and Santees typically identify themselves by dialect and call themselves Lakotas and Dakotas, respectively. The Yanktons and Yanktonais identify themselves as Dakota. Zitkala-Ša was a Yankton Sioux. Although Nakota was her childhood dialect, her Native name – which she gave to herself – is Lakota. Given her three linguistic and cultural identities (Nakota, Dakota, Lakota), I have chosen to refer to her only as a Yankton Sioux.

13. Vallance, "Hiding the Hidden Curriculum" 5–6.

14. Ah-nen-la-de-ni, "Indian Boy's Story" 1780–87; Betzinez and Nye, *I Fought with Geronimo;* Eastman, *From the Deep Woods to Civilization;* La Flesche, *Middle Five;* Lindsey, "Memories of the Indian Territory Mission Field"; Miller, *Mourning Dove;* "Address by Mr. Charles Doxon"; Rogers, *Red World and White;* Standing Bear, *My People the Sioux;* Standing Bear, *Land of the Spotted Eagle;* Webb, *Pima Remembers;* Whitewolf, "Short Story of My Life"; Winnemucca Hopkins, *Life among*

the Piutes. The works of three of these writers – Ah-nen-la-de-ni, Betzinez, Mourning Dove – were subject to some rearrangement and even rewriting by their editors.

15. Alford, *Civilization and the Story of the Absentee Shawnees;* Ball, Henn, and Sánchez, *Indeh;* Goodbird, *Goodbird the Indian;* Marriott and Rachlin, *Dance around the Sun;* Scott, *Karnee;* Frisbie and McAllester, *Navajo Blessingway Singer;* Seaman, *Born a Chief;* Stands in Timber and Liberty, *Cheyenne Memories;* Bass, *Arapaho Way;* Simmons, *Sun Chief;* Yava, *Big Falling Snow.*

16. Bloodworth, "Varieties of American Indian Autobiography" 68–69; Bataille and Sands, *American Indian Women* 15–16; Brumble, *American Indian Autobiography* 17; McBeth, "Myths of Objectivity" 149–50; Coleman, *American Indian Children at School* 7–8; Murray, *Forked Tongues* 66–67.

17. Pratt, "Arts of the Contact Zone" 35.

I. ENGLISH AND COLONIALIST DISCOURSES

1. Zitkala-Ša, "School Days of an Indian Girl"; "White's Institute, Indiana," *Minutes of the Indiana Yearly Meeting of Friends* (Richmond IN: Yarmon, 1883) 19; Winger, *Brief Centennial History of Wabash County* 6; Zitkala-Ša, "Impressions of an Indian Childhood" 45.

2. Parker and Parker, *Josiah White's Institute* 36; Lambert, "Culture and Language as Factors in Learning and Education" 67.

3. Cheyfitz, *Poetics of Imperialism* 112; Viswanathan, *Masks of Conquest;* Pennycook, *Cultural Politics of English as an International Language;* Ngũgĩ wa Thiong'o, *Decolonising the Mind* 11; Noriega, "American Indian Education in the United States."

4. Kaestle, "Ideology and American Educational History" 125, 134; Hoare and Smith, *Selections from the Prison Notebooks of Antonio Gramsci* 12.

5. Battey, *Life and Adventures of a Quaker among the Indians* 318.

6. Prucha, *American Indian Policy in Crisis* 18; Report to the President by the Indian Peace Commission, January 7, 1868, Report of the Commissioner of Indian Affairs, *Executive Documents Printed by Order of the House of Representatives during the Third Session of the Fortieth Congress, 1868–'69* (Washington: GPO, 1869) 502–04; Fletcher, *Indian Education and Civilization* 167. References to annual reports of the Commissioner of Indian Affairs, published in the annual reports of the Secretary of the Interior, are hereafter cited as *RCIA.*

7. Fletcher, *Indian Education and Civilization* 167, 289; Burleigh, "Yancton Sioux Agency, Dakota Territory, October 12, 1863," *RCIA* (1863) 276; P. H. Conger,

"Yancton Agency, Dakota Territory, September 7, 1868," RCIA (1869) 648; John W. Douglas, "Yankton Agency, Dakota. August 26, 1878," RCIA (1878) 543. *Note:* The spelling of *Yancton* was later changed to *Yankton.*

8. Edward P. Smith, RCIA (1873) 377; John G. Gasmann, "Yankton Agency, Dakota Territory, September 20, 1873," RCIA (1873) 606 Gasman[n], "Yancton Agency, Dak., September 17, 1874," RCIA (1874) 567; Fletcher, *Indian Education and Civilization* 167. After 1873, the mission schools drew their funds from their own religious societies, from tribal annuities, or through special contracts with the federal government.

9. Williamson, "Yancton Agency, Dakota Territory, August 9, 1870," RCIA (1871) 678; Douglas, RCIA (1878) 543.

10. "Captain Pratt's Campaign," *Southern Workman* (Dec. 1878) 91; Richard Henry Pratt, RCIA (1881) 247; Gump, *Dust Rose Like Smoke* 102. With the exception of the peaceful Yankton Sioux, various Sioux bands resisted United States forces until the 1890 massacre of women and children at Wounded Knee. Utley, *Last Days of the Sioux Nation* 5; Hoover and Bruguier, *Yankton Sioux* 22.

11. Pratt, *Battlefield and Classroom* 222–23; Hyde, *Spotted Tail's Folk* 286, 290–92.

12. Samuel Armstrong to Richard Henry Pratt, August 27, 1878, Richard Henry Pratt Papers, Yale Collection of Western Americana, Beinecke Rare Book and Manuscript Library, Yale University; Guimond, "'Vanishing Red'"; Malmsheimer, "'Imitation White Man.'"

13. Welsh, *Four Weeks among Some of the Sioux Tribes of Dakota and Nebraska* 21; Adams, "Fundamental Considerations" 6; Washington, *Up from Slavery.* Washington became head of the Tuskegee Institute in 1881.

14. Kutzleb, "Educating the Dakota Sioux" 208; Burgess, "Goddess, the School Book, and Compulsion" 201; Laurence, "Indian Education" 395–96; W. D. E. Andrus, "Yankton Agency, Dakota, August 3, 1881," RCIA (1881) 119.

15. Samuel J. Kirkwood, *Report of the Secretary of the Interior,* vol. 1 (Washington DC: GPO, 1881) iii; RCIA (1887) 18; Hiram Price, RCIA (1881) 27; M. C. Wilkinson, "Training School for Indian Youth, Forest Grove, Oregon, October 4, 1881," RCIA (1882) 257.

16. Price, RCIA (1882) 26; John H. Oberly, "Report of the Indian School Superintendent," RCIA (1885) 75, 123.

17. Morgan, *Studies in Pedagogy;* Thomas J. Morgan, RCIA (1891) ix, cxl; Hendrick, "Federal Campaign for the Admission of Indian Children Into Public Schools" 20; Hoxie, "Redefining Indian Education" 9. The three-year term was extended to five years in some schools. Eventually, school principals began to hold students against their will beyond the three-to-five-year commitment they had made

to attend boarding school. See, for example, the correspondence between Richard Henry Pratt and parents in the Richard Henry Pratt Papers, Yale Collection of Western Americana, Beinecke Rare Book and Manuscript Library, Yale University.

18. Hewes, "Those First Good Years of Indian Education" 63–64, 73; W[illiam] N. Hailmann, "Report of the Superintendent of Indian Schools," RCIA (1897) 344–45, 339; Superintendent of Indian Schools, *Syllabus of Language Work.*

19. Hailmann, RCIA (1897) 345; Hailmann, RCIA (1896) 344; Reel, *Report of the Superintendent of Indian Schools* 19; Holm, "Racial Stereotypes and Government Policies" 19–20.

20. Hoxie, *Final Promise* 190–91, 199–200; Littlefield, "Learning to Labor" 44; Szasz, "Listening to the Native Voice" 48.

21. Institute for Government Research, *Problem of Indian Administration* 392–93. One example of the relationship between sexual harassment and literacy acquisition was reported by Annie Miner Peterson. On the first day of school at the Alsea Subagency in 1873, her teacher put her on his lap and fondled her. Fourteen years old at the time, and knowing that this behavior was inappropriate, Peterson quit school within a few days. She never learned to read and write. Youst, *She's Tricky Like Coyote* 91.

22. Andrus, "Yankton Agency, Dakota, August 10, 1880," RCIA (1880) 181; Beard and Beard, *American Spirit* 292–93; Adams, "Fundamental Considerations" 5.

23. Vaughn, "From White Man to Redskin" 919, 922–23, 949; Berkhofer, *White Man's Indian* 55; Horsman, *Race and Manifest Destiny* 2, 5.

24. Welsh, *Four Weeks among Some of the Sioux Tribes of Dakota and Nebraska* 23–24; Bannan, "Idea of Civilization and American Indian Policy Reformers in the 1880s" 788; Morgan, "Indian Question" 332.

25. "Government Manual Labor Boarding School, Yankton Agency, D. T.," *Iapi-Oaye – Word Carrier* (hereafter *Word Carrier*) Sept. 1882: 72; Horsman, *Race and Manifest Destiny* 140; Harmon, "When Is an Indian Not an Indian?" 111, 107.

26. John B. Riley, Report of the Superintendent of Indian Schools, RCIA (1887) 791.

27. J. D. C. Atkins, RCIA (1886) 99; Fiske, "'Manifest Destiny'" 578, 588. This essay was also published in Fiske, *American Political Ideas;* Atkins, RCIA (1887) 19.

28. Atkins, RCIA (1887) 19; Heath, "English in Our Language Heritage" 6–7.

29. Atkins, RCIA (1887) 19; Leibowitz, *Educational Policy and Political Acceptance* 4, 10–11, 13, 15–16.

30. Atkins, RCIA (1887) 20; Riggs, "Sunset to Sunset" 255; *Word Carrier* July 1887: 1; *Word Carrier* Aug.–Sept. 1887: 1.

31. Atkins, RCIA (1887) 21; Commissioner Atkins's Order [from the *New York*

Times]," *Word Carrier* Nov. 1887: 2; Left Handed, "Letter to the Commissioner," *Word Carrier* Dec. 1887: 1.

32. Barton, *John P. Williamson* 155; United States Indian Office, *Correspondence on the Subject of Teaching the Vernacular in Indian Schools;* Oberly, RCIA (1888) xvii.

33. Olsen, "Problem of Language in the Indian Schools of Dakota Territory" 57; Sam T. Leavy, "Report of Yankton Agency, Yankton Agency, Greenwood, Dak., August 24, 1889," RCIA (1890) 171.

34. J. F. Kinney, "Report of the Yankton Agency, Yankton Agency, Dakota, August 20, 1888," RCIA (1888) 73; Morgan, RCIA (1890) 3.

35. William M. Ridpath, "Yankton Agency, Dakota, September 6, 1882," RCIA (1882) 109; Morgan, RCIA (1892) 53.

36. "Rules for Indian Schools," RCIA (1891) cxlvi–clxv; Office of Indian Affairs, *Rules for Indian Schools;* Daniel Dorchester, "The Care of Indian Schools," RCIA (1893) 613; Williamson, "Report of the Missionary, Yankton Reservation, Yankton Agency, S. Dak., August 11, 1893," RCIA (1894) 315–16.

37. Knepler, "Education in the Cherokee Nation"; Davis, "Life and Work of Sequoya"; Perdue, *Cherokee* 57–59, 64. A community of approximately a thousand Cherokees remained in North Carolina.

38. John B. Jones, "United States Agency for Cherokees, Tahlequah, Cherokee Nation, September 1, 1972," RCIA (1872) 620; McLoughlin, *After the Trail of Tears* 317.

39. McLoughlin, *After the Trail of Tears* 95; Mihesuah, *Cultivating the Rosebuds.* The histories of Choctaw, Chickasaw, and Creek education followed a similar path. See Debo, "Education in the Choctaw Country after the Civil War"; Noley, "Choctaw Bilingual and Bicultural Education in the 19th Century" 25–39; Spring, *Cultural Transformation of a Native American Family and Its Tribe;* Cobb, *Listening to Our Grandmothers' Stories;* Bass, *The Story of Tullahassee.*

40. S[amuel] C. Armstrong, "Hampton Normal and Agricultural Institute," RCIA (1880) 307.

41. Jos. W. Cook, "Yancton Agency, August 17, 1870," RCIA (1871) 679; La Flesche, *Middle Five* 24; Armstrong, RCIA (1880) 306–07; Leap, "American Indian Languages" 132–33.

42. Betzinez and Nye, *I Fought with Geronimo;* Ball, *In the Days of Victorio;* Ball, Henn, and Sánchez, *Indeh* 135.

43. Thompson, *Navajos' Long Walk for Education* 26–27; Frisbie and McAllester, *Navajo Blessingway Singer* 57.

44. Yava, *Big Falling Snow* 10–11.

45. Kloss, *American Bilingual Tradition* 283.

1. Berrol, "Public Schools and Immigrants" 32–33; Bettman, *Good Old Days* 168; P. F. Burke, "Albuquerque Indian Industrial School," RCIA (1887) 332.

2. Burke RCIA (1887) 332; R. H. Pratt, "Report of School at Carlisle PA," RCIA (1896) 399.

3. John H. Oberly, Report of the Indian School Superintendent, RCIA (1885) 121; Kneale, *Indian Agent* 48.

4. John B. Riley, Report of the Indian School Superintendent, RCIA (1887) 763; Daniel Dorchester, Report of the Indian School Superintendent, RCIA (1892) 482; W[illiam] N. Hailmann, Report of Superintendent of Indian Schools, RCIA (1895) 360–64.

5. Kneale, *Indian Agent;* Jenkins, *Girl from Williamsburg;* Brown, *Stubborn Fool;* Gage, "Romance of Pioneering"; Golden, *Red Moon Called Me;* Iliff, *People of the Blue Water.*

6. S[amuel] C. Armstrong, "Hampton, VA., September 1, 1886," RCIA (1886) 242.

7. Young, "An Approach to the Study of Curricula as Socially Organized Knowledge."

8. Williamson, "Early Missions to the Dakota Indians in Minnesota" 3, 5; "Sketches of the Dakota Mission," *Word Carrier* Nov. 1873: 44; Riggs, *Mary and I* 38–39; Barton, *John P. Williamson* 102. One of the earliest Dakota language texts was Riggs and Pond, *Dakota First Reading Book* [*Dakota Oyawa Wowapi*].

9. A[lfred] L. Riggs, "Notes concerning the Christianization and Civilization of the Dakotas," RCIA (1872) 684; Barton, *John P. Williamson* 136; Williamson, "Yankton Agency, Dakota Territory, September 20, 1870," RCIA (1871) 677–78; Williamson, "Dakota Qa Wasicun Iapi Wicisakim Ehnakapi/Dakota and English Parallel Lessons," *Word Carrier* Jan. 1880: 6; Eastman, *From the Deep Woods to Civilization* 30; Riggs, *Wicoie Wowapi Kin* [*The Word Book*]; Riggs and Riggs, *Maka-oyakapi* [*Guyot's Elementary Geography in the Dakota Language*]; "English or Indian," *Word Carrier* Mar. 1873: 4.

10. Tinker, *Missionary Conquest* 6; Craig, "Christianity and Empire" 4; Sneve, *Completing the Circle* 60.

11. "Santee Normal School" 4.

12. Battey, *Life and Adventures of a Quaker among the Indians* 8, 30–31.

13. Battey, *Life and Adventures of a Quaker among the Indians* 73.

14. Battey, *Life and Adventures of a Quaker among the Indians* 122–23.

15. Battey, *Life and Adventures of a Quaker among the Indians* 124, 192.

16. Pratt, *Battlefield and Classroom* 97, 138–44.

17. Hoxie, *Final Promise* 55; Stowe, "Indians at St. Augustine" 345; Pratt, *Battlefield and Classroom* 121.

18. Pratt, "Advantages of Mingling Indians with Whites" 45–46.

19. Samuel Chapman Armstrong to Emma Armstrong, April 19, 1878, Samuel Chapman Armstrong Collection, 1826–1947, Williams College Library Archives and Special Collections, Williamstown MA.

20. Hoxie, *Final Promise* 55; "An Indian Raid on Hampton Institute," *Southern Workman* May 1878: 36.

21. Campbell, *Colonel Francis W. Parker* 129–30; Patridge, *"Quincy Methods" Illustrated* xii–xiii, 86.

22. "Report of the Principal," *Southern Workman* June 1878: 44; "Anniversary Day at Hampton," *Southern Workman* June 1878: 46; Ezra A. Hayt, RCIA (1878) 473; Richard Henry Pratt, "Official Report," *Southern Workman* Dec. 1878: 90.

23. Ludlow, *Ten Years' Work for Indians at the Hampton Normal and Agricultural Institute* 13; B[ooker] T. W[ashington], "Incidents of Indian Life at Hampton," *Southern Workman* Oct. 1880: 103; "Scholarship Letters," *Southern Workman* Apr. 1879: 44; J[ames] C. R[obbins], "Incidents of Indian Life at Hampton," *Southern Workman,* Sept. 1879: 93; Ludlow, "Incidents of Indian Life at Hampton," *Southern Workman* Feb. 1880: 19. For an analysis of the (good and bad) relations between African American and Native students at Hampton, see Lindsey, *Indians at Hampton Institute.*

24. Washington, "Incidents of Indian Life at Hampton," *Southern Workman* Oct. 1880: 103; "Incidents of Indian Life at Hampton," *Southern Workman* Aug. 1879: 85; Washington, "Incidents of Indian Life at Hampton," *Southern Workman* Jan. 1881: 7. According to Donal Lindsey, it was also financially advantageous for Armstrong to send the children away during the summer months. *Indians at Hampton Institute* 37.

25. Hultgren and Molin, *To Lead and to Serve* 21–22; Ludlow, "Incidents of Indian Life at Hampton," *Southern Workman* Apr. 1879: 44.

26. "Scholarship Letters," *Southern Workman* Mar. 1879: 29; Cora M. Folsom, "Forty Years After: More Sioux Hamptonians," *Southern Workman* Aug. 1925: 359; Armstrong, RCIA (1883) 226; Armstrong, RCIA (1885) 466; "Incidents of Indian Life at Hampton," *Southern Workman* Jan. 1885: 8.

27. "Incidents of Indian Life at Hampton, " *Southern Workman* Mar. 1879: 31; Armstrong, RCIA (1885) 465; Armstrong, RCIA (1888) 281.

28. H[ollis] B. Frissell, "Hampton Normal and Agricultural Institute, Thirtieth

Annual Report of the Principal for the School and Fiscal Year Ending June 30th, 1898," *Southern Workman* May 1898: 92; Hultgren and Molin, *To Lead and to Serve* 50.

29. Carpenter, Baker, and Scott, *Teaching of English in the Elementary and the Secondary School* 199, 145; "Indian Report of Miss H. W. Ludlow. The Talking Class," *Southern Workman* June 1882: 68. When Hampton students had achieved at least moderate levels of proficiency in speaking, listening, and reading, they began to learn about the structure of the language, using grammar books written for first-language learners of English. However, teachers used these texts with discretion, "omitting what seemed adapted only to native English speaking children." Among the many grammars used over the years were the following books, whose titles reflect their contents: Reed and Kellogg, *An Elementary English Grammar, Consisting of One Hundred Practical Lessons, Carefully Graded and Adapted to the Class Room;* and Patterson, *Elements of Grammar and Composition Including Analysis and Synthesis of Sentences, and a Complete System of Diagrams.*

30. Robbins, "Incidents of Indian Life at Hampton," *Southern Workman* Jan. 1879: 7; Armstrong, RCIA (1884) 241; Armstrong, RCIA (1883) 228.

31. Armstrong, RCIA (1884) 241; the Worman series is mentioned in Armstrong, RCIA (1882) 241. One book in the series was Worman, *First French Book after the Natural or Pestalozzian Method: For Schools and Home Instruction.* See also Downs, *Heinrich Pestalozzi* 132; Cuban, *How Teachers Taught* 39; "Indian Report of Miss H. W. Ludlow" 68.

32. Cuban, *How Teachers Taught* 39; Armstrong, RCIA (1882) 241; Peet, *Language Lessons* vii. The full title of Peet's book was *Language Lessons: Designed to Introduce Young Learners, Deaf Mutes and Foreigners to a Correct Understanding and Use of the English Language, on the Principle of Object Teaching.*

33. The Guyot series is mentioned in Armstrong, RCIA (1882) 242. One book in the series was *Elementary Geography for Primary Classes.* For current theory on content-based language learning, see Brinton, Snow, and Wesche, *Content-Based Second Language Instruction.*

34. Cuban, *How Teachers Taught* 30; Robbins, "Incidents of Indian Life at Hampton," *Southern Workman* May 1880: 55; Ludlow, "Incidents" Apr. 1879: 44; Armstrong, RCIA (1883) 228.

35. Robbins, "Incidents" Mar. 1880: 31; "Indian Report of Miss H. W. Ludlow" 68; "Indian Report of Miss Laura E. Tileston. Geography," *Southern Workman* June 1882: 68.

36. Robbins, "Incidents of Indian Life at Hampton," *Southern Workman* Apr.

1880: 43; "Indian Report of Miss Laura E. Tileston" 68; Armstrong, RCIA (1882) 241; RCIA (1883) 227; RCIA (1885) 465.

37. Washington, "Incidents of Indian Life at Hampton," *Southern Workman* Sept. 1880: 93; Ludlow, "Indian Education " 664–65; J. E., "Incidents of Indian Life at Hampton," *Southern Workman* Jan. 1884: 7.

38. RCIA (1882) 245; RCIA (1883) 227; "Incidents of Indian Life at Hampton," *Southern Workman* Nov. 1881: 111; Ludlow, "Indian Education at Hampton and Carlisle" 664; Tileston, "Report on English," *Southern Workman* June 1885: 70; Armstrong, RCIA (1883) 227; "Indian Report of Miss Laura E. Tileston" 68.

39. Armstrong, RCIA (1881) 253; Engs, *Educating the Disfranchised and Disinherited;* Armstrong, RCIA (1890) 315.

40. Elaine Goodale, "The Indians of To-day," Anniversary Exercises of the Hampton Normal and Agricultural Institute, Thursday, May 20th, 1886. Samuel Chapman Armstrong Collection, 1826–1947, Williams College Library Archives and Special Collections, Williamstown MA.

41. Ludlow, "The Charm of a Book," *Southern Workman* June 1879: 67; Washington, "Incidents of Indian Life at Hampton," *Southern Workman* Dec. 1880: 125; Armstrong, *Indian Question* 8; Samuel C. Armstrong, "Indian Education in the East: An Address," *Southern Workman* Nov. 1880: 114.

42. Harris, Rickoff, and Bailey, "From the Authors to the Teacher" 2; Ludlow, "Incidents" Apr. 1879: 44.

43. Ludlow, "Charm" 67; Ludlow, "Incidents" Apr. 1879: 44; Washington, "Incidents" Oct. 1880: 103.

44. Armstrong, RCIA (1885) 467; "Indian Report of Miss Josephine Richards: History," *Southern Workman* June 1882: 68.

45. Armstrong, RCIA (1883) 225–26; Ludlow, "Indian Education" 663; Armstrong, RCIA (1888) 282. The Dawes bill, known as the Allotment Act, was promoted by reformers as beneficial to Native populations, but it had a devastating effect on tribal communal life, for it resulted in the loss of most of the land protected by treaties and thus undermined self-sufficiency. Prucha, *American Indian Policy in Crisis* 227–64; Child, *Boarding School Seasons* 9–12.

46. Ludlow, "Incidents," Apr. 1879: 44; Nietz, *Old Textbooks* 324.

47. Armstrong, RCIA (1892) 601.

48. "A Set of Scholarship Letters," *Southern Workman* Feb. 1880: 17; Armstrong, Indian Education in the East," *Southern Workman* Nov. 1880: 114.

49. Graber, *Sister to the Sioux* 20; "Incidents of Indian Life at Hampton," *Southern Workman* Aug. 1882: 85; Armstrong, RCIA (1880) 305.

50. Armstrong, *RCIA* (1892) 599; Morris, *Reading, 'Riting, and Reconstruction* 156–57.

51. Armstrong, *RCIA* (1890) 315; Ludlow, "Results of English Teaching at Hampton," *Southern Workman* June 1882: 64.

52. Armstrong, *RCIA* (1884) 241–42.

53. Swinton, *Introductory Geography in Readings and Recitations* 19–20; "Our World: Work and Fun in the Geography Class," *Southern Workman* Feb. 1885: 20. For discussions of the treatment of Native people in nineteenth-century schoolbooks, see Elson, *Guardians of Tradition* 71–81; Hauptman, "Mythologizing Westward Expansion" 272–75; Hauptman, "Westward the Course of Empire" 432–37.

54. "Our World" 20; Armstrong, *RCIA* (1885) 464–65; Joseph E. Estes, "Indian Debating Society," *Southern Workman* Apr. 1884: 42.

55. Lindsey, *Indians at Hampton Institute* 213; Folsom, "Record of Returned Indian Students"; Engs, *Educating the Disfranchised and Disinherited* 132; Lindsey, *Indians at Hampton Institute* 217.

56. "Indian Report of Miss Josephine Richards" 68; Armstrong, *RCIA* (1887) 352; Graber, *Sister to the Sioux* 19. For current theory and practice related to second-language acquisition, see Krashen, *Principles and Practices in Second Language Acquisition;* Peregoy and Boyle, *Reading, Writing, and Learning in* ESL. For the application of these principles to the teaching of Native students today, see Reyhner, *Teaching American Indian Students.*

57. Armstrong, *RCIA* (1884) 241. According to Donal Lindsey, Folsom was the only teacher at Hampton who attempted to learn a Native language. Lindsey, *Indians at Hampton Institute* 252. Elaine Goodale learned Dakota after she left Hampton to teach in Dakota Territory. She later married Dakota physician Charles Eastman. Graber, *Sister to the Sioux* 35.

58. Armstrong, *RCIA* (1884) 243; Zallie Rulo, "The Indian Woman," *Southern Workman* June 1885: 62; Folsom, "Record" 376.

3. REPRODUCTION AND RESISTANCE

1. Riggs, *Mary and I* 301; Williamson, "Early Missions to the Dakota Indians in Minnesota" 7; "Return of the Indian Students from Hampton," *Southern Workman* Mar. 1882: 33; Sneve, *Completing the Circle* 98.

2. W[illiam] N. Hailmann, Report of the Superintendent of Indian Schools, *RCIA* (1897) 351; S[amuel] C. Armstrong, "Report of Normal and Agricultural Institute, at Hampton VA.," *RCIA* (1893) 701; Armstrong, "Report of Hampton Normal and Agricultural Institute," *RCIA* (1892) 602.

3. James Garvie, "Translation and Writing," *Word Carrier* June–July 1886: 2; Gilman, *Conquest of the Sioux* 43.

4. Lindsey, "Memories of the Indian Territory Mission Field"; Alford, *Civilization and the Story of the Absentee Shawnees;* Winnemucca Hopkins, *Life among the Piutes;* Standing Bear, *My People the Sioux;* Standing Bear, *Land of the Spotted Eagle. Note:* Thomas Wildcat Alford's *Civilization and the Story of the Absentee Shawnees* is an "as told to" autobiography, but his file at the Hampton Archives, which is filled with his letters, essays and speeches, indicates that he was an accomplished writer in English.

5. Littlefield, "B.I.A. Boarding School" 435–36.

6. McNickle, "American Indians Who Never Were" 6–7.

7. Bass, *Story of Tullahassee* 19, 23–26, 29–30, 240–41, 251. Lilah Denton Lindsey's family had come to Indian Territory from Georgia with the first Creek group. Foreman, "Yuchi" 495.

8. Lindsey, "Memories of the Indian Territory Mission Field" 181; Lauderdale, "Tullahassee Mission" 290, 295; Bass, *Story of Tullahassee* 241, 255–57.

9. Lindsey, "Memories of the Indian Territory Mission Field" 182, 188–89; 194; Misch, "Lilah D. Lindsey" 194; "Reminiscences of Lilah D. Lindsey," rpt. in Misch, "Lilah D. Lindsey" 200. Lindsey uses the name "Highland Institute," but Misch calls it "Hillsboro-Hyland Institute."

10. Lindsey, "Memories of the Indian Territory Mission Field" 195–96; Misch, "Lilah D. Lindsey" 194; "Reminiscences" 201. *Note:* There are conflicting dates in these sources related to when Lindsey taught at different schools. The chronology I have created may not be accurate.

11. Lindsey, "Memories of the Indian Territory Mission Field" 196–97.

12. Misch, "Lilah D. Lindsey" 199; Lindsey, "Memories of the Indian Territory Mission Field" 197–98.

13. Foreman, "Yuchi" 496; Misch, "Lilah D. Lindsey" 193, 198; "Reminiscences" 199; Lindsey, "Memories of the Indian Territory Mission Field" 188–89. *Note:* I did not uncover information about Lindsey's father's education.

14. Alford, *Civilization and the Story of the Absentee Shawnees* 1, 7, 13–14.

15. Alford, *Civilization and the Story of the Absentee Shawnees* 21, 26, 79, 73.

16. Alford, *Civilization and the Story of the Absentee Shawnees* 75–76, 78–79.

17. Alford, *Civilization and the Story of the Absentee Shawnees* 80, 82–83, 85, 87, 90, 89.

18. Alford, *Civilization and the Story of the Absentee Shawnees* 100–01, 106, 109; *Minutes of Indiana Yearly Meeting of Friends* (Richmond IN: Yarmon, 1882) 46;

"Hampton Students' Own," *Southern Workman* June 1881: 71; "Graduating Address of Thomas Wildcat Alford," *Southern Workman* July 1882: 78.

19. Alford, *Civilization and the Story of the Absentee Shawnees* 111–13, 121.

20. Alford, *Civilization and the Story of the Absentee Shawnees* 120, 122, 117, 126–27.

21. Alford, *Civilization and the Story of the Absentee Shawnees* 127–28.

22. Alford, *Civilization and the Story of the Absentee Shawnees* 129–30.

23. Alford, *Civilization and the Story of the Absentee Shawnees* 132, 23, 101–02.

24. Alford, *Civilization and the Story of the Absentee Shawnees* 198.

25. When not quoting nineteenth-century material, I use the contemporary spelling of Paiute.

26. Winnemucca Hopkins, *Life among the Piutes* 5, 11.

27. Winnemucca Hopkins, *Life among the Piutes* 18, 58, 70.

28. Winnemucca Hopkins, *Life among the Piutes* 115–18, 123, 134.

29. Winnemucca Hopkins, *Life among the Piutes* 209, 215–16, 234.

30. Howard, *My Life and Experiences among Our Hostile Indians* 432; Winnemucca Hopkins, *Life among the Piutes* 241–42, 244–45.

31. Canfield, *Sarah Winnemucca of the Northern Paiutes* 200–01, 226–28.

32. Qtd. in Canfield, *Sarah Winnemucca of the Northern Paiutes* 239; Qtd. in Ronda, *Letters of Elizabeth Palmer Peabody* 397; Peabody, *Piutes* 13.

33. Peabody, *Piutes* 15–16.

34. Qtd. in Canfield, *Sarah Winnemucca of the Northern Paiutes* 239; Peabody, *Sarah Winnemucca's Practical Solution to the Indian Problem* 11.

35. Winnemucca Hopkins, *Life among the Piutes* 51.

36. Standing Bear, *My People the Sioux* preface; *Land of the Spotted Eagle* 227; *My People the Sioux* 68, 3, 27; *Land of the Spotted Eagle* 15.

37. Standing Bear, *My People* 98.

38. Marianna Burgess to Richard Henry Pratt, October 21, 1879. Richard Henry Pratt Papers, Yale Collection of Western Americana, Beinecke Rare Book and Manuscript Library, Yale University; Standing Bear, *My People the Sioux* 139, 146, 152.

39. Standing Bear, *My People the Sioux* 161–64.

40. Standing Bear, *My People the Sioux* 172, 175, 179.

41. Standing Bear, *My People the Sioux* 189–90.

42. Standing Bear, *My People the Sioux* 192–93, 241; *Land of the Spotted Eagle* 240–41.

43. Standing Bear, *My People the Sioux* 239; *Land of the Spotted Eagle* 241–42.

44. Standing Bear, *Land of the Spotted Eagle* 242; *My People the Sioux* 193–94; *Land of the Spotted Eagle* 234.

45. Standing Bear, *Land of the Spotted Eagle* 249, 227–28, 27.

46. Standing Bear, *Land of the Spotted Eagle* 255.

47. Standing Bear, *Land of the Spotted Eagle* 236.

4. TRANSLINGUAL IRONIES

1. Coleman, *American Indian Children at School.* Coleman's own research aids were H. David Brumble's *Annotated Bibliography of American Indian and Eskimo Autobiographies* and its supplement, appended to Brumble's *American Indian Autobiography,* which together list more than six hundred published autobiographies, ranging from fragments to full books. One book considered here, *Born a Chief: The Nineteenth Century Hopi Boyhood of Edmund Nequatewa,* is not included in Coleman's study.

2. Bloodworth, "Varieties of American Indian Autobiography" 69–70; Bataille and Sands, *American Indian Women* 3–4; Krupat, *For Those Who Come After* 28–30; Ruoff, "Three Nineteenth-Century American Indian Autobiographers" 251–52; Krupat, *Ethnocentrism* 201–31; Wong, *Sending My Heart Back across the Years* 12–17; O'Brien, *Plains Indian Autobiographies* 6.

3. Lyons, "Rhetorical Sovereignty" 449; Weaver, "From I-Hermeneutics to We-Hermeneutics" 16. The first works published by a Native writer in English were Samson Occom's sermons in the 1770s. The first full-life narrative by a Native writer published in English was William Apes's *Son of the Forest* in 1829. Ruoff, "American Indian Authors" 190–91.

4. Gee, "Orality and Literacy" 719–20; Zamel and Spack, *Negotiating Academic Literacies* xi; Brown, *Principles of Language Learning and Teaching* chaps. 5–7; Savignon, "Communicative Language Teaching"; Peirce, "Social Identity, Investment, and Language Learning." See also the autumn 1997 issue of the *TESOL Quarterly,* devoted to language and identity.

5. Coleman, *American Indian Children at School;* Adams, *Education for Extinction;* Lyons, "Rhetorical Sovereignty" 461. Other scholars have reported on students' positive experiences at school, especially among peers in United States government boarding schools. Littlefield, "B.I.A. Boarding School" 438–39; McBeth, *Ethnic Identity and the Boarding School Experience of West-Central Oklahoma American Indians* 118–20; Trennert, *Phoenix Indian School* 119; Lomawaima, *They Called It Prairie Light* 159–66; Adams, *Education for Extinction* 261–63. In at least one English-only school run by the Cherokee Nation, positive reactions dominated the

experiences of students whose families had embraced European American values. Mihesuah, *Cultivating the Rosebuds* 72–84.

6. Liu, *Translingual Practice*.

7. Berkhofer, *White Man's Indian* 28, 16.

8. Murray, *Forked Tongues* 70.

9. Ebersole, *Captured by Texts* 3–6, 12; Harris, "Mary White Rowlandson" 340; Lyons, "Captivity Narrative" 88.

10. Faery, *Cartographies of Desire* 16, 123–24; Lepore, *Name of War* 125–26.

11. Sewell, "'So Unstable and Like Mad Men They Were'" 39, 42; Ebersole, *Captured by Texts*.

12. Ebersole, *Captured by Texts* 7; La Flesche, *Middle Five* 3; Ah-nen-la-de-ni, "Indian Boy's Story" 1782.

13. Ball, Henn, and Sánchez, *Indeh* 151; La Flesche, *Middle Five* 3; Zitkala-Ša, "School Days of an Indian Girl" 187; Eastman, *From the Deep Woods to Civilization* 16; Miller, *Mourning Dove* 25–27.

14. Ah-nen-la-de-ni, "Indian Boy's Story" 1782, 1784–85.

15. Simmons, *Sun Chief* 89–90.

16. Gump, *Dust Rose Like Smoke* 102; Seaman, *Born a Chief* 157; Yava, *Big Falling Snow* 9–11.

17. Ebersole, *Captured by Texts* 7, 27; Goodbird, *Goodbird the Indian* 65; Zitkala-Ša, "School Days of an Indian Girl" 187; Ball, Henn, and Sánchez, *Indeh* 144.

18. Standing Bear, *My People the Sioux* 159; RCIA (1887) 341; RCIA (1888) 278; Ball, *In the Days of Victorio* 200; Levchuk, "Leaving Home for Carlisle Indian School" 178.

19. Ebersole, *Captured by Texts* 8, 159, 166, 8; La Flesche, *Middle Five* 58; Simmons, *Sun Chief* 130; Ah-nen-la-de-ni, "Indian Boy's Story" 1783; Seaman, *Born a Chief* 125–27.

20. Ah-nen-la-de-ni, "Indian Boy's Story" 1787.

21. La Flesche, *Middle Five* xv.

22. Lepore, *Name of War* 128; Standing Bear, *My People the Sioux* 124; Standing Bear, *Land of the Spotted Eagle* 235.

23. Cheyfitz, *Poetics of Imperialism* 104; Venuti, *Scandals of Translation* 11, 83.

24. Rosenwald, "*Last of the Mohicans* and the Languages of America"; Sossing, "Our Barbarian Brethren" 800; Venuti, *Scandals of Translation* 68; Standing Bear, *Land of the Spotted Eagle* 251.

25. Bass, *Arapaho Way* 65; Eastman, *From the Deep Woods to Civilization* 46; Ball, *In the Days of Victorio* 200.

26. Quackenbos, *Elementary History of the United States* xx.

27. La Flesche, *Middle Five* xix; Winnemucca Hopkins, *Life among the Piutes* 91; Standing Bear, *My People the Sioux* 167–68.

28. La Flesche, *Middle Five* xix, xvi–xvii; Alford, *Civilization and the Story of the Absentee Shawnees* 66–67.

29. La Flesche, *Middle Five* 22, xvii, 35, 29, 76, 20, 11.

30. Bass, *Arapaho Way* 5; Eastman, *From the Deep Woods to Civilization* 22; Miller, *Mourning Dove* 25; Frisbie and McAllester, *Navajo Blessingway Singer* 66, 65.

31. La Flesche, *Middle Five* xviii; Greenblatt, "Learning to Curse" 569; Simmons, *Sun Chief* 117; Webb, *Pima Remembers* 71–72; Standing Bear, *My People the Sioux* 182; Stands in Timber and Liberty, *Cheyenne Memories* 290.

32. La Flesche, *Middle Five* xix; Webb, *Pima Remembers* 73.

33. Yava, *Big Falling Snow* 82, 72, 74, 79.

34. Cheyfitz, *Poetics of Imperialism* 112; La Flesche, *Middle Five* xvii; Ah-nen-la-de-ni, "Indian Boy's Story" 1783.

35. La Flesche, *Middle Five* xviii; Ah-nen-la-de-ni, "Indian Boy's Story" 1783; Ball, Henn, and Sánchez, *Indeh* 144.

36. La Flesche, *Middle Five* 6; Frisbie and McAllester, *Navajo Blessingway Singer* 66.

37. Ashcroft, Griffiths, and Tiffin, *Empire Writes Back* 10; Pratt, "Arts of the Contact Zone" 36.

38. Peyer, *Tutor'd Mind;* Achebe, "English and the African Writer" 29.

39. Ashcroft, Griffiths, and Tiffin, *Empire Writes Back* 5–6; Whitewolf, "Short Story of My Life" 31; "Address by Mr. Charles Doxon" 425; Betzinez and Nye, *I Fought with Geronimo* 199; Bass, *Arapaho Way* 67.

40. Hertzberg, *Search for an American Indian Identity* 135; Bass, *Arapaho Way* 76.

41. Eastman, *From the Deep Woods to Civilization* 47.

42. Eastman, *From the Deep Woods to Civilization* 23, 29, 16, 165.

43. Eastman, *From the Deep Woods to Civilization* 67–68, 194–95.

44. Rogers, *Red World and White* 73, 108, 142.

45. Simmons, *Sun Chief* 88–89, 94, 116, 134, 299, 99.

46. Scott, *Karnee* 58–59, 67–68, 90, 83, 109.

47. Marriott and Rachlin, *Dance around the Sun* 4, 22, 40–41, 76, 99.

48. Miller, *Mourning Dove* 30–31, 182, 189, 12.

49. Yava, *Big Falling Snow* 10; Bass, *Arapaho Way* 3–4, 64–65, 67.

50. Goodbird, *Goodbird the Indian* 42–44, 59, 68, 73–74.

1. Zitkala-Ša, "Indian Teacher among Indians" 386; Lincoln, *Indi'n Humor* 20; Rosaldo, *Culture and Truth* 21.

2. Zitkala-Ša, "School Days of an Indian Girl" 190; Ezra A. Hayt, RCIA (1879) 11; Richard Henry Pratt, "United States Indian Service, Training School for Indian Youths," RCIA (1881) 247; Lomawaima, "Domesticity in the Federal Indian Schools" 231; Pratt, RCIA (1881) 247; "White's Institute," Report of Committee on Indian Affairs, *Minutes of Indiana Yearly Meeting* (Richmond IN: Yarmon, 1891) 17.

3. Zitkala-Sa File, Lilly Library, Earlham College Archives, Richmond IN; Gertrude E. Simmons to Susan Unthank, April 25, 1898, Susan B. Unthank Collection, Indiana State Library, Indianapolis; Parker and Parker, *Josiah White's Institute* 60, 72; Tatum, *Our Red Brothers and the Peace Policy of President Ulysses S. Grant* 332.

4. *Indian Helper,* Sept. 24, 1897: n.pag.; *Indian Helper,* July 9, 1897: n.pag.; "Wants Indian Stories," *Indian Helper* Mar. 18, 1898: 1.

5. A. J. Standing to Miss Gertrude Simmons, January 23, 1899, Richard Henry Pratt Papers, Yale Collection of Western Americana, Beinecke Rare Book and Manuscript Library, Yale University; Tatum, *Our Red Brothers and the Peace Policy of President Ulysses S. Grant* 331–32; "People Who Interest Us," *Harper's Bazaar* April 1900: 330; Cook, "Representative Indian" 80–83.

6. "School Days of an Indian Girl," *Red Man* Feb. 1900: 8; "Zitkala Sa in the Atlantic Monthly," *Red Man* June 1900: 1 (reprinted from *Word Carrier*); Cary, "Recent Writings by American Indians" 24. For a discussion of Zitkala-Ša's musical work, see Dominguez, "Zitkala-Sa (Gertrude Simmons Bonnin)" 83–97; Hafen, "Cultural Duet" 102–11.

7. Willard, "Zitkala Sa" 11–16; Johnson and Wilson, "Gertrude Simmons Bonnin"; Bell, "'If This Is Paganism . . .'" 67, 61; Warrior, *Tribal Secrets* 10, 19–20.

8. Stout, "Zitkala-Sa" 74; Fisher, "Zitkala-Ša" vi–vii.

9. Lukens, *Creating Cultural Spaces* 162–96; Susag, "Zitkala-Sa (Gertrude Simmons Bonnin)" 3–24; Smith, "'A Second Tongue'" 46–60; Cutter, "Zitkala-Sä's Autobiographical Writings" 31–44; Smith, "Cheesecake, Nymphs, and 'We the People'" 120–40; Bernardin, "Lessons of a Sentimental Education" 212–38; Diana, "'Hanging in the Heart of Chaos'" 154–72.

10. Cheyfitz, *Poetics of Imperialism* 126–27. Cheyfitz draws on Frantz Fanon's 1952 *Black Skin, White Masks*.

11. Kehoe, "Shackles of Tradition" 54, 56–57, 64.

12. Weist, "Beasts of Burden and Menial Slaves" 29–31, 37–38. Weist borrows the phrase from Welter's "Cult of True Womanhood."

13. Qtd. in Kolodny, *Lay of the Land* 4; Green, "Pocahontas Perplex" 701–02, 711. Green notes that the Indian princess as the symbol of American civilization was replaced with the male Uncle Sam because she "confronted America with too many contradictions" (714).

14. Fisher, "Zitkala-Ša" v; Wexler, "Tender Violence" 173; Okker, "Native American Literatures and the Canon" 89; Sedgwick, *History of the "Atlantic Monthly"* 310.

15. Sedgwick, *History of the "Atlantic Monthly"* 308; W. H. Page to Mr. Chamberlin, August 14, 1899. Houghton Mifflin Business Records: Editorial Department Pressed Letter Books, Houghton Library, Harvard University; J. E. Chamberlin to Major R. H. Pratt, March 9, 1900, Richard Henry Pratt Papers, Yale Collection of Western Americana, Beinecke Rare Book and Manuscript Library, Yale University; Sedgwick, *History of the "Atlantic Monthly"* 310, 279.

16. That she chose her name from the Lakota dialect of the Teton Sioux rather than the Nakota dialect of the Yanktons suggests that Zitkala-Ša wanted to link herself with the Lakotas – the last Sioux holdouts against the United States cavalry – rather than with the Yanktons, who were peaceful. (In the Nakota dialect the name would have been "Zitkana-Ša.")

17. Susag, "Zitkala-Sa (Gertrude Simmons Bonnin)" 7.

18. Zitkala-Ša, *American Indian Stories,* hereafter cited as AIS.

19. Barton, *John P. Williamson* 217; S[amuel] C. Armstrong, RCIA (1885): 478–79; Folsom, "Record of Returned Indian Students" 342–43. "Dawée" may have been Zitkala-Ša's baby pronunciation of her brother's name. I have found no evidence that he had any name other than David.

20. Gilman, *Conquest of the Sioux* 47; Parker and Parker, *Josiah White's Institute* 60; Picotte, foreword, *Old Indian Legends* xv.

21. Okker, "Native American Literatures and the Canon" 95; Adams, *Telling Lies in Modern American Autobiography* 6. There is evidence that Zitkala-Ša had attempted to write an autobiographical work at the turn of the century. In fact the editorial board of the *Atlantic Monthly* encouraged her to write a full-length autobiography along the lines of Lucy Larcom's *A New England Girlhood,* and they sent her a copy. Their responses to her letters from 1900 to 1903 indicate that she began the project but then abandoned it. Houghton Mifflin Business Records: Editorial Department Pressed Letter Books, Houghton Library, Harvard University.

22. AIS 7–9, 36–37; Weist, "Beasts of Burden and Menial Slaves" 31–32; Lukens, *Creating Cultural Spaces* 169.

23. DeMallie, "Male and Female in Traditional Lakota Culture" 238; Albers, "Sioux Women in Transition" 218; Allen, *Sacred Hoop* 32; Weist, "Beasts of Burden and Menial Slaves" 37; *AIS* 19; Schneider, "Women's Work" 109–10; *AIS* 20, 76.

24. *AIS* 40; Albers, introduction, *Hidden Half* 14.

25. *AIS* 8, 47–48; "Zitkala Sa in the Atlantic Monthly," *Red Man* June 1900: 1; Lukens, *Creating Cultural Spaces* 175.

26. *AIS* 59, 55, 67.

27. DeMallie, "Male and Female in Traditional Lakota Culture" 240, 241; Green, *Women in American Indian Society* 28–29; *AIS* 66–67, 75.

28. Cheyfitz, *Poetics of Imperialism* 126; *AIS* 80.

29. *AIS* 98, 95, 65, 64, 17, 77; Tinker, *Missionary Conquest* 2–3.

30. "White's Institute, Indiana," Report of the Committee on Indian Affairs, *Minutes of Indiana Yearly Meeting of Friends* (Richmond IN: Nicholson, 1887) 18; Samuel B. Hill, "Thirty-sixth Annual Report of the Trustees of White's Indiana Manual Labor Institute," *Minutes of Indiana Yearly Meeting of Friends* (Richmond IN: Yarmon, 1888) 14; "White's Manual Labor Institute," Report of Executive Committee on Indian Affairs, *Minutes of Indiana Yearly Meeting of Friends* (Richmond IN: Yarmon, 1892) 29; Nathan Coggeshall, "Thirty-fourth Annual Report of the Trustees of White's Indiana Manual Labor Institute," *Minutes of Indiana Yearly Meeting of Friends* (Richmond IN: Yarmon, 1886) 15; Martha H. Bales, "Report of White's Institute Household Committee," *Minutes of Indiana Yearly Meeting of Friends* (Richmond IN: Yarmon, 1891) 22.

31. R[ichard] H. Pratt, "Report of School at Carlisle PA.," *RCIA* (1895) 408; *Indian Helper* Jan. 1898: n.pag.; Pearce, *Savagism and Civilization* 19–22; Williams, "Documents of Barbarism" 247–50; Lepore, *Name of War*.

32. Photographic History Collection, National Museum of American History, Smithsonian Institution, Washington DC. Gertrude Käsebier, whose studio was in New York City, was one of the preeminent photographers of her day. Zitkala-Ša was a guest in Käsebier's home during her summer vacation in 1898. The violin was not just a symbol, for Zitkala-Ša was taking violin lessons with a Professor Taube of Harrisburg, Pennsylvania, who was a "Leipsic graduate," according to the Carlisle School newspaper. This may be the violin Zitkala-Ša borrowed from Susan and Joe Unthank, whom she had known at White's Institute, and whom the children called "Aunt Sue" and "Uncle Joe." Michaels, *Gertrude Käsebier; Indian Helper* Aug. 12, 1898: n.pag.; *Indian Helper* July 1, 1898: n.pag; Gertrude E. Simmons to Aunt Sue and Uncle Joe, April 25, 1898, Susan Unthank Collection, Indiana State Library, Indiana Division.

33. Merial Dorchester, "Report of Special Agent in Indian School Service," RCIA (1890) 343.

34. AIS 107, 31–32.

35. Zitkala-Ša sent her own son to a Catholic boarding school. Zitkala-Ša to Carlos Montezuma, June 23, 1913, Carlos Montezuma Papers, Division of Archives and Manuscripts, State Historical Society of Wisconsin, Madison. Jane Hafen provides documentation that Zitkala-Ša practiced both Catholicism and Mormonism. Hafen, "Zitkala Ša" 38; AIS 107.

36. The previously published stories are "The Soft-Hearted Sioux," *Harper's Monthly Magazine* Mar. 1901: 505–09; "The Trial Path," *Harper's Monthly Magazine* Oct. 1901: 741–44; and "A Warrior's Daughter," *Everybody's Magazine* Apr. 6, 1902: 346–52. The new stories are "A Dream of Her Grandfather" and "The Widespread Enigma of Blue-Star Woman."

37. Allen, *Sacred Hoop* 205; Green, *Women in American Indian Society* 21; AIS 111–12, 94; DeMallie, "Male and Female in Traditional Lakota Culture" 261.

38. Zitkala-Ša to Carlos Montezuma, March 5, 1901, Carlos Montezuma Papers; Allen, *Sacred Hoop* 205. For a more detailed analysis of Zitkala-Ša's correspondence with Carlos Montezuma, see Spack, "Dis/engagement"; AIS 134–35.

39. Green, "Pocahontas Perplex" 699, 704; Medicine, "'Warrior Women'" 275; AIS 137; AIS 142. For an excellent analysis of the perpetuation of the Pocahontas image, see Tilton, *Pocahontas*.

40. AIS 151, 153, 137; Smith, "'A Second Tongue'" 53–54; Medicine, "'Warrior Women'" 270; Allen, *Sacred Hoop* 203.

41. AIS 143; DeMallie, "Male and Female in Traditional Lakota Culture" 250; Weist, "Beasts of Burden and Menial Slaves" 44; Zallie Rulo, "The Indian Woman," *Southern Workman* June 1885: 62; Zitkala-Ša to Carlos Montezuma, March 1901, Carlos Montezuma Papers; Parker and Parker, *Josiah White's Institute* 71.

42. AIS 155–57; Albers, "Sioux Women in Transition" 191; DeMallie, "Male and Female in Traditional Lakota Culture" 240.

43. AIS 159–60.

44. AIS 163.

45. AIS 162, 159, 164.

46. Smith, "'A Second Tongue'" 52; AIS 177, 165, 168; Gump, *Dust Rose Like Smoke* 102.

47. Zitkala-Ša, "America's Indian Problem" 4–6, 10; AIS 185–86.

48. Hertzberg, *Search for an American Indian Identity* 174.

49. *AIS* 99.

EPILOGUE

1. Joseph Abeyta, introduction, *One House, One Voice, One Heart;* Patricia L. Jiron, Santa Fe Indian School, personal communication.

2. Child, *Boarding School Seasons* 14–15; St. Clair and Leap, *Language Renewal among American Indian Tribes;* Reyhner, *Teaching Indigenous Languages;* Churchill and Morris, "Key Indian Laws and Cases" 15–17.

3. Bowker, *Sisters in the Blood* 43, 283–84.

4. Bowker, *Sisters in the Blood* 276–79.

5. Bowker, *Sisters in the Blood* 282–90; Swisher, "Why Indian People Should Be the Ones to Write about Indian Education"; Lomawaima, "Tribal Sovereigns" 3–4.

6. Bowker, *Sisters in the Blood* 80; Leap, *American Indian English* 163; Reyhner, *Teaching American Indian Students;* Charleston, "Toward True Native Education" 30–31; Urion, "Changing Academic Discourse about Native Education" 7. *Note:* In addition to being offered through subscription, *Tribal College Journal* is provided free to contributors to the American Indian College Fund.

7. Mihesuah, *American Indians;* Lyons, "Rhetorical Sovereignty" 458–61, 448–49; *Indian Voices* 1; Warrior, *Tribal Secrets* 96–97; Weaver, "From I-Hermeneutics to We-Hermeneutics" 22; Cook-Lynn, "Who Stole Native American Studies?" 22.

8. Weaver, *That the People Might Live.*

Bibliography

ARCHIVAL MATERIALS

American Tract Society, Garland, Tex.

Cumberland Historical Society, Carlisle, Pa.

Earlham College, Lilly Library, Richmond, Ind.: Zitkala-Sa File

Hampton University, University Archives, Hampton, Va.: Native American Collection

Harvard University, Houghton Library, Cambridge, Mass.: Houghton Mifflin Business Records: Editorial Department Pressed Letter Books

Indiana State Library, Indiana Division, Indianapolis, Ind.: Susan Unthank Collection

National Archives, Washington, D.C.: Office of Indian Affairs, Record Group 75

National Museum of American History, Washington, D.C.: Photographic History Collection; National Anthropological Archives

Nevada Historical Society, Reno, Nev.

Oklahoma Historical Society, Oklahoma City, Okla.

Santa Fe Indian School, Santa Fe, N.M.

Smithsonian Institution, Smithsonian Anthropological Library, Washington, D.C.

State Historical Society of Wisconsin, Division of Manuscripts and Archives, Madison, Wis.: Carlos Montezuma Papers

United States Department of Education, Educational Research Library, Washington, D.C.

Williams College, Library Archives and Special Collections, Williamstown, Mass.:
  Samuel Chapman Armstrong Collection, 1826–1947
Yale University, Beinecke Rare Book and Manuscript Library, New Haven, Conn.:
  Yale Collection of Western Americana, Richard Henry Pratt Papers

PRIMARY SOURCES

Iapi-Oaye – The Word Carrier
The Indian Helper
Minutes of Indiana Yearly Meeting of Friends
The Red Man
Reports of the Commissioner of Indian Affairs to the Secretary of the Interior (RCIA),
  reprinted in the annual reports of the secretary of the interior
Southern Workman

SECONDARY SOURCES

Abeyta, Joseph. Introduction. *One House, One Voice, One Heart: Native American Education at the Santa Fe Indian School.* Sally Hyer. Santa Fe: Museum of New Mexico Press, 1990.

Achebe, Chinua. "English and the African Writer." *Transition* 18 (1964): 27–30.

Adams, David Wallace. *Education for Extinction: American Indians and the Boarding School Experience, 1875–1928.* Lawrence: UP of Kansas, 1996.

———. "Fundamental Considerations: The Deep Meaning of Native American Schooling, 1880–1900." *Harvard Educational Review* 58.1 (1988): 1–28.

Adams, Timothy Dow. *Telling Lies in Modern American Autobiography.* Chapel Hill: U of North Carolina P, 1990.

"Address by Mr. Charles Doxon." *Red Man* 5 (1913): 423–26.

Ah-nen-la-de-ni. "An Indian Boy's Story." *Independent* July 1903: 1780–87.

Albers, Patricia. Introduction; New Perspectives on Plains Indian Women. Albers and Medicine 1–26.

———. "Sioux Women in Transition: A Study of Their Changing Status in Domestic and Capitalist Sectors of Production." Albers and Medicine 175–234.

Albers, Patricia, and Beatrice Medicine, eds. *The Hidden Half: Studies of Plains Indian Women.* Lanham, Md.: UP of America, 1983.

Alford, Thomas Wildcat, as told to Florence Drake. *Civilization and the Story of the Absentee Shawnees.* 1936. Norman: U of Oklahoma P, 1979.

Allen, Paula Gunn. *The Sacred Hoop: Recovering the Feminine in American Indian Traditions.* 2nd ed. Boston: Beacon, 1992.

Armstrong, Samuel C. *The Indian Question.* Hampton, Va.: Normal School Steam P, 1883.

Ashcroft, Bill, Gareth Griffiths, and Helen Tiffin. *The Empire Writes Back: Theory and Practice in Post-colonial Literatures.* London: Routledge, 1989.

Axtell, James. *The European and the Indian: Essays in the Ethnohistory of Colonial North America.* New York: Oxford UP, 1981.

Ball, Eve. *In the Days of Victorio: Recollections of a Warm Springs Apache.* Tucson: U of Arizona P, 1970.

Ball, Eve, with Nora Henn and Lynda Sánchez. *Indeh: An Apache Odyssey.* 1980. Norman: U of Oklahoma P, 1988.

Bannan, Helen M. "The Idea of Civilization and American Indian Policy Reformers in the 1880's." *Journal of American Culture* I (1978): 787–99.

Barton, Winifred W. *John P. Williamson: A Brother to the Sioux.* New York: Revell, 1919.

Bass, Althea, ed. *The Arapaho Way: A Memoir of an Indian Boyhood.* New York: Potter, 1966.

———. *The Story of Tullahassee.* Oklahoma City: Semco, 1960.

Bataille, Gretchen M., and Kathleen Mullen Sands. *American Indian Women: Telling Their Lives.* Lincoln: U of Nebraska P, 1984.

Battey, Thomas C. *The Life and Adventures of a Quaker among the Indians.* 1875. Norman: U of Oklahoma P, 1968.

Beard, Charles A., and Mary R. Beard. *The American Spirit: A Study of the Idea of Civilization in the United States.* New York: Collier, 1942.

Bell, Betty Louise. "'If This Is Paganism . . .': Zitkala-Sa and the Devil's Language." Weaver, *Native American Religious Identity* 61–68.

Berkhofer, Robert F., Jr. *The White Man's Indian: Images of the American Indian from Columbus to the Present.* New York: Vintage, 1978.

Bernardin, Susan. "The Lessons of a Sentimental Education: Zitkala-Ša's Autobiographical Narratives." *Western American Literature* 32.3 (1997): 212–38.

Berrol, Selma. "Public Schools and Immigrants: The New York City Experience." *American Education and the European Immigrant, 1840–1940.* Ed. Bernard J. Weiss. Urbana: U of Illinois P, 1982. 31–43.

Bettman, Otto L. *The Good Old Days – They Were Terrible!* New York: Random, 1974.

Betzinez, Jason, with William Sturtevant Nye. *I Fought with Geronimo*. 1959. Lincoln: U of Nebraska P, 1987.

Bloodworth, William. "Varieties of American Indian Autobiography." MELUS 5 (1978): 67–81.

Bowden, Henry Warner. *American Indians and Christian Missions: Studies in Cultural Conflict*. Chicago: U of Chicago P, 1981.

Bowker, Ardy. *Sisters in the Blood: The Education of Women in Native America*. Newton, Mass.: WEEA, 1993.

Brinton, Donna, Marguerite Ann Snow, and M. B. Wesche. *Content-Based Second Language Instruction*. Boston: Heinle, 1989.

Brown, Estelle Aubrey. *Stubborn Fool: A Narrative*. Caldwell, Idaho: Caxton, 1952.

Brown, H. Douglas. *Principles of Language Learning and Teaching*. 2nd ed. Englewood Cliffs, N.J.: Prentice, 1987.

Brumble, H. David, III. *American Indian Autobiography*. Berkeley: U of California P, 1988.

———. *An Annotated Bibliography of American Indian and Eskimo Autobiographies*. Lincoln: U of Nebraska P, 1981.

Burgess, Charles. "The Goddess, the School Book, and Compulsion." *Harvard Educational Review* 46.2 (1976): 199–216.

Campbell, Jack K. *Colonel Francis W. Parker: The Children's Crusader*. New York: Teachers College P, 1967.

Canfield, Gae Whitney. *Sarah Winnemucca of the Northern Paiutes*. Norman: U of Oklahoma P, 1983.

Carpenter, Charles. *History of American Schoolbooks*. Philadelphia: U of Pennsylvania P, 1963.

Carpenter, George C., Franklin T. Baker, and Fred N. Scott. *The Teaching of English in the Elementary and the Secondary School*. 1903. New York: Longmans, 1927.

Cary, Elizabeth Luther. "Recent Writings by American Indians." *Book Buyer: A Monthly Review of American and Foreign Literature* 24 (1902): 23–25.

Charleston, G. Mike. "Toward True Native Education: A Treaty of 1992." Final Report of the Indian Nations at Risk Task Force. *Journal of American Indian Education* 33.2 (1994): 7–56.

Cheyfitz, Eric. *The Poetics of Imperialism: Translation and Colonization from "The Tempest" to "Tarzan."* Expanded ed. New York: Oxford UP, 1991.

Chiappelli, Fredi, Michael J. B. Allen, and Robert L. Benson, eds. *First Images of America: The Impact of the New World on the Old*. Berkeley: U of California P, 1976.

Child, Brenda. *Boarding School Seasons: American Indian Families, 1900–1940*. Lincoln: U of Nebraska P, 1998.

Churchill, Ward, and Glenn T. Morris. "Key Indian Laws and Cases." Jaimes 13–17.

Cobb, Amanda J. *Listening to Our Grandmothers' Stories: The Bloomfield Academy for Chickasaw Females, 1852–1949*. Lincoln: U of Nebraska P, 2000.

Coleman, Michael C. *American Indian Children at School, 1850–1930*. Jackson: UP of Mississippi, 1993.

Cook, Jessie W. "The Representative Indian." *Outlook* May 1900: 80–83.

Cook-Lynn, Elizabeth. "A Centennial Minute from Indian Country, or Lessons in Christianizing the Aboriginal Peoples of America from the Example of Bishop William Hobart Hare." *Why I Can't Read Wallace Stegner and Other Essays: A Tribal Voice*. Elizabeth Cook-Lynn. Madison: U of Wisconsin P, 1996. 41–59.

———. "Who Stole Native American Studies?" *Wicazo Sa Review* 12.1 (1997): 9–28.

Craig, Robert. "Christianity and Empire: A Case Study of American Protestant Colonialism and Native Americans." *American Indian Culture and Research Journal* 21.2 (1997): 1–41.

Crawford, James. *Bilingual Education: History, Politics, Theory, and Practice*. Trenton, N.J.: Crane, 1989.

Cuban, Larry. *How Teachers Taught: Constancy and Change in American Classrooms, 1890–1990*. 2nd ed. New York: Teachers College P, 1993.

Cutler, Charles L. *O Brave New Words! Native American Loanwords in Current English*. Norman: U of Oklahoma P, 1994.

Cutter, Martha J. "Zitkala-Sä's Autobiographical Writings: The Problems of a Canonical Search for Language and Identity." *MELUS* 19.1 (1994): 31–44.

Darian, Steven G. *English as a Foreign Language: History, Development, and Methods of Teaching*. Norman: U of Oklahoma P, 1972.

Davis, John B. "The Life and Work of Sequoya." *Chronicles of Oklahoma* 8.1 (1930): 149–80.

Debo, Angie. "Education in the Choctaw Country after the Civil War." *Chronicles of Oklahoma* 10 (1932): 383–91.

DeJong, David. *Promises of the Past: A History of Indian Education in the United States*. Golden, Colo.: North American P, 1993.

DeMallie, Raymond J. "Male and Female in Traditional Lakota Culture." Albers and Medicine 237–65.

Diana, Vanessa Holford. "'Hanging in the Heart of Chaos': Bi-cultural Limbo,

Self-(Re)presentation, and the White Audience in Zitkala-Sa's *American Indian Stories.*" *Cimarron Review* 121.4 (1997): 154–72.

Dominguez, Susan. "Zitkala-Sa (Gertrude Simmons Bonnin), 1876–1938: (Re)discovering *The Sun Dance.*" *American Music Research Center Journal* 5.1 (1995): 83–97.

Downs, Robert B. *Heinrich Pestalozzi: Father of Modern Pedagogy.* Boston: Twayne, 1975.

Eastman, Charles A. [Ohiyesa]. *From the Deep Woods to Civilization: Chapters in the Autobiography of an Indian.* 1916. Lincoln: U of Nebraska P, 1977.

———. *Indian Boyhood.* New York: McClure, 1907.

Ebersole, Gary L. *Captured by Texts: Puritan to Postmodern Images of Indian Captivity.* Charlottesville: UP of Virginia, 1995.

Edgerton, Franklin. "Notes on Early American Work in Linguistics." *Proceedings of the American Philosophical Society* 87.1 (1943): 25–34.

Ellis, Clyde. *To Change Them Forever: Indian Education at the Rainy Mountain Boarding School, 1893–1920.* Norman: U of Oklahoma P, 1996.

Elementary Geography for Primary Classes. Guyot's Geography Series. New York: Scribner's, 1879.

Elson, Ruth Miller. *Guardians of Tradition: American Schoolbooks of the Nineteenth Century.* Lincoln: U of Nebraska P, 1964.

Engs, Robert Francis. *Educating the Disfranchised and Disinherited: Samuel Chapman Armstrong and Hampton Institute, 1839–1893.* Knoxville: U of Tennessee P, 1999.

Faery, Rebecca Blevins. *Cartographies of Desire: Captivity, Race, and Sex in the Shaping of an American Nation.* Norman: U of Oklahoma P, 1999.

Fanon, Frantz. *Black Skin, White Masks: The Experiences of a Black Man in a White World.* 1952. Trans. Charles Lam Markmann. New York: Grove, 1967.

Ferguson, Charles A., and Shirley Brice Heath, eds. *Language in the USA.* Cambridge: Cambridge UP, 1981.

Fisher, Dexter. "Zitkala-Ša: The Evolution of a Writer." *American Indian Stories.* Zitkala-Ša. Lincoln: U of Nebraska P, 1985. v–xx.

Fiske, John. *American Political Ideas Viewed from the Standpoint of Universal History: Three Lectures Delivered at the Royal Institution of Great Britain in May 1880.* New York: Harbor, 1885.

———. "'Manifest Destiny.'" *Harper's New Monthly Magazine* Mar. 1885: 578–90.

Fletcher, Alice C. *Indian Education and Civilization.* Washington, D.C.: GPO, 1888.

Folsom, Cora. "Record of Returned Indian Students." Ludlow, *Twenty-two Years' Work* 325–493.

Foreman, Carolyn Thomas. "The Yuchi: Children of the Sun." *Chronicles of Oklahoma* 37.4 (1959–60): 480–96.

Frisbie, Charlotte J., and David P. McAllester, eds. *Navajo Blessingway Singer: The Autobiography of Frank Mitchell, 1881–1967.* Tucson: U of Arizona P, 1978.

Gage, Lucy. "A Romance of Pioneering." *Chronicles of Oklahoma* 29 (1951): 284–313.

Gee, James Paul. "Orality and Literacy: From *The Savage Mind* to *Ways with Words*." *TESOL Quarterly* 20.4 (1986): 719–46.

Gidley, Mick. *Edward S. Curtis and the North American Indian, Incorporated.* Cambridge: Cambridge UP, 1998.

Gilman, S[amuel] C. *The Conquest of the Sioux.* Rev. ed. Indianapolis: Carlon, 1897.

Golden, Gertrude. *Red Moon Called Me: Memoirs of a Schoolteacher in the Government Indian Service.* San Antonio: Naylor, 1954.

Goodbird, Edward, as told to Gilbert L. Wilson. *Goodbird the Indian: His Story.* 1914. St. Paul: Minnesota Historical Society P, 1985.

Graber, Kay, ed. *Sister to the Sioux: The Memoirs of Elaine Goodale Eastman, 1885–91.* Lincoln: U of Nebraska P, 1978.

Green, Rayna. "The Pocahontas Perplex: The Image of Indian Women in American Culture." *Massachusetts Review* 16.4 (1975): 698–714.

———. "The Tribe Called Wannabee: Playing Indian in America and Europe." *Folklore* 99.1 (1988): 30–55.

———. *Women in American Indian Society.* New York: Chelsea, 1992.

Greenblatt, Stephen J. "Learning to Curse: Aspects of Linguistic Colonialism in the Sixteenth Century." Chiappelli, Allen, and Benson 561–80.

Guimond, James K. "The 'Vanishing Red': Photographs of Native Americans at Hampton Institute." *Princeton Library Chronicle* (1988): 235–55.

Gump, James O. *The Dust Rose Like Smoke: The Subjugation of the Zulu and the Sioux.* Lincoln: U of Nebraska P, 1994.

Hafen, P. Jane. "A Cultural Duet: Zitkala Ša and *The Sun Dance* Opera." *Great Plains Quarterly* 18.2 (1998): 102–11.

———. "Zitkala Ša: Sentimentality and Sovereignty." *Wicazo Sa Review* 12.2 (1997): 31–41.

Harmon, Alexandra. "When Is an Indian Not an Indian? The 'Friends of the Indian' and the Problem of Indian Identity." *Journal of Ethnic Studies* 18.2 (1990): 95–123.

Harris, Sharon M. "Mary White Rowlandson, 1637?–1711." *The Heath Anthology of American Literature,* 2nd ed. Vol. 1. Ed. Paul Lauter et al. Lexington, Mass.: Heath, 1994. 340–42.

Harris, William T., Andrew J. Rickoff, and Mark Bailey. "From the Authors to the Teacher." *Appletons' School Readers: The Second Reader.* 1877, 1878. New York: American, 1902. 2.

Hauptman, Laurence M. "Mythologizing Westward Expansion: Schoolbooks and the Image of the American Frontier before Turner." *Western Historical Quarterly* 8 (1977): 269–82.

———. "Westward the Course of Empire: Geography Schoolbooks and Manifest Destiny." *Historian* 40 (1978): 423–40.

Heath, Shirley Brice. "English in Our Language Heritage." Ferguson and Heath 6–20.

Heckewelder, John. *History, Manners, and Customs of the Indian Nations Who Once Inhabited Pennsylvania and the Neighboring States.* 1819, 1876. Philadelphia: Historical Society of Pennsylvania, 1990.

Hendrick, Irving G. "The Federal Campaign for the Admission of Indian Children into Public Schools, 1890–1934." *American Indian Culture and Research Journal* 5.3 (1981): 13–32.

Herriman, Michael, and Barbara Burnaby, eds. *Language Policies in English-Dominant Countries.* Clevedon, Eng.: Multilingual, 1996.

Hertzberg, Hazel W. *The Search for an American Indian Identity: Modern Pan-Indian Movements.* Syracuse: Syracuse UP, 1971.

Hewes, Dorothy. "Those First Good Years of Indian Education: 1894–1898." *American Indian and Culture and Research Journal* 5.2 (1981): 63–82.

Hoare, Quentin, and Geoffrey Nowell Smith, eds. and trans. *Selections from the Prison Notebooks of Antonio Gramsci.* New York: International, 1971.

Holm, Tom. "Racial Stereotypes and Government Policies regarding the Education of Native Americans, 1879–1920." Regents of the U of California. 15–24.

Hoover, Herbert T., and Leonard R. Bruguier. *The Yankton Sioux.* New York: Chelsea, 1988.

Horsman, Reginald. *Race and Manifest Destiny: The Origins of American Racial Anglo-Saxonism.* Cambridge: Harvard UP, 1981.

Howard, O[liver] O. *My Life and Experiences among Our Hostile Indians: A Record of Personal Observations, Adventures, and Campaigns among the Indians of the Great West, with Some Account of Their Life, Habits, Traits, Religion, Ceremonies,*

Dress, Savage Instincts, and Customs in Peace and War. Hartford, Conn.: Worthington, 1907.

Howatt, A. P. R. *A History of English Language Teaching.* Oxford: Oxford UP, 1984.

Hoxie, Frederick E. *A Final Promise: The Campaign to Assimilate the Indians, 1880–1920.* Lincoln: U of Nebraska P, 1984.

———. "Redefining Indian Education: Thomas J. Morgan's Program in Disarray." *Arizona and the West* 24.1 (1982): 5–18.

Hultgren, Mary Lou, and Paulette Fairbanks Molin. *To Lead and to Serve: American Indian Education at Hampton Institute.* Virginia Beach, Va.: Virginia Foundation for the Humanities, 1989.

Hyde, George E. *Spotted Tail's Folk: A History of the Brulé Sioux.* Norman: U of Oklahoma P, 1961.

Iliff, Flora Gregg. *People of the Blue Water: A Record of Life among the Walapai and Havasupai Indians.* 1954. Tucson: U of Arizona P, 1985.

Indian Voices: The First Convocation of American Indian Scholars. San Francisco: Indian Historian P, 1970.

Institute for Government Research. *The Problem of Indian Administration.* 1928. New York: Johnson, 1971.

Jaimes, M. Annette, ed. *The State of Native America: Genocide, Colonization, and Resistance.* Boston: South End, 1992.

Jenkins, Minnie Braithwaite. *Girl from Williamsburg.* Richmond, Va.: Dietz, 1951.

Johnson, David L., and Raymond Wilson. "Gertrude Simmons Bonnin, 1876–1938: 'Americanize the First American.'" *American Indian Quarterly* 12.1 (1988): 27–40.

Kaestle, Carl F. "Ideology and American Educational History." *History of Education Quarterly* 22 (1982): 123–37.

Kehoe, Alice B. "The Shackles of Tradition." Albers and Medicine 53–73.

Kloss, Heinz. *The American Bilingual Tradition.* Rowley, Mass.: Newbury, 1977.

Kneale, Albert H. *Indian Agent.* Caldwell, Idaho: Caxton, 1950.

Knepler, Abraham E. "Education in the Cherokee Nation." *Chronicles of Oklahoma* 21.4 (1943): 378–401.

Knobel, Dale T. *America for the Americans: The Nativist Movement in the United States.* New York: Twayne, 1996.

———. "Know-Nothings and Indians: Strange Bedfellows?" *Western Historical Quarterly* 15 (1984): 175–98.

Kolodny, Annette. *The Lay of the Land: Metaphor as Experience and History in American Life and Letters.* Chapel Hill: U of North Carolina P, 1975.

Krashen, Stephen. *Principles and Practices in Second Language Acquisition.* New York: Pergamon, 1982.

Krupat, Arnold. *Ethnocriticism: Ethography, History, Literature.* Berkeley: U of California P, 1992.

———. *For Those Who Come After: A Study of Native American Autobiography.* Berkeley: U of California P, 1985.

Kutzleb, Charles R. "Educating the Dakota Sioux: 1876–1890." *North Dakota History* 32 (1965): 197–215.

La Flesche, Francis. *The Middle Five: Indian Schoolboys of the Omaha Tribe.* 1900. Madison: U of Wisconsin P, 1963. (Originally published as *The Middle Five: Indian Boys at School.*)

Lambert, Wallace, E. "Culture and Language as Factors in Learning and Education." *Education of Immigrant Students: Issues and Answers.* Ed. Aaron Wolfgang. Toronto: Ontario Institute, 1975. 55–83.

Larcom, Lucy. *A New England Girlhood.* Boston: Houghton, 1892.

Lauderdale, Virginia E. "Tullahassee Mission." *Chronicles of Oklahoma* 25 (1948): 285–300.

Laurence, Robert. "Indian Education: Federal Compulsory School Attendance Law Applicable to American Indians: The Treaty-Making Period: 1857–1871." *American Indian Law Review* 6 (1977): 393–413.

Leap, William L. *American Indian English.* Salt Lake City: U of Utah P, 1993.

———. "American Indian Languages." Ferguson and Heath 116–44.

Leibowitz, Arnold H. *Educational Policy and Political Acceptance: The Imposition of English as the Language of Instruction in American Schools.* Washington, D.C.: ERIC, 1971.

Lepore, Jill. *The Name of War: King Philip's War and the Origin of American Identity.* New York: Knopf, 1998.

Levchuk, Berenice. "Leaving Home for Carlisle Indian School." *Reinventing the Enemy's Language: Contemporary Native Women's Writings of North America.* Ed. Joy Harjo and Gloria Bird. New York: Norton, 1997. 175–86.

Lincoln, Kenneth. *Indi'n Humor: Bicultural Play in Native America.* New York: Oxford UP, 1993.

Lindsey, Donal F. *Indians at Hampton Institute, 1877–1923.* Urbana: U of Illinois P, 1995.

Lindsey, Lilah Denton. "Memories of the Indian Territory Mission Field." *Chroni-*

cles of Oklahoma 36 (1958): 181–98. (Originally published in *Indian Pioneer History* 109 [1938]: 226–65, in the Indian Archives, Oklahoma Historical Society.)

Littlefield, Alice. "The B.I.A. Boarding School: Theories of Resistance and Social Reproduction." *Humanity and Society* 13.4 (1989): 428–41.

———. "Learning to Labor: Native American Education in the United States, 1880–1930." *The Political Economy of North American Indians.* Ed. John H. Moore. Norman: U of Oklahoma P, 1993. 43–59.

Liu, Lydia H. *Translingual Practice: Literature, National Culture, and Translated Modernity – China, 1900–1937.* Stanford: Stanford UP, 1995.

Lomawaima, K. Tsianina. "Domesticity in the Federal Boarding Schools: The Power of Authority over Mind and Body." *American Ethnologist* 20.2 (1993): 227–40.

———. *They Called It Prairie Light: The Story of Chilocco Indian School.* Lincoln: U of Nebraska P, 1994.

———. "Tribal Sovereigns: Reframing Research in American Indian Education." *Harvard Educational Review* 70.1 (1999): 1–21.

Ludlow, Helen [W.]. "Indian Education at Hampton and Carlisle." *Harper's Magazine* Apr. 1881: 662–68.

———, ed. *Ten Years' Work for Indians at the Hampton Normal and Agricultural Institute at Hampton, Virginia, 1878–1888.* Hampton, Va.: Hampton, 1888.

———, ed. *Twenty-two Years' Work of the Hampton Normal and Agricultural Institute at Hampton, Virginia.* Hampton, Va.: Normal School P, 1893.

Lukens, Margaret Austin. *Creating Cultural Spaces: The Pluralist Project of American Women Writers, 1843–1902 (Margaret Fuller, Harriet Jacobs, Sarah Winnemucca, and Zitkala-Sa).* Diss. U of Colorado at Boulder, 1991. Ann Arbor: UMI, 1992. 9200618.

Lyons, Scott Richard. "A Captivity Narrative: Indians, Mixedbloods, and 'White' Academe." *Outbursts in Academe: Multiculturalism and Other Sources of Conflict.* Ed. Kathleen Dixon. Portsmouth, N.H.: Boynton/Cook, 1998. 87–108.

———. "Rhetorical Sovereignty: What Do American Indians Want from Writing?" *College Composition and Communication* 51.3 (2000): 447–86.

Malmsheimer, Lonna M. " 'Imitation White Man': Images of Transformation at the Carlisle Indian School." *Studies in Visual Communication* 2.4 (1985): 54–75.

Marriott, Alice, and Carol K. Rachlin. *Dance around the Sun: The Life of Mary Little Bear Inkanish, Cheyenne.* New York: Crowell, 1977.

McBeth, Sally. *Ethnic Identity and the Boarding School Experience of West-Central Oklahoma American Indians.* Lanham, Md.: UP of America, 1983.

———. "Myths of Objectivity and the Collaborative Process in Life History Research." *When They Read What We Write: The Politics of Ethnography.* Ed. Caroline B. Brettell. Westport, Conn.: Bergin, 1993. 145–62.

McLoughlin, William G. *After the Trail of Tears: The Cherokees' Struggle for Sovereignty, 1839–1880.* Chapel Hill: U of North Carolina P, 1993.

McNickle, D'Arcy. "American Indians Who Never Were." *Indian Historian* 3.3 (1970): 4–7.

Medicine, Beatrice. "The Anthropologist as the Indian's Image Maker." *Indian Historian* 4.1 (1971): 27–29.

———. "'Warrior Women': Sex Role Alternatives for Plains Indian Women." Albers and Medicine 267–80.

Michaels, Barbara L. *Gertrude Käsebier: The Photographer and Her Photographs.* New York: Abrams, 1992.

Mihesuah, Devon A. *American Indians: Stereotypes and Realities.* Atlanta: Clarity, 1996.

———. *Cultivating the Rosebuds: The Education of Women at the Cherokee Female Seminary, 1851–1909.* Urbana: U of Illinois P, 1993.

Miller, Jay, ed. *Mourning Dove: A Salishan Autobiography.* Lincoln: U of Nebraska P, 1990.

Misch, Mrs. J. O. "Lilah D. Lindsey." *Chronicles of Oklahoma* 33.2 (1955): 193–201.

Morgan, Lewis Henry. "The Indian Question." *Nation* Nov. 1878: 332–33.

Morgan, Thomas J. *Studies in Pedagogy.* Boston: Silver, 1889.

Morris, Robert C. *Reading, 'Riting, and Reconstruction: The Education of Freedmen in the South, 1861–1870.* Chicago: U of Chicago P, 1981.

Murray, David. *Forked Tongues: Speech, Writing and Representation in North American Indian Texts.* Bloomington: Indiana UP, 1991.

Ngũgĩ wa Thiong'o. *Decolonising the Mind: The Politics of Language in African Literature.* London: Currey, 1986.

Nietz, John A. *Old Textbooks: Spelling, Grammar, Reading, Arithmetic, Geography, American History, Civil Government, Physiology, Penmanship, Art, Music, as Taught in the Common Schools from Colonial Days to 1900.* Pittsburgh: U of Pittsburgh P, 1961.

Noley, Grayson. "Choctaw Bilingual and Bicultural Education in the 19th Century." Regents of the U of California 25–39.

Noriega, Jorge. "American Indian Education in the United States: Indoctrination for Subordination to Colonialism." Jaimes 371–402.

O'Brien, Lynne Woods. *Plains Indian Autobiographies.* Boise: Boise State College, 1973.

Office of Indian Affairs. *Rules for Indian Schools, with Course of Study, List of Textbooks, and Civil Service Rules.* Washington, D.C.: GPO, 1892.

Okker, Patricia. "Native American Literatures and the Canon: The Case of Zitkala-Ša." *American Realism and the Canon.* Ed. Tom Quirk and Gary Scarnhorst. Newark: U of Delaware P, 1994. 87–101.

Olsen, Louise P. "The Problem of Language in the Indian Schools of Dakota Territory, 1885–88." *North Dakota History* 20.1 (1953): 47–57.

Park, James. "Historical Foundations of Language Policy: The Nez Percé Case." St. Clair and Leap 49–67.

Parker, John W., and Ruth Ann Parker. *Josiah White's Institute: The Interpretation and Implementation of His Vision.* Dublin: Prinit, 1983.

Patridge, Lelia E. *The "Quincy Methods" Illustrated: Pen Photographs from the Quincy Schools.* New York: Kellogg, 1885.

Patterson, Calvin. *Elements of Grammar and Composition Including Analysis and Synthesis of Sentences, and a Complete System of Diagrams.* New York: Sheldon, 1886.

Peabody, Elizabeth P. *The Piutes: Second Report of the Model School of Sarah Winnemucca.* Cambridge, Mass.: Wilson, 1887.

————. *Sarah Winnemucca's Practical Solution to the Indian Problem.* Cambridge, Mass.: Wilson, 1886.

Pearce, Roy Harvey. *Savagism and Civilization: A Study of the Indian and the American Mind.* 1953. Baltimore: Johns Hopkins UP, 1967.

Peet, Isaac L. *Language Lessons: Designed to Introduce Young Learners, Deaf Mutes and Foreigners to a Correct Understanding of the English Language, on the Principle of Object Teaching.* New York: Baker, 1875.

Peirce, Bonny Norton. "Social Identity, Investment, and Language Learning," *TESOL Quarterly* 29.1 (1995): 9–31.

Pennycook, Alistair. *The Cultural Politics of English as an International Language.* London: Longman, 1994.

————. *English and the Discourses of Colonialism.* London: Routledge, 1998.

"People Who Interest Us." *Harper's Bazaar* Apr. 1900: 330.

Perdue, Theda. *The Cherokee.* New York: Chelsea, 1989.

Peregoy, Suzanne F., and Owen F. Boyle. *Reading, Writing, and Learning in ESL: A Resource Book for K 12 Teachers.* 2nd ed. New York: Longman, 1997.

Peyer, Bernd. *The Tutor'd Mind: Indian Missionary-Writers in Antebellum America.* Amherst: U of Massachusetts P, 1997.

Phillipson, Robert. *Linguistic Imperialism.* Oxford: Oxford UP, 1992.

Picotte, Agnes M. Foreword. *Old Indian Legends.* Zitkala-Ša. Lincoln: U of Nebraska P, 1985. xi–xviii.

Pratt, Mary Louise. "Arts of the Contact Zone." *Profession '91* (1991): 33–40.

Pratt, Richard Henry. "The Advantages of Mingling Indians with Whites." *Proceedings of the National Conference of Charities and Correction* (1892): 45–59.

———. *Battlefield and Classroom: Four Decades with the American Indian, 1867–1904.* Ed. Robert Utley. New Haven: Yale UP, 1964.

Prucha, Francis Paul. *American Indian Policy in Crisis: Christian Reformers and the Indian, 1865–1900.* Norman: U of Oklahoma P, 1976.

———. *The Churches and the Indian Schools, 1888–1912.* Lincoln: U of Nebraska P, 1979.

Quackenbos, G[eorge] P. *Elementary History of the United States: With Numerous Illustrations and Maps.* 1860. Rev. ed. New York: Appleton, 1884.

Reed, Alonzo, and Brainerd Kellogg. *An Elementary English Grammar, Consisting of One Hundred Practical Lessons, Carefully Graded and Adapted to the Class Room.* New York: Clark, 1880.

Reel, Estelle. *Report of the Superintendent of Indian Schools.* Washington, D.C.: GPO, 1900.

Regents of the U of California, eds. *Multicultural Education and the American Indian.* Los Angeles: American Indian Studies Center, 1979.

"Reminiscences of Lilah D. Lindsey." Misch 199–200. (Originally published in *Indian Pioneer History* 61 [n.d.]: 333–38, in the Foreman Collection, Indian Archives Division, Oklahoma Historical Society.)

Reyhner, Jon, ed., *Teaching American Indian Students.* Norman: U of Oklahoma P, 1992.

———. *Teaching Indigenous Languages.* Proceedings of the Fourth Annual Stabilizing Indigenous Language Symposium, May 1997, Northern Arizona University. Flagstaff: Division of Educational Services, 1998.

Reyhner, Jon, and Jeanne Eder. *A History of Indian Education.* Billings: Eastern Montana College, 1989.

Riggs, Alfred L. *Wicoie Wowapi Kin [The Word Book].* New York: American Tract Society, 1877.

Riggs, Stephen Return. "The Dakota Mission." *Minnesota Historical Collections* 3 (1870–89): 115–28.

————. *Mary and I: Forty Years with the Sioux.* Chicago: Holmes, 1880.

Riggs, Stephen R[eturn], and Gideon H. Pond. *The Dakota First Reading Book* [*Dakota Oyawa Wowapi*]. Cincinnati: Kendall, 1839.

Riggs, Stephen R[eturn], and Alfred L. Riggs. *Maka-oyakapi* [*Guyot's Elementary Geography, in the Dakota Language*]. New York: Scribner, 1876.

Riggs, Thomas Lawrence, as told to Margaret Kellogg Howard. "Sunset to Sunset: A Lifetime with My Brothers, the Dakotas." *South Dakota Historical Collections* 29 (1958): 87–306.

Riney, Scott. *The Rapid City Indian School, 1898–1933.* Norman: U of Oklahoma P, 1999.

Rogers, John [Chief Snow Cloud]. *Red World and White: Memories of a Chippewa Boyhood.* 1957. U of Oklahoma P, 1996. (Originally published as *A Chippewa Speaks.*)

Ronda, Bruce A., ed. *Letters of Elizabeth Palmer Peabody, American Renaissance Woman.* Middletown, Conn.: Wesleyan UP, 1984.

Rosaldo, Renato. *Culture and Truth: The Remaking of Social Analysis.* 2nd ed. Boston: Beacon, 1993.

Rosenwald, Lawrence. "*The Last of the Mohicans* and the Languages of America." *College English* 60.1 (1998): 9–30.

Ruoff, A. LaVonne Brown. "American Indian Authors, 1774–1899." *Critical Essays on Native American Literature.* Ed. Andrew Wiget. Boston: Hall, 1985. 190–202.

————. "Three Nineteenth-Century American Indian Autobiographers." *Redefining American Literary History.* Ed. A. LaVonne Brown Ruoff and Jerry W. Ward Jr. New York: MLA, 1990. 250–69.

St. Clair, Robert, and William Leap, eds. *Language Renewal among American Indian Tribes: Issues, Problems, and Prospects.* Rosslyn, Va.: National Clearinghouse for Bilingual Education, 1982.

"The Santee Normal School." *The Dakota Missions Past and Present.* Minneapolis: Tribune, 1886. 22–24.

Savignon, Sandra J. "Communicative Language Teaching: State of the Art." *TESOL Quarterly* 25.2 (1991): 261–77.

Schneider, Mary Jane. "Women's Work: An Examination of Women's Roles in Plains Indian Arts and Crafts." Albers and Medicine 101–21.

Scott, Lalla, ed. *Karnee: A Paiute Narrative.* Greenwich, Conn.: Fawcett, 1966.

Seaman, P. David, ed. *Born a Chief: The Nineteenth Century Hopi Boyhood of Edmund Nequatewa,* as told to Alfred F. Whiting. 1967. Tucson: U of Arizona P, 1993.

Sedgwick, Ellery. *A History of the "Atlantic Monthly," 1857–1909: Yankee Humanism at High Tide and Ebb.* Amherst: U of Massachusetts P, 1994.

Selinker, Larry. "Interlanguage." *International Review of Applied Linguistics* 10 (1972): 209–36.

Sewell, David R. "'So Unstable and Like Mad Men They Were': Language and Interpretation in Early American Captivity Narratives." *A Mixed Race: Ethnicity in Early America.* Ed. Frank Shuffelton. New York: Oxford UP, 1993. 39–55.

Simmons, Leo W., ed. *Sun Chief: The Autobiography of a Hopi Indian.* New Haven: Yale UP, 1942.

Smith, Jeanne. "'A Second Tongue': The Trickster's Voice in the Works of Zitkala-Ša." *Tricksterism in Turn-of-the-Century American Literature: A Multicultural Perspective.* Ed. Elizabeth Ammons and Annette White-Parks. Hanover: U of New England P, 1994. 46–60.

Smith, Raoul N. "The Interest in Language and Languages in Colonial and Federal America." *Proceedings of the American Philosophical Society* 123.1 (1979): 29–46.

Smith, Sidonie. "Cheesecake, Nymphs, and 'We the People': Un/National Subjects about 1900." *Prose Studies* 17.1 (1994): 120–40.

Sneve, Virginia Driving Hawk. *Completing the Circle.* Lincoln: U of Nebraska P, 1995.

Sossing, Benson J. "Our Barbarian Brethren." *Harper's New Monthly Magazine* May 1870: 793–811.

Spack, Ruth. "Dis/engagement: Zitkala-Ša's Letters to Carlos Montezuma, 1901–1902." *MELUS* 26.1 (2001: 173–204).

———. "English, Pedagogy, and Ideology: A Case Study of the Hampton Institute, 1878–1900." *American Indian Culture and Research Journal* 24.1 (2000): 1–24.

———. "Re-visioning Sioux Women: Zitkala-Ša's Revolutionary *American Indian Stories.*" *Legacy: A Journal of American Women Writers* 14.1 (1997): 25–42.

Spring, Joel. *The Cultural Transformation of a Native American Family and Its Tribe, 1763–1995: A Basket of Apples.* Mahwah, N.J.: Erlbaum, 1996.

Standing Bear, Luther. *Land of the Spotted Eagle.* Boston: Houghton, 1933.

———. *My People the Sioux.* Ed. E. A. Brininstool. 1928. Lincoln: U of Nebraska P, 1975.

Stands in Timber, John, and Margot Liberty. *Cheyenne Memories.* 1967. Lincoln: U of Nebraska P, 1972.

Stout, Mary. "Zitkala-Sa: The Literature of Politics." *Coyote Was Here: Essays on*

Contemporary Native American Literary and Political Mobilization. Ed. Bo Scholer. Aarhus, Den.: SEKLOS, 1984. 70–78.

Stowe, Harriet Beecher. "The Indians at St. Augustine." *Christian Union* Apr. 1877: 345.

Superintendent of Indian Schools. *Syllabus of Language Work and Suggestions to Teachers concerning Lessons in Speaking, Reading, Writing, Spelling, and Grammar for the Use of Indian Day Schools and Reservation Boarding Schools.* Washington, D.C.: GPO, 1894.

Susag, Dorothea M. "Zitkala-Sa (Gertrude Simmons Bonnin): A Power(full) Literary Voice." *Studies in American Indian Literatures* 5.4 (1993): 3–24.

Swisher, Karen. "Why Indian People Should Be the Ones to Write about Indian Education." *American Indian Quarterly* 20 (1996): 83–90.

Swinton, Willliam. *Introductory Geography in Readings and Recitations.* New York: Ivison, 1882.

Szasz, Margaret Connell. *Indian Education in the American Colonies, 1607–1783.* Albuquerque: U of New Mexico P, 988.

———. "Listening to the Native Voice: American Indian Schooling in the Twentieth Century." *Montana: The Magazine of Western History* 30.1 (1989): 43–53.

Tatum, Lawrie. *Our Red Brothers and the Peace Policy of President Ulysses S. Grant.* 1899. Lincoln: U of Nebraska P, 1970.

Taylor, Allan R. "Indian Lingua Francas." Ferguson and Heath 175–95.

Thompson, Hildegard. *The Navajos' Long Walk for Education: A History of Navajo Education.* Tsaile Lake, Ariz.: Navajo Community College P, 1975.

Tilton, Robert S. *Pocahontas: The Evolution of an American Narrative.* Cambridge: Cambridge UP, 1994.

Tinker, George E. *Missionary Conquest: The Gospel and Native American Cultural Genocide.* Minneapolis: Fortress, 1993.

Trennert, Robert A. *The Phoenix Indian School: Forced Assimilation in Arizona, 1891–1935.* Norman: U of Oklahoma P, 1988.

Tuttle, Edward F. "Borrowing versus Semantic Shift: New World Nomenclature in European Languages." Chiappelli, Allen, and Benson 595–605.

United States Indian Office. *Correspondence on the Subject of Teaching the Vernacular in the Schools, 1887–'88.* Washington, D.C.: GPO, 1888.

Urion, Carl. "Changing Academic Discourse about Native Education: Using Two Pairs of Eyes." *Canadian Journal of Education* 18.1 (1991): 1–9.

Utley, Robert M. *The Last Days of the Sioux Nation.* New Haven: Yale UP, 1963.

Vallance, Elizabeth. "Hiding the Hidden Curriculum: An Interpretation of the Language of Justification in Nineteenth-Century Educational Reform." *Curriculum Theory Network* 4.1 (1973–74): 5–21.

Vaughn, Alden. "From White Man to Redskin: Changing Anglo-American Perceptions of the American Indian." *American Historical Review* 87.4 (1982): 917–53.

Venuti, Lawrence. *The Scandals of Translation: Towards an Ethics of Difference.* London: Routledge, 1998.

Viswanathan, Gauri. *Masks of Conquest: Literary Study and British Rule in India.* New York: Columbia UP, 1989.

Warrior, Robert Allen. *Tribal Secrets: Recovering American Indian Intellectual Traditions.* Minneapolis: U of Minnesota P, 1995.

Washington, Booker T. *Up from Slavery: An Autobiography.* New York: Burt, 1900.

Weatherford, Jack. *Native Roots: How the Indians Enriched America.* New York: Fawcett, 1991.

Weaver, Jace. "From I-Hermeneutics to We-Hermeneutics: Native Americans and the Post-colonial." Weaver, *Native American Religious Identity* 1–25.

———. *That the People Might Live: Native American Literatures and Native American Community.* New York; Oxford UP, 1997.

———, ed. *Native American Religious Identity: Unforgotten Gods.* Maryknoll, N.Y.: Orbis, 1998.

Webb, George. *A Pima Remembers.* Tucson: U of Arizona P, 1959.

Weist, Katherine M. "Beasts of Burden and Menial Slaves: Nineteenth Century Observations of Northern Plains Indian Women." Albers and Medicine 29–52.

Welsh, Herbert. *Four Weeks among Some of the Sioux Tribes of Dakota and Nebraska Together with a Brief Consideration of the Indian Problem.* Philadelphia: McCann, 1882.

Welter, Barbara. "The Cult of True Womanhood: 1820–1860," *American Quarterly* 18 (1966): 151–74.

Wexler, Laura. "Tender Violence: Literary Eavesdropping, Domestic Fiction, and Educational Reform." *Yale Journal of Criticism* 5.1 (1991): 151–87.

White Hat, Albert, Sr. *Reading and Writing the Lakota Language: Lakȟóta Iyapi uŋ Wowapi nahaŋ Yawapi.* Ed. Jael Kampfe. Salt Lake City: U of Utah P, 1999.

Whitewolf, Howard. "A Short Story of My Life." *American Indian Magazine* Jan.–Mar. 1917: 29–31.

Willard, William. "Zitkala Sa: A Woman Who Would Be Heard!" *Wicazo Sa Review* 1.1 (1985): 11–16.

Williams, Robert A., Jr. "Documents of Barbarism: The Contemporary Legacy of

European Racism and Colonialism in Narrative Traditions of Federal Indian Law." *Arizona Law Review* 31.2 (1989): 231–78.

Williamson, John P. "Early Missions to the Dakota Indians in Minnesota." *The Dakota Missions Past and Present.* Minneapolis: Tribune, 1886. 3–8.

Wilson, Raymond. *Ohiyesa: Charles Eastman, Santee Sioux.* Urbana: U of Illinois P, 1983.

Winger, Otho. *A Brief Centennial History of Wabash County, 1835–1935.* North Manchester, Ind.: Winger, 1935.

Winnemucca Hopkins, Sarah. *Life among the Piutes: Their Wrongs and Claims.* Ed. Mrs. Horace Mann. Boston: Cupples, 1883.

Wong, Hertha Dawn. *Sending My Heart Back across the Years: Tradition and Innovation in Native American Autobiography.* New York: Oxford UP, 1992.

Worman, James H. *First French Book after the Natural or Pestalozzian Method: For Schools and Home Instruction.* New York: American, 1881.

Yava, Albert. *Big Falling Snow: A Tewa-Hopi Indian's Life and Times and the History and Traditions of His People.* Ed. and annotated Harold Courlander. 1978. Albuquerque: U of New Mexico P, 1992.

Young, Michael F. D. "An Approach to the Study of Curricula as Socially Organized Knowledge." *Knowledge and Control: New Directions for the Sociology of Education.* Ed. Michael F. D. Young. London: Collier, 1971. 19–46.

Youst, Lionel. *She's Tricky Like Coyote: Annie Miner Peterson, an Oregon Coast Indian Woman.* Norman: U of Oklahoma P, 1997.

Zamel, Vivian, and Ruth Spack. *Negotiating Academic Literacies: Teaching and Learning across Languages and Cultures.* Mahwah, N.J.: Erlbaum, 1998.

Zitkala-Ša. *American Indian Stories.* Washington, D.C.: Hayworth, 1921.

———. *American Indian Stories.* 1921. Lincoln: U of Nebraska P, 1985.

———. [Mrs. Gertrude Bonnin]. "America's Indian Problem." *Edict* Dec. 1921: 1–2.

———. "Impressions of an Indian Childhood." *Atlantic Monthly* Jan. 1900: 37–47.

———. "An Indian Teacher among Indians." *Atlantic Monthly* Mar. 1900: 381–86.

———. *Old Indian Legends.* 1901. Lincoln: U of Nebraska P, 1985.

———. "The School Days of an Indian Girl." *Atlantic Monthly* Feb. 1900: 185–94.

———. "Why I Am a Pagan." *Atlantic Monthly* Dec. 1902: 801–03.

Index

civilizing project, 25, 26–27, 144, 146; and Native teachers, 81–82, 89, 90–91
civil rights, 20
Civil War, 17, 83, 85, 87
Cleveland, Grover, 34–35, 97
Cockenoe, 2, 3
colleges, tribal, 175
colonialism, 4, 117; of English-only education, 9, 14, 29, 48; and language, 3, 128–29, 148–49; of mission schools, 51–52
Colville Reservation, 116, 138
Comanches, 54, 132
contact zone, 7
Cooper, James Fenimore: *The Last of the Mohicans,* 122
Correspondence on the Subject of Teaching the Vernacular in Indian Schools, 35
Coweta Indian Boarding School, 84
Creek National Council, 83, 84
Creeks, 17, 82–83, 85
Crow Creek Agency, 49–50
cultural genocide, 51
culture change, 82
curricula, 8, 27, 48; appropriateness of, 24–25, 177; as ideology, 71–73; Native teachers and, 80, 90–91
Custer, 101, 163

Daklugie, Asa, 10, 40, 118, 129–30; *Indeh,* 115
Dakota language, 35, 37, 57, 62; school use of, 18–19, 49, 126; teacher training in, 79
Dakota Mission, 15, 18, 30, 47, 79, 80, 145, 146; bilingual education at, 50, 51, 52, 116; language use at, 34, 35
Dakotas, 40, 49–50; female power among, 155–56; language use, 35, 126; as teachers, 79, 80; uprising of, 49, 163; women's lives among, 153–55
Dakota Territory, 15, 56–57
Dance around the Sun (Inkanish), 137
Darlington Agency, 139
Dartmouth College, 134
Darwinism, 29, 20

Dawes bill, 68, 188 n.45
Dawson, Anna, *142*
day schools, 18, 29, 88, 90, 117; Creek, 84–85
debating society: at Hampton Institute, 64
Diné (Navajos), 40–41, 126
discourse, 7, 110, 170; of colonialism, 29, 30, 48, 113, 132, 152, 174; educational, 14–15; European American, 112, 149; Native, 169, 176; political, 167; religious, 158
disease, 118
division of labor: Dakota, 154–55
dominance: European American, 71–72
Dorchester, Daniel, 37
Dorchester, Merial, 161
Douglas, John, 19
Doxon, Charles, 10, 65; "Address by Mr. Charles Doxon," 132
"A Dream of Her Grandfather" (Zitkala-Ša), 163, 166
dropout rates, 174

Earlham College, 145
Eastman, Charles, 10, 50, 123, 126; *From the Deep Woods to Civilization,* 116, 133–35; *Indian Boyhood,* 133
Eastman, Elaine Goodale, 69, 74, 133. *See also* Goodale, Elaine
Edict (journal), 168
education, 2, 19, 49, 83, 100, 174, 183 n.21; of Thomas Alford, 87–89; Caddo, 52–53; Cherokee Nation, 38–39; by colonists, 3–4; consistency of, 27–28; English language and, 28–29, 50, 99, 169–70; gender and, 19, 112, 138–39; goals of, 26–27, 130–31; at Hampton Institute, 47–48, 55–76; of Kiowas, 53–54; level of, 54–55; multiculturalism and, 139–40; Native American, 113, 135–36, 154; Native discourse in, 176–77; and opportunity, 69–70; resistance to, 39–42; and self-determination, 175–76; Luther Standing Bear on, 104–7; transcultural, 133–38; as treaty requisite, 40–41
educational reform, 4, 100

grammar school education, 28
Grant, Ulysses S., 15, 16, 52, 170
Great Britain, 6, 14
Great Plains, 7, 39
"The Great Spirit" (Zitkala-Ša), 162
Guyot's Geographical Series, 50, 61

Hailmann, William N., 25, 79, 99; *Syllabus of Language Work*, 26
Hampton Normal and Agricultural Institute, 19, 20, 22, 80, *108, 142*, 186 n.24; Dakota students at, 39, 40; education at, 55–57, 89, 187 n.29; ideology taught at, 71–73, 75–76; language use at, 58–59; literacy training at, 69–70; outing system of, 57–58; teaching at, 47–48, 59–60, 61–69, 74–75, 189 n.57
Hare, William, 18, 33–34
Harper's Monthly Magazine, 122, 161
Haskell Institute, 25
Hawaii, 65
Hayt, Ezra, 144
Hayworth Publishing House, 162
Heckewelder, John: *History, Manners, and Customs of the Indian Nations . . .* , 3
hegemony, 16
heredity, 31, 70, 76
Hidatsas, 140
Highland Institute (Ohio), 84
history: European American, 75–76, 123; Native American, 106, 107, 135–36, 139, 167–68
History, Manners, and Customs of the Indian Nations . . . , (Heckewelder), 3
Holbrook, Harriet, 58, 67
Hopis, 41, 117, 128, 136
Hotevilla, 117
Howard, O. O., 96
Howling Wolf, 54–55
hunger, 118

Iapi Oaye (*Word Carrier;* newspaper), 34, 50
idcntity: 41, 118, 129; Americanization and,

37–38; and captivity, 120–21; language and, 14, 70; Native, 85, 87, 134–35, 166–68; racial paradigms and, 72–73; retaining, 132–33
ideology, 6, 9, 122, 166; assimilationist, 103; curriculum as, 48, 71–73; of dominance, 75–76; European American, 81–82, 85, 89, 90–91, 165; racial, 119–20; and social institutions, 15–16
I Fought with Geronimo (Betzinez), 132
Iktomi, 165
Illinois Federation of Women's Clubs, 168
immigrants, 26, 27, 36, 42, 45
immigration: Americanization and, 36–37
imperialism, 71, 121–22, 129; cultural and linguistic, 48
"Impressions of an Indian Childhood" (Zitkala-Ša), 152; themes in, 153–56
In the Days of Victorio (Kaywaykla), 118
Indeh (Daklugie), 115
Indian Boyhood (Eastman), 133
"An Indian Boy's Story" (Ah-nen-la-de-ni), 115, 116, 119–20
Indian Child Welfare Act, 174
Indian Citizenship Day (Hampton Institute), *108*
Indian Helper, 145, 160
Indian Nations at Risk Task Force, 176
Indian Office. *See* Office of Indian Affairs
Indian princess, 97, 150, 164–65, 168, 169, 196 n.13
Indian Reorganization Act, 4, 174
Indian Self-Determination and Educational Assistance Act, 174
Indian service. *See* Office of Indian Affairs
Indiana, 145
"Indians of To-day" (Goodale), 65
"An Indian Teacher among Indians" (Zitkala-Ša), 143, 146, 152, 163, 169; themes in, 158–61
Indian Territory, 38–39, 54, 84, 83, 87
Indian Welfare Committee, 148
individualism, 29

religion, 53, 158, 165; and Native writers, 11, 93, 106, 112, 115, 126, 129, 148, 156
Richards, Josephine, 60, 62, 67, 72–73, 74
Ridpath, William M., 36
Riggs, Alfred L., 34, 50
Riggs, Stephen, 49
Riggs, Thomas L., 33
Riley, John B., 31, 46
Robbins, James, 57, 59–60
Robertson, Ann Augusta, 83
Robertson, William, 83
Rogers, John, 10; *Red World and White*, 135–36
role playing, 63–64
Rosebud Agency, 20, 103
Rowlandson, Mary: *The Soveraignty and Goodness of God*, 114, 120, 121
"Rules for Indian Schools" (Morgan), 37
Rulo, Zallie, 58, 75–76, 165

Salish, 138
SAI. *See* Society of American Indians
Santa Fe Indian School, *172, 173*
Santee Agency, 50–51
Santee dialect, 49
Santee Normal School, 50–51, 79, 145
Sauk and Fox Agency, 88
scholarship: Native American, 177
schoolbooks, 66
"The School Days of an Indian Girl" (Zitkala-Ša), 13, 116, 152; themes in, 156–58
schools, 4, 22, 27–28, 174, 182 n.8; curricula of, 24–25; establishment of, 17–18; Native teachers at, 79–80, 95; Sara Winnemucca's, 97, 99–100
Schurz, Carl, 96
second-language acquisition, 61, 74, 110–11, 189 n.56
self-determination, 175–76
self-reliance, 29
Senecas, 16
sexual harassment, 28, 183 n.21
Shawnee language, 125

Shawnees, 87–88, 89, 90–91, 93
Shawnee Town, 88
Sherman Institute, 136
"A Short Story of My Life" (Whitewolf), 132
Silver State (Nevada), 97, 100
Simmons, David, 57, 58, 152, 196 n.19
Simmons, Gertrude. *See* Zitkala-Ša
sign language, 2, 40, 139; students' use of, 58–59, 122, 123
Sioux, 180 n.12, 182 n.10; culture of, 152, 162, 163, 165, 166, 167; reservation, 102; women, 154, 156, 161, 164, 165, 168. *See also* Dakotas; Lakotas; Nakotas
Smith, Edward P., 18
Smith, John, 164
social Darwinism, 29, 30
social institutions: and ideology, 15–16
Society of American Indians (SAI), 133, 146, 148, 169
Society of Friends (Quakers), 16, 89, 159; schools run by, 13, 47, 52–54, 88
"The Soft-Hearted Sioux" (Zitkala-Ša), 163, 164
Southern Workman (newspaper), 47, 55, 67, 89; racist ideology in, 72, 73; student letters in, 68–69
The Soveraignty and Goodness of God (Rowlandson), 114, 120
Spencer method, 68
Spotted Tail, 20
Standing Bear, Luther, 10, *78,* 81, 122, 127, 177; on American Indian education, 104–7; captivity of, 118, 120–21; education of, 101–3, 124; *Land of the Spotted Eagle,* 101, 105; *My People the Sioux,* 101, 118; teaching career of, 103–4
Stands in Timber, John, 10; *Cheyenne Memories,* 127
stereotypes, 48, 75, 122; of European Americans, 119, 156–57; of Native men, 112–13
Stowe, Harriet Beecher, 54, 55
St. Augustine FL, 54
St. Paul's School for Boys, 18, 30